"*Pivot* is a book you will turn to again and again, whether you're seeking a new career direction, a second career after retirement, or just on the lookout for new ways to use your talents. Jenny Blake takes a strength-based approach to managing the risk that comes with making a change, and provides tons of helpful examples and exercises."
—Daniel H. Pink,
author of *To Sell is Human* and *Drive*

"Nontraditional career journeys are not only the new normal, they're how innovators throughout history changed their world and ours. With actionable insights and lucid prose, Jenny Blake illuminates the path to building your own destiny."
—Shane Snow, author of *Smartcuts*
and cofounder of Contently

"Wondering what your next move is? Read this book! Jenny Blake is one of the wisest and freshest voices on the subject of career development, and this is her best work yet. In *Pivot*, you will hear the good news: that you can get paid to do what you love. It may not look like what you thought, and it may require some personal growth, but you can find the work you were meant to do. You just have to pivot."
—Jeff Goins, author of *The Art of Work*

"Are the tectonic plates below your sturdy career suddenly splitting into a deep abyss of unknown? Let this book be your rope ladder out."
—Neil Pasricha, author of *The Happiness Equation*
and the 1,000 Awesome Things blog

"If you think life is a highway, then you've got it wrong. It's more like a winding path through an unpredictable forest. Not only do you have to wade the swamp and battle the beasts, but time after time you come to a crossroads. Left? Right? Straight ahead? Jenny Blake's new book will help you find the wisdom and resources to make the best choices, move into the sunlight, and end up where you want to be."
—Michael Bungay Stanier, author of
The Coaching Habit and *Do More Great Work*

"We live in a time of rapid evolution, and we develop skills quickly now by absorbing many shorter term work experiences, so we can become what Jenny Blake calls *impacters* in our careers. This book gives you a solid roadmap to making the right call about career changes that will help you discover what you're truly built for. Courage, consciousness, and competence—that's what *Pivot* offers you. It's excellent!"

—Penney Peirce, author of *The Intuitive Way*,
Frequency, and *Leap of Perception*

"The book is fantastic. No matter where you are in your career, *Pivot* is provokingly relevant." —Dr. Tom Guarriello, founder of RoboPsych and founding
faculty at New York's School of Visual Arts, Masters in Branding

"Today, the average person has eleven jobs and three to six careers, which is why *Pivot* is essential reading for every professional. Let Jenny be your coach, giving you the confidence and tools required to make your next career transition. Whether you're an employee, freelancer, or entrepreneur, this book will help you identify the skills you have or need that will lead to your next opportunity. Jenny has been through career transitions and has successfully navigated them on her own, which makes her the perfect spokesperson for helping you do the same. *Pivot* is the book that you'll need to read multiple times through your life because change is constant and often times unexpected!" —Dan Schawbel, author of *Promote Yourself* and *Me 2.0*

"Whether you're considering a career change or job change, or figuring out what to do next, Jenny Blake's *Pivot* is the book you need. It's a comprehensive, practical, must-have guide to your pivot."

—Susan RoAne, keynote speaker and author of *How to Work a Room*

PIVOT

PIVOT

THE ONLY MOVE THAT MATTERS IS YOUR NEXT ONE

Jenny Blake

Portfolio / Penguin

Portfolio / Penguin
An imprint of Penguin Random House LLC
375 Hudson Street
New York, New York 10014

LIBRARY OF CONGRESS CATALOGING-IN-PUBLICATION DATA
Names: Blake, Jenny, author.
Title: Pivot : the only move that matters is your next one / Jenny Blake.
Description: New York : Portfolio, 2016.
Identifiers: LCCN 2016011437 | ISBN 9781591848202 (hardback)
  | ISBN 9780698406704 (ebook) | ISBN 9780399564383 (international edition)
Subjects: LCSH: Career development. | Career changes. | BISAC: BUSINESS &
  ECONOMICS / Careers / General. | BUSINESS & ECONOMICS / Motivational.
Classification: LCC HF5381 .B455 2016 | DDC 650.14—dc23 LC record available at
  https://lccn.loc.gov/2016011437

Printed in the United States of America
10 9 8 7 6 5 4 3 2 1

Set in Warnock Pro with Open Sans and League Gothic
Book design by Daniel Lagin

*To my grandma Janice Deino, who pivoted her entire life
at eighty years old with strength and grace.
You are an unwavering source of support and inspiration,
and the most agile, resilient person I know.
Thank you for everything.*

How should we be able to forget those ancient myths that are at the beginning of all peoples, the myths about dragons that at the last moment turn into princesses; perhaps all the dragons of our lives are princesses who are only waiting to see us once beautiful and brave. . . .

So you must not be frightened . . . if a sadness rises up before you larger than any you have ever seen; if a restiveness, like light and cloud-shadows, passes over your hands and over all you do. You must think that something is happening with you, that life has not forgotten you, that it holds you in its hand; it will not let you fall.

—**Rainer Maria Rilke,** *Letters to a Young Poet*

CONTENTS

INTRODUCTION: PIVOT IS THE NEW NORMAL 1

Pivot or Get Pivoted 4

Changing Careers in the Age of the App 8

Connect the Dots Looking Backward 10

Pivot Method at a Glance 13

HIGH NET GROWTH 18

Career Operating Modes 23

Trust Your Risk Tolerance 25

Two (Many) Steps Ahead, One Step Back 29

STAGE ONE: PLANT 33

PLANT OVERVIEW 35

CHAPTER 1: CALIBRATE YOUR COMPASS 39

What Are Your Guiding Principles? What Is Your Happiness Formula?

Create Your Compass 40

Identify Your Happiness Formula   46

Your Body Is Your Business   47

Reduce Decision Fatigue   49

Meditate to Activate Your Best Instincts   50

CHAPTER 2: PUT A PIN IN IT 53

What Excites You Most?
What Does Success Look Like One Year from Now?

Avoid the Tyranny of the Hows   55

Vision Cloudy? Start Somewhere.   56

Clarify Your Vision Statement   60

Summarize Knowns and Unknowns   62

CHAPTER 3: FUEL YOUR ENGINE 65

What Is Working? Where Do You Excel?

Identify Your Strengths   67

Work-History Highlights   70

CHAPTER 4: FUND YOUR RUNWAY 75

What Is Your Timeline? How Can You Earn Extra Income?

Build a Solid Financial Foundation   76

Pivot Finance 101   77

Income-Anxiety Seesaw Awareness   84

STAGE TWO: SCAN
87

SCAN OVERVIEW
89

CHAPTER 5: BOLSTER YOUR BENCH
91

Who Do You Already Know? Who Can Provide Advice?
What Can You Give in Return?

Expand Your Sphere of Influence   93

Build a Network of Collective Brainpower   94

Career Karma: Seek Reciprocal Success   104

CHAPTER 6: BRIDGE THE GAPS
107

What Skills and Expertise Will Take You to the Next Level?

Mind the Gap   108

Learn How to Learn   108

Limit Linear Thinking   111

Investigative Listening   114

Be Discerning About Your Learning   119

CHAPTER 7: MAKE YOURSELF DISCOVERABLE
123

How Can You Add Unique Value and Build Visibility?

Define Your Project-Based Purpose   124

Platform and Leverage   125

Revel in the Work Others Reject   130

Leapfrog: Work Backward from Two Moves Ahead   130

Let Others Know You Are Looking   133

STAGE THREE: PILOT

139

PILOT OVERVIEW   141

CHAPTER 8: GET SCRAPPY   143
What Small Experiments Can You Run?
What Real-World Data Can You Collect?

Aim First for Quantity, Not Quality   145

What Makes a Strong Pilot?   146

Incremental Pilots Within Organizations   152

Reduce Risk with Redundancy   153

Travel Pilots to Shake Up Stagnant Thinking   157

CHAPTER 9: PAUSE, REVIEW, REPEAT   161
What Worked? What Didn't? What Could You Do Differently?

Pause and Review   163

Take Incrementally Bigger Risks   164

STAGE FOUR: LAUNCH

169

LAUNCH OVERVIEW   171

CHAPTER 10: BUILD FIRST, COURAGE SECOND   173
When Will You Make the Big Move?
What Are Your Linchpin Decision Criteria?

Identify your Launch Timing Criteria   174

Pivot Hexagon   183

Know When to Hold Versus Fold   186

Your Gut Has a Brain   192

Pivot Scales: Comfort Versus Risk   194

CHAPTER 11: FLIP FAILURE   197
What Will Move You into Action?

Rejection as a Stepping-Stone to Success   200

Mine Failure for Strengths   201

You Can't Make Everybody Happy—
So Stop Trying and Start Living   202

Separate Decisions from Difficult Conversations   205

Don't Wait for Perfect Conditions   207

How Do You Know Your Launch Worked?   209

The Continuous Pivot   211

STAGE FIVE: LEAD   215

LEAD OVERVIEW   217

CHAPTER 12: ARE YOU LISTENING?   219
How Can You Facilitate Engaging Career Conversations?

Your Interest Matters More Than You Think   221

How to Use the Pivot Method Within Organizations   226

Pilot Creative Internal-Mobility Programs   229

CONCLUSION: CELEBRATE COMPLEXITY   235

Checking In at the Last Resort   237

The Courageous Life   238

ACKNOWLEDGMENTS   243

POST PIVOT: ONLINE RESOURCES   249

PIVOT METHOD QUICK REFERENCE   251

LAUNCH CRITERIA CHECKLIST   253

RESOURCES FOR COMPANIES   255

PIVOT 201: RECOMMENDED READING   257

NOTES   259

INDEX   265

PIVOT

INTRODUCTION: PIVOT IS THE NEW NORMAL

Chaos is merely order waiting to be deciphered.

—José Saramago

"I think I am going crazy."

"I don't know what's wrong with me."

"Am I asking for too much?"

"I just can't do this anymore."

"I think I am having a midlife crisis."

"Will I ever be happy?"

NO MATTER THEIR AGE, LIFE STAGE, BANK ACCOUNT BALANCE, OR CAREER LEVEL, these are the sentiments I hear from people who are looking for more in their lives, even if they have found career success by traditional standards.

Many have perfect-on-paper jobs, but have hit a plateau and feel an inexplicable urge to do things differently. They may be considering walking away from a robust salary, folding or starting their own business, or taking time off altogether. Some are unsatisfied or frustrated with their work for other reasons: they have outgrown their position or business, or they feel drawn to a new area that better suits their values and interests, where they can make a greater contribution.

Through their confusion and self-doubt, one thing remains clear: the way they have been working is no longer working. Maybe you can relate to some of the following stories of people who reached a career crossroad:

- Amy Schoenberger had been working as a senior creative strategist in a public relations firm for four years. She was starting to feel uninspired by the work, but had no desire to leave the company and coworkers she loved.

- After several tumultuous years in his late twenties, Adam Chaloeicheep hit a point of physical and emotional burnout. He wondered, *Is this all there is?* Adam needed time to reflect and reset, so he left his lucrative job as creative director of a real estate development firm, sold nearly all his possessions, and moved from Chicago to Thailand to study meditation in a monastery.

- Tara Adams had been at Google for eleven years running educational outreach programs when she felt the urge to slow the frenetic pace of her career and start a family, perhaps even take a break from work.

- After graduating from UCLA, Marques Anderson spent four years in the NFL as a safety. He started playing for the Green Bay Packers, then after three years got traded to the Oakland Raiders before a final trade to the Denver Broncos one year later. Though he loved his time in the league, Marques also knew that it was important to have a transition plan for what would follow.

- Kyle Durand was on active duty in Iraq, practicing international and operational law, when he found out he had been passed over for promotion after seventeen years of service. After receiving the news in a brief phone call with his commanding officer, he left his office (located at the time in Saddam Hussein's palace) and walked back to his tent in the middle of the night. While he pondered his fate, a rocket suddenly shot over his head, hit a fuel bladder on a nearby runway, and exploded. At that moment, Kyle knew it was time to return home. He was devastated by the phone call, and no longer wanted to risk his life for an organization that did not seem to value his efforts.

- As John Hill and Bud Bilanich approached big birthdays—sixty and sixty-five years old, respectively—friends, family, and colleagues repeatedly asked if they would retire. As they considered how the next phase of their careers might unfold, one constant remained strong: neither had any interest in clichéd notions of retirement that involved stopping work completely.

- Brian Jones (not his real name) and Julie Clow were executives who had outgrown their senior-level leadership roles at prestigious companies and felt capped in their trajectories. However, with families to support and large financial packages at their current jobs, leaving would not be an easy choice.

- I had been working at Google in training, coaching, and career development for over five years when I took a sabbatical to launch my first book, *Life After College*, in 2011. Even though I loved working there and had a perfect-on-paper role myself, something was still missing.

From the outside, it may have looked like we were all undergoing quarter-life or midlife crises. Onlookers might have wrongly assumed we were falling apart or going crazy for seeming unsatisfied with our current paths and leaving our stable jobs behind.

However, on the inside we all knew we had hit a plateau, or *pivot point*, in our careers. We were talented, hardworking, and committed to making a positive impact—and yet we all felt called to do things differently than how we had been doing them. Tackling these massive changes felt disorienting but right. For whatever uncertainties lay ahead, each of us knew that staying in the same place would have been the greater risk.

Calling such career aspirations a crisis, shaming and blaming people for wanting to prioritize meaningful work in a volatile economy by saying they are "entitled" or "too picky," means we are missing a huge opportunity to celebrate and support those who seek to make a greater contribution to their workplaces, society, and the lives of everyone around them.

We do not have a productive description for this type of career transition. Or at least we didn't, until now.

PIVOT OR GET PIVOTED

People are no longer working at the same jobs for forty years with the safety of pension plans waiting at the end. The average employee tenure in America is now four to five years and job roles often change dramatically *within* those four to five years. Among workers twenty-five to thirty-four years old, the average tenure drops to three years.

Many jobs that disappeared during the last recession are not coming back. Every day, breakthroughs in technology generate greater automation in the workplace, threatening positions held by hardworking people and the stability of companies large and small. Job security has become an antiquated idea, a luxury most people today do not enjoy, whether they are aware of it or not.

Corporate loyalty has given way to uncertainty; companies that seem too big to fail have collapsed, along with many smaller ones. New ones take their place. With the advent of app marketplaces, crowdfunding, the maker revolution, and sharing economies, we now see billion-dollar valuations for companies that would not have existed ten years ago, and many smaller businesses cropping up in parallel.

To add to the upheaval, a recent Gallup study revealed that almost 90 percent of workers are either "not engaged" or "actively disengaged from their jobs."

But you do not need to read any of the statistics, books, or articles to have a visceral sense of this volatility. "Virtually everything about jobs and work and careers has changed," said Scott Uhrig, an executive recruiter for technology firms and author of *Navigating Successful Job Transitions*. "Just like the boiling frog, we may not fully appreciate the magnitude of the change even though we are completely immersed in it." Perhaps you are currently experiencing this boiling frog feeling in your career—if you have not already jumped out of the pot.

Some say the word *career* itself is dead—a throwback to a bygone era—as we move increasingly toward a project-based economy. Certainly, we can expect to experience significant changes every few years, much more often than was socially acceptable in the past. Because our careers are so fundamentally tied to our livelihood and sense of confidence, meaning, and purpose, these transitions can be traumatic without a road map for traversing them.

But this doesn't all have to be bad news. Navigating this accelerated pace of change and this transitional career state, learning to embrace it instead of resisting it, *can* become an edge and advantage. You can learn to enjoy calculated risk and uncertainty in exchange for adventure, flexibility, freedom, and opportunity.

By approaching their career transitions in a positive, methodical way, each of the people whose stories I shared earlier recalibrated toward more resonant trajectories:

- Amy sought to prove her value at her PR firm by taking on the projects that no one else wanted to do. In 2009, when it became increasingly clear that social media and blogger outreach were important for PR strategy, she volunteered to learn more about it—a job others in the company avoided, for fear of lowering their status by working with bloggers instead of marquee clients. Amy soon developed a reputation as the company's social media expert, consulting on all the biggest accounts and parlaying this expertise into a new role as director of digital entertainment.

- When he returned to the States after eight months abroad, Adam knew he wanted to combine his interests in fashion, technology, brand strategy, and entrepreneurship. He applied and was accepted into Parsons Business of Design graduate program, which helped build his skills, business acumen, and network over the following two years. After graduation, Adam remained in New York City, where he and his company, ABC Design Lab, are thriving.

- Tara had never lived outside of California, but had a hunch that moving to and working remotely from New Orleans, where she had been volunteering annually since Hurricane Katrina, would be the exact refresh her life needed. Within one year, Tara met a man, got engaged, and made the tough decision to quit her job. After taking off a year to have a baby, she returned to work as a consultant in the nonprofit sector for large-scale social impact programs.

- Inspired by a fortuitous meeting with a soon-to-be mentor on the day he was traded from the Raiders to the Broncos, Marques decided to pursue his master's degree in Adult Learning and Global Change at a university in Sweden after retiring from the NFL. A few years later he founded the World Education Foundation, and now travels the world launching initiatives in developing nations to create "improved human experiences in health, education, infrastructure, and sports."

- When Kyle first returned home to the States after serving in the Middle East in 2006, he said, "I was completely lost. That transition was like someone dropping me off in the middle of the desert. I didn't know what the hell to do with myself." He downshifted his military involvement, switching to part time in the reserves, and resolved to work for himself so that he could take control of his life and "never let someone else determine his future." Kyle went on to build a suite of companies, including an IT hardware company, a tax law and accounting practice, and a scalable contracts service for entrepreneurs called OurDeal.

- When the company he was working for got acquired, having served as a chief information officer for twenty-two years, John said he was looking forward to a next phase in his career, but had no plans to retire. Within five months of exploring, and allowing himself the freedom to focus more time on his love of travel and photography, he accepted a role as chief operations officer at a global cloud computing software company, his largest role to date. Bud was in a similar position, having spent twenty-five years on the road and ready for a transition that wasn't retirement. He shifted his consulting business online to spend more time at home. "This is legacy time," Bud said, noting that he, too, plans to continue working for at least another ten years.

- After Brian and Julie exhausted their options internally and opened themselves up to pushing past their career plateaus by switching companies, job offers for full-time leadership roles seemed to fall from the sky. Both were "poached"—sought out by recruiters based on their reputation and work history—for dream roles: Brian as senior vice president of engineering for a start-up company, and Julie as head of global people development for Chanel.

■ In 2011, I made the difficult decision to leave Google after my sabbatical and launch a full-time business based on my blog and recently released book. People reacted as if I were breaking up with Brad Pitt. *"You really think* you *can do better than Gooooogle?!"* I wasn't sure, but I knew I would forever regret not trying. So I rented out my condo, packed a suitcase, and moved from Silicon Valley to New York City. I have been running my own company in the years since as a career and business strategist, writer, and keynote speaker. I am the happiest and healthiest I have ever been. Even as my business goes through ups and downs, I feel calm and engaged with my work.

As much as we began from similar places of dissatisfaction, our stories all have something in common with how we proceeded, too. We each shifted to new, related work by leveraging our *existing* base of strengths, interests, and experience. Though it might seem as if each of us made drastic changes, we were not starting from scratch. In Silicon Valley parlance, we *pivoted*.

Eric Ries, author of the business bible *The Lean Startup* defines a business pivot as "a change in strategy without a change in vision."

I define a *career pivot* as doubling down on what is working to make a purposeful shift in a new, related direction. Pivoting, as we will refer to it in this book, is an intentional, methodical process for nimbly navigating career changes.

Typically when the word *pivot* is applied to a business strategy shift, it is considered Plan B: changing directions to save a business from dwindling profits or a dismal forecast. Pivoting was a response to failing at Plan A, the original goal. But when it comes to our careers, learning to pivot *is* Plan A. Pivoting, within our roles and throughout our careers, is the new normal.

Punctuated moments of career success—promotions, launches, and financial windfalls—are nice, but they are only a tiny fraction of our overall experience. By doubling down on what is working best while thinking about how to develop into what's next, you accelerate the experimentation and change process. You can proceed with confidence, knowing that you already have what it takes to get where you want to go.

Your choice, today and in the future, is to pivot or get pivoted. Pivoting is a mindset and a skill set, and you *can* get better at both. In this book I will share a framework to help you manage the process with focus, fulfillment, and—*dare I say*—fun.

CHANGING CAREERS IN THE AGE OF THE APP

Careers are no longer straightforward, linear, and predictable like ladders. They are now much more modular, customizable, and dynamic, like smartphones. Our education and our upbringing are the out-of-the-box model. After that, it is up to us to download the apps—for skills, interests, experiences, and education—that we want and need to feel fulfilled.

But what do you do when your entire operating system needs an upgrade? It is not as easy as clicking "update now" and waiting five minutes for shiny new features to set in. We are not machines; we are flawed, fear-prone, desire-driven, sometimes irrational, endlessly creative human beings.

Career changes seem to threaten our most fundamental needs on Maslow's hierarchy: food, shelter, clothing, and safety, in addition to higher-level needs for belonging, esteem, and even self-actualization. We are afraid that if we make one wrong move, we will soon become homeless (or forced to live in our parents' basement) and unemployed, unable to fend for our very survival. Perceiving this potential threat to our primary needs, we freeze, flee, or fight the nagging voice within us that seeks greater fulfillment.

As Stephen Grosz writes in *The Examined Life*, "All change involves loss." It is natural to fear change when we know that we must grieve what we may leave in its wake. Even the most exciting changes can be bittersweet, as they often involve letting something else go.

But many of us fear change for a more irrational reason: we anticipate worst-case scenarios, which may or may not occur. To remain calm and to have access to our most creative faculties, we must learn to see the new career change landscape as normal, expected, and part of a revolution ripe with opportunity. As my friend Monica's mother advises when she worries about the future, "Don't suffer twice."

In the career-as-smartphone analogy, pivoting is about learning to download apps one by one—or a few smaller apps simultaneously—so you can reduce risk, experiment with ideas, and enhance your career operating system without sending yourself into a panic by trying to make moves that are too drastic, too far removed from what you are doing right now.

You will never see the entire pivot path at the outset, nor would you want to. If the next steps were obvious and manageable with a simple spreadsheet, you would either already be taking them or you would be bored. The exhilarating part of tackling new opportunities is the inherent risk and uncertainty involved. It is the "call to adventure" from Joseph Campbell's Hero's Journey archetype, which necessitates that we venture into the land of the unknown and become bigger, more fully expressed versions of ourselves in the process.

What Is the Difference Between a Crisis and a Pivot?

There are certain life events that are all consuming; they rock us to the core, break us down, and torch the world as we knew it. The death of a loved one, disease, divorce, getting fired—all of these can be extremely traumatic. To call them pivot points would be a gross understatement.

A pivot is change you make of your own volition when you have reached a point in your career when you are ready for increased challenge and impact. Traumatic events, ones that leave you with the feeling that you are crawling out of your own skin, are most often not voluntary.

Certain events happen *to* us and they require space for patience, compassion, grief, and sometimes therapy or spiritual guidance in order to heal. These events demand a period of time to retreat, process, and regroup. Sometimes just waking up and making it through the day is an enormous accomplishment. Crises typically require more processing than planning, though not everyone will have the luxury to do those two things in sequence. It is likely that those in the throes of trauma need time to heal before embarking on the more proactive phases of pivoting.

In many cases, painful experiences also serve as powerful wake-up calls, encouraging us to rebuild in an even more authentic direction. I recommend books for each *Pivot stage* in the Pivot 201 section at the back of the book, but the two I suggest for processing major life events are *When Things Fall Apart* by Pema Chödrön, and *Second Firsts* by Christina Rasmussen.

CONNECT THE DOTS LOOKING BACKWARD

When I was twenty years old, I took a leave of absence from UCLA, where I was studying political science and communications, to join a political polling start-up in Silicon Valley as its first employee. This was my first pivot, and it kicked off my examination of what it takes to switch quickly and successfully from one trajectory to the next, even when it seems to go against the grain of what others are doing.

In hindsight I see my entire career as a series of pivots, within companies and also on my own, where I have made several smaller pivots in my business since:

- After two years at Polimetrix, where my role included managing our Google AdWords accounts, I landed a job at Google in training and development, teaching customer service representatives how to support the AdWords product.

- Next I pivoted within Google, moving from the AdWords product training team to the career development team, a move made easier after having attended the Coaches Training Institute on weekends to become a certified coach. On the career development team, I helped create and launch a global coach training program for managers called Career Guru, which made drop-in coaching available to any Googler—a program still cited as one of the benefits that make Google a top company to work for.

- While I was at Google, I started working on a hobby "side hustle" during nights and weekends—my first blog and book, *Life After College.* This became the springboard to my next big move, even though I had no clue for the first few years that it would eventually become my full-time occupation.

- When I left Google, I pivoted to launch my own career-consulting and speaking business. I shifted the *context* of my work environment, but not the *content*, given that I applied a similar set of strengths and activities. Two years after that, I expanded my platform to a website under my own name, JennyBlake.me, where I focus on systems at the intersection of mind, body, and business.

As Steve Jobs said in his 2005 Stanford commencement speech, "You can't connect the dots looking forward; you can only connect them looking backward." The days of mapping an entire career path are over. You do not have to specify the details of your life five moves or five years out. Consider what you were doing five years ago. Did you have any idea where you would be today? The challenge now is to be present. In doing so, we stay awake to the dots that are right in front of us.

I encourage you to reflect on your work history and connect the dots looking backward to see how you have *already* pivoted from one related area to the next. It is likely that, before even reading this book, many of these concepts will be things you have unknowingly applied in your own career.

I disagree with Jobs on one point: I *do* think it is possible to connect at least one or two dots looking forward. Maybe not with perfect detail, but we can get better at making the connection to our one next career step, and we must, as the economy demands that we all respond to change more deftly. By learning how to connect the dots looking backward *and then* forward, we can get better at making career connections in real time, not waiting too long until we are burned out, unhappy, or forced to make a change.

I have spent the last decade studying and reverse engineering career change, as my own life has been defined by these transitions. By reviewing through the lens of hindsight, examining my career and interviewing others, I uncovered patterns in what makes those transitions successful and what impedes them.

I have worked with people of all ages and career stages. Those who are most successful give themselves permission to explore continually, improving how quickly they spot their next move. They find and create cultures—whether in an office of one or ten thousand—that allow space to shift purposefully from one related area into the next.

While at Google I worked in the People Operations organization for five and a half years as the company skyrocketed from 6,000 to 36,000 employees. I trained over 1,000 people, from recent graduates to senior-level managers and directors, and saw how the feeling of bumping up against a career plateau affected everyone, not just entry-level workers. Moreover, both employees and managers wanted the same things—a happy, engaged, productive workforce—but did not always know how to close the communication gaps that opened between them when clarifying next career steps. When I started coaching entrepreneurs, I noticed how they, too, longed to create success without falling into the pressures of what "everyone else" was doing. They *had* to connect at least a few dots looking forward, on their own terms and based on their existing strengths, in order to stay in business.

Together, we will explore how to get better at this process no matter what work environment you are in. You can already connect your career dots looking backward to see how each related area led to the next; this book will teach you how to become an expert dot connector looking forward, now and in the future.

To operate this way, let go of expectations and fears about what *can* or *should* or *might* happen. Zoom back in to where you are right now, and where you want to go next. That is all you have to do. Once you make your next move, you will collect the experience and real-world data to plan the move after that.

When I was a freshman at UCLA I plotted all four years of required courses on a quarter-by-quarter, year-by-year spreadsheet to figure out how to double-major most efficiently. I printed this one-page, *next-four-years-of-my-life* plan, slipped it into a sheet protector, and followed it to the letter until I graduated, setting the stage for a rude awakening after graduation as I entered the unpredictable real world.

On one hand, my plan-heavy approach gave me the structure to jump at the opportunity to work at a start-up during my junior year, because I was ahead in my course work. However, this plan suffocated day-to-day spontaneity—and I missed out on following threads of exploration outside of checking boxes for maximum efficiency and compliance. After all, the best thing that happened to me in college, the job offer that set the stage for the rest of my career, was the one thing I *didn't* plan for.

PIVOT METHOD AT A GLANCE

Agile development is a collaborative approach to project management that emphasizes continual planning, testing, and launching. One of my favorite sayings from this business practice is "Each time you repeat a task, take one step toward automating it." Given that we will have many more career iterations than previous generations, it behooves us all to become better at the steps involved.

This book is structured around a four-stage process, the *Pivot Method*. Through each of the four stages—Plant, Scan, Pilot, and Launch—you will learn how to systematically bridge the gaps between where you are now and where you want to be.

In basketball, a pivot refers to a player keeping one foot firmly in place while moving the other in any direction to explore passing options. Much like a basketball player, successful pivots start by *planting* your feet—setting a strong foundation—then *scanning* the court for opportunities, staying rooted while exploring options. Scanning alone will not put points on the board, so eventually you start passing the ball around the court—testing ideas and getting feedback, or *piloting*—generating perspectives and opportunities to make a shot—eventually *launching* in the new direction.

Here is an overview of each stage in more detail:

- *Plant* by creating a foundation from your values, strengths, and interests, and your one-year vision for the future. The most successful pivots start from a strong base of who you *already* are, what is *already* working, and how you will define success for this next phase of your life.

- *Scan* by researching new and related skills, talking to others, and mapping potential opportunities. This is the exploration phase: identifying and plugging knowledge and skill gaps, and having a wide variety of conversations.

- Next, you will run a series of *pilots*—small, low-risk experiments to test your new direction. Pilots help gather real-time data and feedback, allowing you to adjust incrementally as you go, instead of relying on blind leaps.

- Eventually it is time for a bigger move, or *launch*. The first three stages of the Pivot Method, repeated as many times as necessary, help reduce risk and give you a greater chance of success, often taking you 80 to 90 percent of the way toward your goal. Launch is when you pull the trigger on the remaining 10 to 20 percent. These are the bigger decisions that require commitment even in the face of remaining uncertainty.

Pivot Cycle

Throughout the book you will find exercises, marked with an **E** *, to apply what you are learning and plan your pivot. All exercises have a corresponding template online that you can personalize at PivotMethod.com/toolkit.*

The book also includes a fifth and final stage, *lead*, that describes how organizations and leaders can apply the Pivot Method as a coaching framework for career conversations. The Pivot Method and mindset creates dynamic cultures that encourage employees to pivot internally and within their roles before looking for opportunities outside of the company, strengthening the organization as a whole through greater transparency and communication.

How Long Should a Pivot Take?

The Pivot Method is a cycle, not a one-and-done process. Some pivots take one month, while others can take years. Sometimes it takes several smaller pivots to reach your destination. Just as an 18-wheeler cannot turn on a dime, bigger pivots often require several smaller turns. Repeat the Plant-Scan-Pilot process as many times as necessary to gain clarity and gather feedback before advancing to the fourth stage, Launch.

Your pivot timing will depend on the scope of your change, how far your ideal end state is from where you are now, your risk threshold, your savings runway, your expertise and reputation, and the complexity of what you are building toward. Ultimately, *results* are the indicator of where you are in your pivot. Are you experiencing momentum and fulfillment? The income and energy that you desire? If not, you will return to the earlier Pivot stages to determine what adjustments to make.

I have worked through the Pivot Method with others in as little as ten minutes when demonstrating it as a coaching tool, and conversely have often spent one month or more on each of the four stages when working with individual coaching clients. The method works just as well when applied within sticking points on projects and business plans as it does for career moves.

I have shared versions of this coaching model in various forms with thousands of people to help them find career clarity. Because the method reveals latent strengths, pivoters will often express sentiments like, "I can't believe I didn't see this sooner, it seems so obvious in hindsight," or "I feel like my whole life and career have been unknowingly preparing me for this."

We might think we are in total control of our careers, but consider that they are working on our behalf behind the scenes. My pivots start shaping me long before I see them coming.

Embracing this reality requires surrender: admitting that we cannot plan in perfect specificity how the next ten, twenty, or thirty years of our lives will unfold. In surrendering, we make way for curiosity and serendipity.

Release the illusion of security within a fixed future and allow life to surprise you instead. The only move that matters is your next one.

A Note Before We Proceed

This book is not a rallying cry for quitting your job and fighting against "the man." There have been plenty of those since people discovered they could start a company from their laptop, live out of a suitcase, outsource every task, and work from a beach in Southeast Asia. And don't get me wrong—I have done all those things and felt alive while doing them. They are just not the whole story.

Nor is this book a caution to stay put, shackled by golden handcuffs, if you have hit a career plateau. I do not believe in resigning yourself to a subpar working life just because friends and family (whose top priority is often to keep us safe) or society tells us so.

It would be a mistake to assume that everyone should follow one path or the other, or to judge one as categorically better or worse. A *Pivot mindset* is not one that proposes reckless job hopping by quitting a job or folding a business at the first sign of displeasure. Rather, it emphasizes shifting naturally within your role and from one position into the next, while remaining open to a wide variety of options along the way.

Many people dip in and out of self-employment. Sometimes they work entirely for themselves or with partners, sometimes they take on longer-term consulting work with bigger companies, and sometimes they go back to work in other organizations full or part time. The most successful entrepreneurs I know are adept at working *with* companies, consulting for them as clients as they build their own businesses. After all, even the most nonconformist, hoodie-wearing coders may end up managing massive companies, becoming "the man" they once rebelled against.

The most successful employees I know are skilled at creative thinking and innovating within the organizations they work for as intrapreneurs. Many pivot within the companies they love, even crafting entirely new positions in the process. They know they can make a huge impact by leveraging the company's resources, while receiving a consistent paycheck to boot. They are able to build a portfolio of skills, experiences, and contacts within these companies that will stay with them for the rest of their careers.

———

There is no doubt that amplified anxiety lurks in the shadows of all this economic upheaval, innovation, and transformation. I will not discount your fears by telling you this career carving will always be easy and fun. It certainly can be, but it can also take work, focus, question asking, problem solving, and adapting to new tools and tactics.

Many of these skills are already in your wheelhouse. The opportunity now is to surface your strengths so that you will be ready and primed to pivot when a compelling opportunity knocks. Through the Pivot process, you can stop taking your struggles and searching personally, as shortcomings in your operating system, and start redirecting your valuable attention and brainpower toward what matters most.

There is no point in sugarcoating the truth: this new terrain can be challenging. But how you meet and interpret that challenge is paramount. You *can* learn to capitalize on risk, fear, insecurity, and uncertainty as the doorways of opportunity. So before we put the Pivot Method into practice, there is one critical element to explore in depth first: the mindset that makes it possible. If change is the only constant, let's get better at it.

HIGH NET GROWTH

I did stand-up comedy for eighteen years. Ten of those years were spent learning, four years were spent refining, and four were spent in wild success.

—Steve Martin, *Born Standing Up*

I WAS SITTING BEHIND A CARD TABLE IN THE STICKY TEXAS HEAT AT THE SOUTH by Southwest Conference in 2011, signing copies of *Life After College* at a small launch party. The books were not even in stores yet—they were truly "hot off the press." The first person in line walked up to the table and, as I started signing, asked, "So . . . what's next?"

I stuttered and stammered through an awkward reply. Even though he had the best intentions, I could not help but feel a bit deflated. It was so strange. Here was this massive project, this life goal embodied in a bound stack of paper, sitting in my hands after three years of staring down my gremlins to write it, and people were already asking *what's next.*

The truth was, I had no idea. I had just started three months of unpaid leave from Google, and as regularly as brushing my teeth, I agonized over my own next career move as the clock on my sabbatical ticked down. Every day I struggled with what the right decision would be: return to Mountain View after my book tour, ask to work part time from New York City, or leave the company altogether? Should I make the safe, secure choice? Or should I take the risk of leaving and do the thing that terrified and excited me most by taking my own business full time?

Though I loved my time at Google—it was the best five-year MBA I could ask for—ultimately I felt I could make the biggest contribution if I pursued a new direction. I ran the numbers: I could support up to 35,000 Googlers at the time through internal career development programs, or I could leave and try to expand my reach and global impact to a far greater number, following my personal mission to be as helpful as possible to as many people as possible.

Some people measure their lives in terms of money, orienting their careers around acquiring wealth and material markers of success. Those who have accumulated financial wealth are considered *high net worth individuals*. But for the vast majority of people I encounter, money is *not* the number one driver of purpose and fulfillment. It is only a partial means to that end. A study by Daniel Kahneman and Angus Deaton confirms this: once people surpass $75,000 in annual net income ($82,000 in today's dollars), they experience no statistically significant bump in their day-to-day emotional well-being.

For many, money is nice to have, but not at the expense of soul-crushing work, if they have the economic flexibility to choose otherwise. The people I am talking about, and the ones for whom this book will resonate most, are those who are unwilling to settle for a career of phoning it in. They are willing to pay dues, but are not prepared to sit stalled for long, unable to see the value or impact of their work.

These individuals optimize for *high net growth* and *impact*, not just high net worth. I call them *impacters* for short. Impacters love learning, taking action, tackling new projects, and solving problems. They are generous and cooperative, and imbued with a strong desire to make a difference.

Impacters aim first and foremost for a sense of momentum and expansion. They ask, "Am I learning?" When their inward desire for growth is being met, they turn their attention outward, seeking to make a positive impact on their families, companies, communities, and global societies. Often these happen in tandem; by seeking problems they can fix and tackling them, impacters meet their needs for exploration and challenge, uncovering callings along the way.

Stanford University psychologist Carol Dweck, author of *Mindset: The Psychology of Success*, discovered in her research that the most successful people are those with a growth mindset. These are people who believe that their basic qualities are things they can cultivate through their efforts, rather than believing their gifts (or lack of them) are fixed traits. The truth, Dweck says, is that brains and talent are just the starting point. "The passion for stretching yourself and sticking to it, even (or especially) when it's not going well, is the hallmark of the growth mindset," Dweck writes. "This is the mindset that allows people to thrive during some of the most challenging times in their lives."

Maintaining a growth mindset is critical to navigating a pivot successfully. By seeing change as an opportunity, rather than a personal shortcoming or obstacle, you will be much more likely to find creative solutions based on what excites you, rather than subpar choices clouded by fear. Making career moves based solely on running from unhappiness and avoiding fear is like trying to fix a gaping wound with a Band-Aid; the solution does not stay in place for long. With a growth mindset, you will be open to new ideas, observant in your experimentation, deliberate in your implementation, and flexible in the face of change.

Fixed *anything* doesn't work for impacters, who are allergic to stagnation and boredom. Author Tim Ferriss captured this sentiment in *The 4-Hour Workweek*, saying, "The opposite of love is indifference, and the opposite of happiness is . . . boredom." It turns out that boredom itself can induce stress, causing the same physical discomfort as too much work: increased heart rate and cortisol levels, as well as muscle tension, stomachaches, and headaches.

For impacters, boredom is a symptom of fulfillment deficiency—of not maximizing for growth and impact—rather than a sign of inherent laziness. As University of Waterloo professor of neuroscience James Danckert wrote, "We tend to think of boredom as someone lazy, as a couch potato. It's actually when someone is motivated to engage with their environment and all attempts to do so fail. It's aggressively dissatisfying."

In her 1997 study, Dr. Amy Wrzesniewski, associate professor of organizational behavior at Yale University's School of Management, proposed that people see their work as a job, career, or calling. Those with a *job* orientation see work as a means to the end of paying the bills; those with a *career* orientation are more likely to emphasize success, status, and prestige; and those with a *calling* describe work as integral to their lives, a core part of their identity and a fulfilling reward in itself. Impacters fall clearly into the second category and aspire to the third, if they are not already there.

Impacters are not just asking *What did I earn?* but *What did I learn? What did I create? What did I contribute?* They measure their quality of life by how much they are learning, challenged, and contributing. If they are doing all three intelligently and intentionally, they work hard to ensure that the money will follow.

It is not that impacters are not interested in money—they are. They have no desire to live as starving artists. They know it is challenging, if not impossible, to focus on others if one's own basic needs are not met first. But when faced with the prospect of a career plateau, they would make the horizontal move, leave the cushy corporate job, or bootstrap their own business to prioritize growth and impact. A person who aims for learning and contribution may rank intellectual capital over financial capital if pressed to choose, but often ends up wealthy in both.

Take Christian Golofaro and John Scaife, who traded coffee and cotton in the open outcry pits on Wall Street for five years. Tired of the daily pressures of their jobs and looking for meaning beyond buying and selling commodities, they pooled their money in 2014 to start an urban farming business in Red Hook, Brooklyn. They sought to help revolutionize food production by bringing fresh, local, pesticide-free produce to New York City year-round. They were more inspired as impacters in their new business, SpringUps, than they ever were in finance.

Though he spent thousands of hours in high school and college preparing for a career in medicine, Travis Hellstrom decided to join the Peace Corps after graduation instead. He gave up his full ride to medical school and moved to Mongolia, where he served in the Peace Corps for over three years, living on two hundred dollars a month. When Travis reflects on the decision, he says, "It took a lot of soul-searching and being okay with disappointing myself and others, but I left my life and found my calling." After he returned, Travis pivoted again to nonprofit coaching and community management. Several years later, he parlayed that independent consulting work into a role as chair of the Mission-Driven Organizations graduate program at Marlboro University.

Impacters continue learning and contributing throughout their working lives, which often extend far past what is traditionally thought of as retirement age. When I asked Kyle Durand about his impending retirement from the military after twenty-seven years of service, his sentiments reflected those of many people I know who have no plans to retire in the traditional sense.

"I think retirement is an antiquated notion. The whole idea that you work for most of your adult life in order to eventually do the things you want is outmoded," Kyle said. "My retirement from the military is simply closing the chapter on that part of my career, but it is not the end of my working days by any stretch. Now I can shift into building my businesses full time. That is my future, part of my legacy. That is how I want to make an impact with the people I care about."

Christian, John, Travis, and Kyle pivoted in new directions that were more aligned with their values, interests, and goals, even though there was not a guarantee of success. As impacters, they saw these changes as opportunities for growth and recognized that their ability to learn and adapt would help them land on their feet no matter what. This helped them maintain a positive outlook throughout their pivots, knowing they would benefit from following their instincts and aspirations instead of societal expectations, no matter the outcome.

As I was writing this book, many of the people I initially interviewed returned six months or one year later and said things like, "Don't bother putting my story in the book. I am pivoting again."

This manifested in a variety of ways: they got poached by another company for an even better role; their company folded, got acquired, or got sold; they decided not to pursue a new skill or industry after all; they realized entrepreneurship was or was not for them; or they shifted their business into a more promising new direction.

Hearing these updates did not surprise me, nor did it mark their initial pivot as a failure. Instead, they are prime examples of what it means to be high net growth and impact individuals. I *expect* to hear that impacters are pivoting and adjusting dynamically at every turn.

For a directory of people featured in this book and what they are up to now, visit PivotMethod.com/people; for audio interviews and episodes from the Pivot Podcast, visit JennyBlake.me/podcast.

CAREER OPERATING MODES

An essential facet of the Pivot mindset is self-awareness. How are you currently showing up in your day-to-day work? Are you operating at your desired energy levels, creative output, and impact? I have observed four primary Career Operating Modes among pivoters: inactive, reactive, proactive, and innovative. The first two are impacter stressors, the latter two are sweet spots:

- **Inactive:** Does not seek changes; paralyzed by fear, uncertainty, and self-doubt; covers up career or life dissatisfaction with unhealthy habits, such as numbing out with excessive amounts of food, alcohol, TV, video games, and so on; feels and acts like a victim of circumstances.

- **Reactive:** Mimics others' models for success without originality; follows instructions to the letter; waits for inspiration to strike; "phones it in" at work; feels unhappy, but does not inquire into why or what to do about it; lets fear overrule planning for the future and subsequent action steps.

- **Proactive:** Seeks new projects; actively learns new skills; is open to change; improves existing programs; makes connections with others; takes ownership even within existing leadership structures; has a giver mentality, willing and interested in helping others. May not be fully using innate talents, but is exploring what they are and how to amplify them.

- **Innovative:** In addition to proactive mode qualities, fully taps into unique strengths; focuses on purpose-driven work and making meaningful contributions; is energized by a strong vision for new projects with a clear plan for making them happen; does not just improve existing structures, but creates new solutions to benefit others.

Impacters thrive in situations where they are able to be *proactive* and, even more so, *innovative* in driving their career forward, implementing new ideas and creatively solving problems, stretching to the edges of what is possible for themselves and the companies they start or work for. When impacters find themselves in *inactive* or *reactive* operating mode, they look to pivot again toward a new, more engaging opportunity.

Although it is true that some people may work in inactive or reactive mode for their entire careers, this is not a life that impacters can stomach. The boredom, anxiety, and feeling of standing still becomes increasingly intolerable, often manifesting in physical symptoms such as headaches, getting sick more frequently, or worse.

At these critical pivot points, impacters must recognize this tension and take action. Otherwise the unhappiness from staying still for too long

Plateau Versus Pivot

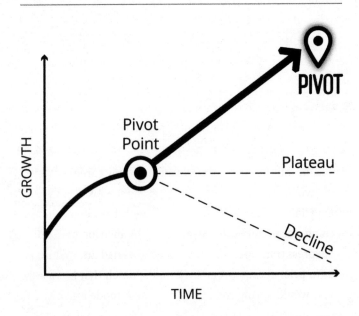

compounds, making the career confusion feel insurmountable, and taking it from conundrum to crisis.

Though they may get restless more easily, impacters do have a distinct advantage: by seeing career boosts *and* setbacks as learning opportunities, all outcomes become fodder for growth. Nassim Nicholas Taleb captures this concept in the six-word title of his book *Antifragile: Things That Gain from Disorder.*

Antifragile organisms do not simply withstand change and survive it; they become better *because* of it. A glass is fragile. If you drop it, it breaks. A tree is resilient. In strong winds, it sways but stays standing, more or less remaining the same. Organisms that are antifragile actually *benefit* from shocks. Taleb invokes Hydra, the creature from Greek mythology: when one of Hydra's many heads is cut off, two grow back in its place. The tough-times cliché is true: what doesn't kill you makes you stronger. According to Taleb, antifragile organisms "thrive and grow when exposed to volatility, randomness, disorder, and stressors," and "love adventure, risk, and uncertainty."

Love risk and uncertainty? *Huh?* Aren't these things to be mitigated, if not entirely eliminated? Not if you want to be antifragile in a world that is ruled by them. Impacters find ways to thrive in uncertainty and disorder. Rather than merely reacting to randomness or becoming paralyzed by it, they look for opportunities to alchemize what is already working into what comes next.

TRUST YOUR RISK TOLERANCE

After much deliberation, I chose not to return to Google after my sabbatical. That is when I first realized that financial security and great benefits were important to me, but not the ultimate drivers of my career decisions.

I knew it would not be fair to Google or to my book to give both projects short shrift by taking on too much. I also knew that I could not sustain the pace of keeping side projects and a full-time job much longer. I was exhausted and on the express train back to burnout, where I had unfortunately been too many times in prior years. Moreover, I had a hunch that leaving to start my own business would spring me out of proactive mode and challenge me to become the innovative impacter I longed to be. So in July 2011, I became a free agent.

Fast-forward one year and once more I was struggling, racking my brain about what's next . . . *again.* I would be turning thirty soon, and although I was proud of *Life After College,* I did not want to talk about it exclusively for the rest of my career. At the same time, in speeches and interviews, I had become known as "the girl who left Google." Even during my time there, I often felt uncomfortable with how much of my identity and professional self-worth was tied up in the company's shadow, and here I was again, facing the same issue from another perspective.

I was defined by *leaving* things, but wanted to look ahead to a more energizing mission. What did I stand for? What problems was I passionate about solving? How could I build a sustainable business that would help me make a meaningful impact on others' lives?

For the next two years I wrestled with these questions, this time without a steady paycheck to fund the exploration. It was much more nerve-racking as my livelihood now depended on the answer.

My tireless brainstorming took me further from myself, not closer. I circled around *big* ideas, *big* bets, and *big* leaps. But really, I kept entertaining options *out there.* Although any one could have been a brilliant idea to pursue over the next six months, they were not going to help me pay my bills *this* month.

I felt like I was on a spinning teacup ride: I was dizzy, tired of circling vague ideas without a clear way forward, and nauseated about how to support myself. *I am a grown adult,* I thought. *There is no excuse for this.*

I understand now that I made the same mistake I see other pivoters making: underestimating what I was capable of, particularly in a sink-or-swim situation, by looking too far outside of myself for answers. I set my sights on next steps that were inaccessible given my starting point and timeline, and that ultimately prevented me from making real progress.

Barring massive events outside of our control, there *is* a sweet spot for when and how to pivot. You probably won't know with 100 percent certainty when to make your next big career move, but you can get a lot smarter about how you reduce the risks and potential margin for error—error in the sense that you end up worse off than you are now.

We all have a different risk tolerance. What is risky for someone else may be a snoozefest for you. Take your risk temperature by identifying which of the four zones you currently fall into on the Riskometer diagram below. Keep these distinctions in mind as you proceed with your pivot. Pay attention to when you start playing it too safe (when you might find yourself slipping from the comfort zone into stagnation), when something feels edgy but exciting (stretch zone), or when a next step seems too overwhelming or extreme (panic zone).

Riskometer

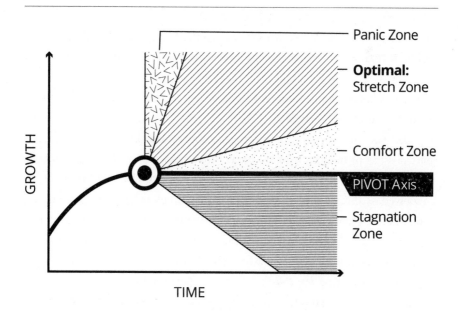

Riskometer Reading

- **Stagnation zone:** Restless, antsy, trapped, anxious, or bored. May start manifesting as physical symptoms and health problems.

- **Comfort zone:** Feeling good about the status quo; daily life doesn't demand much deep thinking about the direction of your career. Work is "fine."

- **Stretch zone:** Challenged, excited, and motivated to get out of bed every day. Actively learning; work may be unpredictable, but you feel engaged.

- **Panic zone:** Anxiety is starting to dominate your thoughts; you are not able to think long term about the future because you are dealing with things that are "on fire" in your day-to-day life. Or, if contemplating next steps, you feel so paralyzed by fear that you end up doing nothing.

Career pivots can stretch us to our maximum capacity, and often even a bit further, but they do not have to be debilitating. Working through the four Pivot stages will help you avoid extremes on the risk spectrum: neither taking a blind leap, nor analyzing yourself into the ground by overcalculating every step. The ideal range for change for impacters is in the stretch zone: the place where you feel challenged, excited, and focused, with a healthy dose of adrenaline propelling you forward.

One way to visualize the amount of risk, reward, and work required for your pivot is to imagine plotting your move on a graph. With time on the x-axis, and growth on the y-axis, the degree, or incline, of your next move can be viewed as the amount of resources it consumes in time, money, energy, and effort. A pivot can be subtle, say a 20-degree turn, such as moving to a new team at work. Or a pivot can be sharper, say 70 degrees, such as switching industries or leaving your job to start a business.

Avoid pivots that are *too* sharp, too far past your stretch zone—what I call 180s. These are dramatic leaps of faith that have little to do with your current role or skill set, which means there are too many unknowns that you would be gambling on when you launch. However, even what sometimes looks like a 180 from the outside might actually be, in execution, a pivot comprising a series of smaller steps that paved the way for larger change.

If your mission makes your heart sing, but the idea of launching into it tomorrow gives you a serious case of anxiety—or *agita*, as Italians would say—build incrementally toward the final Launch stage by planting, scanning, and piloting.

TWO (MANY) STEPS AHEAD, ONE STEP BACK

Thinking too many steps ahead about how to pivot my career and business in those first years after my book was published sent me into my panic zone. I was choked by fear, which was magnified by not knowing how I would consistently cover the basic practicalities of my life. As they say in the financial world, I was about to "blow up." If I blew up, it would be time to get another full-time job. There is nothing objectively wrong with that, but every cell of my body told me that it was not the answer for me, at least not yet.

All of a sudden it hit me: not once did I thoroughly examine my *existing* strengths. My book. My speaking engagements. The websites I had been building for seven years. The work activities I loved, who I knew, how I was already earning income. Any of these assets, if I was to dig deeper into them, could reveal a bounty of ten more related areas to pursue. I was so ready for *the Next Big Thing* that I shut myself off from looking at what was already working.

I realized I had dozens of apps *already* downloaded—skills, interests, and past experiences—all working in my favor, but that I had not been fully using. I had been so focused on what was *not* working, or what I did *not* yet have clarity on, that my transition turmoil lasted longer than necessary.

I felt tremendous relief when I stopped blaming myself for my career confusion and started taking smarter, more focused steps. Combing my past for clues to my future gave me a sense of buoyancy and relief: *I can figure this out.*

I started to celebrate the many things I was proud of and began experimenting with small extensions of the strengths and experiences I had been accumulating throughout my career. This boosted my confidence and empowered me to solve the puzzle sitting right in front of me, with new insight into the pieces already at my disposal.

In January of that key pivot year, I questioned how I would pay my rent. By December, my business was in its most profitable year ever. For the first time, I surpassed six figures, nearly tripling my income from the three years prior. I reconnected with an even stronger sense of focus and flow in my work. Not because a lightning bolt of luck struck me from above—though there were plenty of lucky encounters—but because I was determined to do things differently. I did not just happen upon my confidence again, I aggressively pursued it.

This is the book I wish I'd had during that time: A practical, tactical guide for the trenches of answering what's next. A blueprint for getting unstuck, taking smart risks, and navigating uncertainty now and in the future. A book that would help me, and all of us, stop spinning and refocus all that brilliant energy back where it belongs—on making a positive difference for as many people as we are able to in this lifetime.

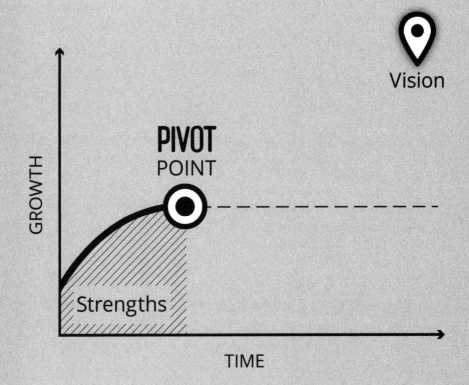

STAGE ONE

PLANT

What Is Working and
Where Do You Want to End Up?

PLANT

SCAN

PILOT

LAUNCH

LEAD

PLANT OVERVIEW

THE PLANT STAGE IS THE CRUX OF YOUR PIVOT, WHERE YOU WILL DEVELOP THE most leverage for the stages that follow. For this reason I encourage you to spend more time with this stage than you might think is necessary, or than you may have given these subjects in the past.

The primary goal of the Plant stage is grounding. Rather than aimlessly searching "out there" or building from scratch, the most successful pivots start from a strong foundation of your core values, a clear understanding of your strengths and interests, and a compelling vision for the future. Without these critical elements, you will be reading, talking, second-guessing, and analyzing ad nauseum without gaining any traction—a car spinning its wheels in mud. Ignoring your existing assets and looking too far ahead will leave you working hard but stuck in place.

Given that earning a living is so closely tied to our most basic needs of food, clothing, and shelter, one of the biggest constraints on a pivot is money. In this stage you will also set a strong financial foundation to help inform your pivot timeline.

Why Start from What's Working?

According to Tom Rath, author of the book *StrengthsFinder 2.0* and accompanying strengths assessment, only one-third strongly agree with the statement, "At work, I have the opportunity to do what I do best every day." Those who *do* have the opportunity to focus on their strengths every day are six times as likely to be engaged in their jobs, and more than three times as likely to report having an excellent quality of life in general.

You have probably found this to be true in your own career. When you invest in what comes naturally and easily to you—in work that makes time fly—your ability to make an impact, and enjoy yourself while doing it, is exponentially higher.

I emphasize what is working because I know you are already tired of what is *not* working. What *isn't* working already keeps you up at night. It is what you are venting to friends and family about, and yes, they are getting as sick of it as you are. What is not working is simply not all that helpful, except as an indicator of what you *do* want. If your mind jumps back to what isn't working throughout the exercises, follow up by asking what the opposite would be. What do you want instead?

Often the more stuck someone is, the more they tell me what is *not* working and what they *don't* want, even when I ask forward-looking questions such as, "What does smashing success look like one year from now?" They might reply, "Well, I don't want to feel stuck. I don't like not having time to myself at the end of the day. I hate feeling so stressed out. I don't want to feel like that anymore."

Although it seems like they are clear on some aspects of how to move forward, this information is not all that useful. These are shallow clues that don't build a life or a game plan. The positive qualities here might be:

Success looks like waking up after a full night's sleep, ideally at 6:30 A.M. I would love to start my day meditating, reading, or going for a run. Work energizes me, and I am collaborating with people in a dynamic, open environment, on projects that match my strengths. I get along with my team and have stimulating conversations throughout the day. I head out around 5 P.M. to go for a walk and cook a healthy dinner. I wind down for a few hours by unplugging completely

from my devices, except for watching a favorite TV show or two. I
head to bed by 10 P.M. unless I am going out with friends.

Which future scenario would motivate you more?

CHAPTER 1: CALIBRATE YOUR COMPASS

What Are Your Guiding Principles?
What Is Your Happiness Formula?

The key to the ability to change is a changeless sense of who you are, what you are about and what you value.

—Stephen R. Covey, *The 7 Habits of Highly Effective People*

WHEN YOU SEARCH FOR A PLACE TO STAY ON AIRBNB, YOU NARROW DOWN THE choices with criteria such as price, location, size, and amenities. Your dream room might be someone else's nightmare. Think about your values as life filters, the search criteria that help clarify your priorities. They are rules of thumb for what makes you most fulfilled, the core operating principles by which you live your life. Even if you have not yet expressed your values in words, they are already a part of who you are and how you make decisions.

In a pivot, your values create boundaries and benchmarks for big decisions. They distill the possibilities of what to pursue, help determine next steps, and reveal how to structure day-to-day activities for maximum happiness and productivity.

Making choices that are in line with what is most important to you feels affirming and satisfying, even when those choices are difficult. Acting in ways that feel disingenuous or deflating let you know a value is being suppressed or actively ignored. For example, telling the truth satisfies a value of integrity, even if it risks making another person upset. Telling a lie or staying quiet to keep the peace does not honor this value, and you end up feeling resentful for neglecting it.

Although they are not likely to change drastically over the course of your life, values may shift in priority at different stages. Major shake-ups can inspire us to take a hard look at what is most important to us, and where the gaps are between what we *say* we believe in and how we are actually spending our time, energy, and resources.

You might think that starting with values and vision is too abstract to be helpful, or that they will be hard to pin down. But I caution you not to skip the exercises in this section. Clarifying your values and vision is one of the biggest accelerators you have during a pivot, and the questions are directly within your control to answer.

CREATE YOUR COMPASS

Justin came to me at a time when he knew he wanted to pivot his career, but was unsure about the direction to take. He lacked confidence after what he felt were a few false starts in his early twenties: resigning from Teach for America, then starting and shuttering a health coaching and personal training practice. He found refuge in a real estate job in his family's business.

But he soon felt stuck in his current situation, and his latent childhood heart problems returned, despite maintaining strong health habits. This may have been an indicator that Justin's work-related stress was manifesting physically, sending him signals to make a more significant change sooner rather than later.

Our first steps were to explore his values and true goals, not what he felt he *should* do based on family expectations or obligations. Justin then identified his top values: financial security, physical fitness and health, feeling alive, loving where he lives, and enjoying relationships with like-minded people. These became a lens through which to explore daily activities and more fulfilling next moves.

Next, Justin and I talked about career options and how they aligned with his values, such as whether to restart his health coaching business or to pursue an MBA. It was important not to immediately discount ideas, like teaching or starting a health camp for teens, that contradicted what he thought his family and friends would approve of.

Our early work together was like a game of hotter/colder, the guessing game many of us played as kids. You hide something and as the other person wanders around looking, you guide them by saying only "cold, colder, FREEZ-ING," or "hot, hotter, ON FIRE!"

Some options felt cold and deflating, particularly when they included the word *should*, such as staying at his job and living on the East Coast. Other ideas felt hot and exhilarating, such as moving to California to attend business school. Earlier false starts, experiences that Justin once viewed as failures, became clues that Justin and I collected to map his values and plan his pivot.

Your next career move speaks to you in much the same way. It may not be able to communicate in words, but as you explore a range of opportunities, if you are paying attention and taking enough quiet time to reflect, each area you explore will provide its own hotter or colder signal in your body. You might speak with someone and feel "HOT, HOT, HOT!" afterward, a magnetic pull to learn more about what he does or where he lives. Or you might find yourself interviewing for a position and feeling freezing, even though the job looks good on paper. Don't let these cold indicators discourage you. Instead, use them to refine your values further.

A few months into our coaching work, Justin was accepted into his first-choice business school with a scholarship. He moved to San Diego, formed a new circle of inspiring friends, and lined up career opportunities for the short term that fit his strengths, with a long-term goal of returning to the family business after graduate school. Each of these elements mapped strongly to his core values. Justin said he finally felt like himself again: strong, confident, grounded, proud of his career path, and ready to tackle anything with a renewed sense of vigor and integrity.

E Values Mining

These exploration exercises will help you build the foundation of your entire Pivot strategy, guiding decisions throughout the process. They progress from high-level ideas to a refined values list by the end.

In Steps One and Two, aim for quantity, not quality. Don't censor yourself. For each question, write whatever first comes to mind, then push yourself to ask follow-up questions such as *What is important to me about that?* and *What else?*

Step One: Free Write

Answer the following questions:

- Describe your ideal day. If money was not an issue, how would you spend your time?
- What excites you most?
- What are you most proud of?
- What is the compliment or acknowledgment you hear most often?
- If someone was to interview your family and/or closest friends, what would they say you value most?
- Think of a peak time in your life—a time of adventure, joy, or peace. It may be a moment in time, or it may have happened over a long period. Describe it with as many vivid details as possible. What makes this memory so powerful? Take yourself back to that time: What do you see? Hear? Taste? Smell? What are you thinking? How do you feel?
- Name three people you admire and list three adjectives for why you chose each person.
- What do you want less of in your life?
- What challenges are you currently facing?
- What are your unanswered questions at the moment?
- Are there any areas in your life where you feel out of balance or as if you are missing something?
- What do you want more of in your life?

Step Two: Values Clusters

Circle or make a list of all of the key words or phrases that jump out at you from the answers above. After you review the initial list, add additional themes you might have missed that are important to you. Here are some values clusters I see often among clients:

- Connection, community, friends, family, intimacy
- Creativity, innovation, ideas, writing, expression
- Courage, risk taking, challenge
- Freedom, independence
- Financial security
- Gratitude, being present, mindfulness, rest and rejuvenation
- Health and wellness routines, sense of balance
- Humor, play, recreation
- Helping others, making a difference, influence, impact, teaching, service, reach
- Learning, growing, exploring, travel, adventure

Step Three: Make a Mind Map

Next, on a sheet of paper, write the word *values* in the middle of a page, circle it, then draw spokes to each of the values you brainstormed above (see example below). Add tertiary spokes radiating from each value with one- to two-word answers to the following questions:

- What is important about each one?
- How is each value most fully expressed in your life?

This exercise will help clarify how your values manifest in your life. For example, from a value of *freedom*, you might draw spokes to phrases such as financial security, flexible schedule, ability to travel, and work autonomy. From a value of *helping others*, you might have teaching, mentoring, sharing experiences, volunteering, and a few groups or organizations that matter to you.

Here is an example of one of my values mind maps:

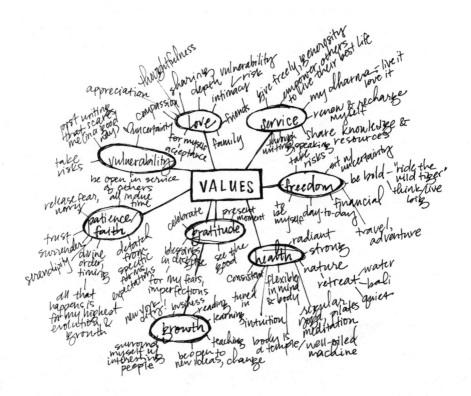

Step Four: Rank Your List

On your mind map, circle the one word or phrase that best represents each value. Write five to ten of these values on their own Post-it Note, stick the notes on a wall or the back of your front door, then rank them in order of importance. If you had to make a choice where two were in conflict, which would you select? In real life we hardly have to make such delineated rankings of our values, but the exercise will help you clarify the ones that matter most.

Group similar themes and eliminate values that are not absolutely critical to your health and happiness, creating a short list that is easy to remember. Reflect over the course of one week, as daily experiences may provide additional clarity.

Step Five: Narrow Down and Rename

Review your mind map and the Post-it ranking exercise to home in on your top five values. These are your oxygen, your must-haves, the elements that are crucial to your well-being. Feel free to get creative with the names; pick labels that make sense to you and that best capture each value's essence. Here are two of my more creatively named values, still relevant, that I shared in *Life After College*:

> *CLEAN-BURNING FIRE—Contribute positive, passionate energy to the world. Bring optimism, good cheer, and a smile to a room or a conversation whenever I can. Be conscious of my impact on others.*

> *RIDE THE WILD TIGER—Live big! Take risks. Do things that make me uncomfortable, that challenge what I think is possible. There is no saddle, there are no reins. Enjoy and adjust to the crazy ups, downs, and surprises that life throws my way.*

Step Six: Create a Visual Reminder

Put 'em where you can see 'em! You might want to write your values list on a small piece of paper to keep in your wallet, make a wallpaper image for your computer or phone, keep a Post-it Note by your desk, or design a more creative visual representation, like a Pinterest board, that you can add to over time. You may refer to this visual reminder often throughout the Pivot process, then at some point the values will become ingrained and you will be able to recall them easily.

Think of this as your own personalized decision scorecard. When you bump up against a particularly tricky dilemma, revisit the list and rank how each option (or even how your life in general) meets each value on a scale of 1 to 5.

IDENTIFY YOUR HAPPINESS FORMULA

One morning I was sitting at my desk, bleary eyed after returning from a week of travel. All of a sudden, I had an out-of-body experience as I watched myself angrily slam my fists on my desk in exasperation because my wireless mouse got disconnected for the umpteenth time. It was a cartoon moment: every item—books, papers, speakers—jumped two inches in the air and scattered back down.

Yikes. *Red flag, much?*

I am not normally an impatient person, but that morning my fuse was short, if not completely blown. I couldn't fix my mood with mental gymnastics or ignore it—clearly that had not been working.

Then it occurred to me: it had been five days since my last bout of vigorous exercise. My eyes darted from my clock, to my to-do list, to my e-mail inbox. I didn't exactly feel like I had the time for a short run, but I certainly did not have the time for hair-trigger frustration and a sour mood the rest of the day either. Everything on my list could wait the twenty minutes it would take to get some endorphins flowing. I laced up my running shoes and headed out the door. Sure enough, after a run and a cup of coffee, my mood and productivity bounced back.

One of the keys to being agile in life is knowing how to quickly find your way back to equilibrium. It is difficult, if not impossible, to pivot from a place of anxiety or unhappiness. Your ability to proceed with the next Pivot stages will be severely hampered if you are weighed down by people, habits, an environment, or activities that drain you.

Your happiness formula is the unique mix of environmental factors and activities that are most likely to invigorate you and reset your energy batteries when they are running low. As you plan your pivot, think of your happiness formula on a micro level—day-to-day routines and five- to twenty-minute habits—and on a macro level of bigger choices like where to live and work.

What micro and macro elements are most important to build into your life? Your happiness formula might contain a mix and match of the following:

Happiness Formula			
	Mental/Emotional/Spiritual	Physical	Social
Micro/Daily	Creating a morning routine Reading Meditating Spiritual practices Journaling	Getting outside Spending time in nature Going for a walk Taking a fitness class	Meeting a friend for coffee or a meal Cooking with others Talking to friends and family on the phone Spending quality time with loved ones
Macro/Lifestyle	Living in an energizing city Creating a comforting home environment Taking weekend trips Working on creative projects	Exercising regularly Getting 7–8 hours of sleep a night Eating healthy meals	Attending cultural or sporting events Volunteering regularly Taking classes Hosting gatherings Long-term traveling

E Define Your Happiness Formula

Translate your values from abstract concepts into real-life practices by filling in your own chart. What daily activities and morning routines are critical to your happiness formula? What macro lifestyle factors are most important? For both categories, note what you are doing well and what you may be missing.

You can even write this out as an actual formula, like my friend Bill Connolly did when I shared this approach with him. His equation is: (Creating) + (Friends and Family) + (Traveling) – (Being Scared) = Happiness.

YOUR BODY IS YOUR BUSINESS

When you are coasting in a comfort zone, you can afford to get a bit lazy. You can overspend, overeat, overdrink, or skip your workout for a few days and you will still have some flex in your system to absorb it. There is more margin for error. But when you are in the middle of a pivot, you need every cell in your body to be high functioning. You will already be on overdrive during this time, asking and answering life's biggest questions.

Willpower is a limited resource. While grappling with important decisions, you have less mental bandwidth available for other things. You will already be prone to feeling more sensitive, so health swerves that did not affect you much in the past will have a greater impact now.

In times of stress, our bodies are often among the first things we neglect, if not actively abuse. But your body is your most valuable asset during a pivot. With so much change, it is important to actively recruit all your natural feel-good chemicals—serotonin, oxytocin, dopamine, and endorphins—while minimizing spikes in cortisol, the stress hormone.

This is a time to guard against numbing out with food, alcohol, drugs, TV, video games, social media, or a smorgasbord of all of the above. Numbing out is an impulse many of us have when life gets more intense than we can bear, but there are significant benefits to breaking these habits, even when it seems toughest to do.

Do not just take my word for it—test things for yourself. Pay close attention to what elevates your mood, performance, creativity, and physical and emotional resilience, and what kills them. The second glass of wine might *seem* completely harmless—and maybe it has been throughout your adult life—until it becomes a slippery slope to the third, and you wake up the next morning feeling foggy headed or downbeat on a day you need to grapple with complex pivot questions.

You be the judge. If something works, it stays. If it detracts from your optimal mood and performance, it's gotta go, no matter how tough the habit is to break. Kick the crutch. Once you have made it through the belly of the pivot beast, you can reintroduce these indulgences, but you may feel so good without them that you no longer want to.

If you find yourself discombobulated at any stage of your pivot, you will benefit from returning to the health fundamentals of nutrition, sleep, and exercise. Strip your life down to the most productive and healthy habits so that you have a clean system from which to operate. If you are hitting a wall, troubleshoot your physical foundation first to find mental clarity. Go for a walk or run, eat healthier for a week (or month), meditate for ten minutes, take a nap, or go outside. Peace of mind is the dividend we collect from paying for the day with supportive habits.

REDUCE DECISION FATIGUE

Your existing routines are likely to get shaken up through the Pivot process, so it is imperative to reestablish anchors in your day. Without habits and routines to systematize your well-being, decision fatigue will set in.

In a *Harvard Business Review* article, Roger Martin wrote that many companies today have stopped making widgets and are instead producing decisions; we have become "decision factories." Our working hours are spent coming up with ideas and strategies, talking about them in meetings, building consensus, and implementing them to achieve results. And just as willpower is proven to be a finite resource, so, too, are our cognitive abilities for complex thinking.

Decision fatigue, also referred to as ego depletion, refers to the dwindling effectiveness of our decision-making abilities throughout the day without proper recharging. In a *New York Times* article, journalist John Tierney summarized the consequences: "Virtually no one has a gut-level sense of just how tiring it is to decide. Big decisions, small decisions, they all add up . . . ego depletion manifests itself not as one feeling but rather as a propensity to experience everything more intensely."

When you are in the middle of a pivot, big decisions regularly weigh on your mind: *Should I stay at my job or quit? Should I fold my business or keep at it? Should I move to a new city, or just take an extended trip?* It is no wonder that with these questions gobbling up the lion's share of our mental bandwidth, we become exhausted sorting through smaller daily questions like what to eat, what to wear, or when to exercise.

There is a reason Steve Jobs wore a black turtleneck and jeans every day—it saved him the mental energy of having to make at least *one* decision.

Similarly, I default to making my mom's chili soup recipe (provided in the *Pivot toolkit* online) for the majority of my meals when I am deep in the zone on my business. It is one less thing for me to think about. For exercise, I schedule my yoga and Pilates classes on their own calendar as non-negotiables. It saves me the trouble of debating *if* or *when* I am going to work out every day, or inefficiently planning and replanning the anchors in my schedule each week.

If decision fatigue is an ailment of the overtaxed mind, then what is the cure?

One of the most powerful allies you have for making clearheaded choices throughout your pivot is one that is readily accessible to you at any moment: getting quiet enough to connect with the part of you that already has the answers.

MEDITATE TO ACTIVATE YOUR BEST INSTINCTS

Despite the many articles and books touting the benefits of meditation—*Improved sleep! Health! Gratitude! Focus! Productivity!*—for the longest time I could not get into it. I got bored, restless, and I never "had the time." *Meditation, schmeditation.*

"Does walking count? Running? Biking? Swimming? Yoga? What about journaling?" I asked my friend Adam, who studied meditation while living in a monastery in Thailand. His answer was a resounding *no* to all of the above. "Get quiet," he said. "Those other activities are just more forms of doing."

It was not until my life flipped upside down, two years into running my own business full time, that I turned to the final frontier of what might soothe my deep discomfort: meditation. Adam taught me a simple practice to start with: sit with eyes closed and maintain steady even breathing, while repeating the mantra, "Rising. Falling. Sitting." I committed to a daily practice of five to thirty minutes. I reinforced the new habit by adding it to my to-do list every day, downloading the Insight Timer app, and holding myself accountable by aiming for unbroken streaks: mediating for ten, twenty, thirty, and—just once—a hundred days in a row.

Soon I felt an enormous sense of relief that even for just ten to twenty minutes a day I could find a quiet, calm center, and access my inner wisdom. These sessions recharged the battery of my brain from blinking red empty back up to a bright green 100 percent. Meditation has since become the most important part of my day.

Many successful people, including Arianna Huffington, Kobe Bryant, Russell Simmons, and Gisele Bündchen, have cited meditation as a critical component of their daily routine and a major success factor behind their thriving careers. Dan Harris, author of *10% Happier*, found meditation after having a panic attack on live national television while anchoring a *Good Morning America* segment. Many companies, hospitals, and the military also promote meditation with quiet rooms, classes, and group sessions for employees.

Even if meditation practice has eluded you until now, I encourage you to experiment with at least ten minutes of quiet, eyes-closed time in the morning; studies show that as little as ten to twelve minutes a day improves attention and working memory. When pivoting, practices like these will sharpen your focus, reduce stress, and provide the creative edge you need.

Give your inner wisdom the respect of inquiry.

E A Basic Meditation Practice to Start With

Since that early conversation, Adam and I polled over three hundred people who identify as "meditation curious" about what gets in the way of starting a practice. We found that many beginners get overwhelmed by some very practical and understandable questions: *How should I sit? What do I do once I close my eyes? What if I am the type that just can't sit still?*

If you are motivated to experiment with your own sitting practice but you are not sure where to begin, here are a few pointers from Casey Gramaglia, cofounder of the Asian Center for Applied Mindfulness.

- **Sit in a chair with your feet planted directly beneath your knees, or cross-legged on the floor:** Keep a cushion available to elevate your hips above your knees to help with comfort and circulation.

- **Straighten your spine, lifting the crown of your head up:** Rest your palms in your lap, right hand on top of the left, thumb tips gently touching, shoulders relaxed.

- **Start by observing your solar plexus area, putting your attention on your belly:** Note when your breath moves in ("rising") and when the breath moves out ("falling").

- **The mind will naturally wander:** There will be moments when you get distracted by hearing, seeing, smelling, tasting, feeling, and thinking. When any of these break your concentration, note it, such as "thinking" or "hearing," then bring your attention back to the rising and falling of your breath.

- **If you feel the need to move, scratch, or fidget, simply note it as "feeling":** Do your best to stay put and return to your practice. Remember, meditation is a checking-in, a seeing what's going on with the mind and body. Sometimes the need to fidget is an indication of just how unsettled we are in our lives.

Make your meditation practice your own. Try different approaches until you find one that works for you. "Remember not to judge yourself, just keep coming back to the practice, and your focus point of concentration," Casey says. "The more often you practice, the better you will get, and the quicker you will be able to bring the mind back to attention, cultivating a refined state of concentration and peace."

In this chapter we homed in on your values and happiness formula. You learned how to get your body primed to pivot, reduce decision fatigue, and quiet your mind to activate your best thinking. But what should you be thinking *about*? Where are you trying to go?

CHAPTER 2: PUT A PIN IN IT

What Excites You Most? What Does Success Look Like One Year from Now?

A man should learn to detect and watch that gleam of light which flashes across his mind from within. . . . Trust thyself: every heart vibrates to that iron string. . . . Nothing is at last sacred but the integrity of your own mind.

—Ralph Waldo Emerson, "Self-Reliance"

MOST PEOPLE—INCLUDING OUR CLOSEST FAMILY AND FRIENDS—DO NOT ASK US the big questions on a regular basis, if ever. They don't typically start end-of-day debriefs with: *What is working best in your life right now? What are you most excited about? What does smashing success look like one year from now?* Casual conversations more often hover around stories and daily drama: *This is what happened to me this week. This is how I felt about it. This is what is bugging me.* Although we sometimes share the most exhilarating moments, we lean toward discussing what troubles us because that's what is top of mind.

If your values are your compass, your vision is your desired destination. Once you know where you are going, the Pivot process can take you there—but first, you need to pinpoint where you want to end up. Your vision attaches a specific future-based form to your values. Both will help you course-correct as you experiment throughout your pivot, while you steer toward a motivating future. Impacters are highly resourceful; once they are clear on *where* they want to end up, they are quite creative about making their vision happen.

The more captivating your vision, the more it will recharge you during uncertain times. It is the difference between a vague sweeping statement such as, "I value travel and teaching" to an alluring invitation from your future self like, "One year from now I am living in London, working from a coffee shop as I prepare for a class I am teaching on international business law." Your vision, though it may shift as you gain more clarity and information, keeps you focused when making big decisions.

When it comes to crafting a powerful vision, I hate the question, "Where do you see yourself in five years?" It is based on an outdated paradigm and halts rather than generates conversation. *Who knows?!* New job fields are emerging at breakneck speed. The iPhone launched in 2007. Do you think that in 2006, the founders of Instagram or Snapchat would have said, "In five years, I would like to have created an app—for an app store and technology that doesn't exist yet—that will be valued at billions of dollars"? *No!* So we should not expect to know exactly what job or even industry we will want to pursue in five years.

Even if we could guess, we would probably sell ourselves short. Studies show that we are quite ineffective at predicting what is going to make us happy in the future. As poet David Whyte puts it, "What you can plan is too small for you to live."

John Hill has been a chief information officer for twenty-two years. As a specialist in emerging technologies, John's career vision is to help lead large organizations through systems upgrades that allow them to stay current, while continually learning and challenging himself. But he can never predict too far out what that might look like, given that the specific technology solutions are frequently changing.

John could sense this conundrum early on, so he adopted the following motto when choosing his college major: "What I want to do doesn't exist yet." This has remained true for most of his career. John never knows exactly what technologies will emerge, but he has become skilled at learning and staying ahead of the curve. His vision carries him forward even when he is uncertain about what his day-to-day work will entail years from now.

Given that so much of what impacters may end up doing in five years does not yet exist, it is most effective to focus vision planning on a shorter time frame and consider what success looks like even just one year from now. Most people have an easier time focusing on a one- or two-year vision than on creating a specific five-year plan. If you happen to have a clear longer-term vision, that is welcome, though not necessary.

The exercises in this chapter will help you articulate how you want your life and career to unfold in the near term.

AVOID THE TYRANNY OF THE HOWS

One common mistake I see among people tackling a big decision is jumping straight into the *how*. This is a surefire way to send yourself into panic mode. One of my first coaches, Jeff Jacobson, called this the "tyranny of the hows."

The problem-solving spiral tends to go something like this: "I am unhappy at work. How will I tell my manager? How could I find a new role within the company? How should I look for a job at another company while I am still here? If I decide to work for myself, how will I earn money? How will I ensure this all works out? What if things don't go as planned? Will I have regrets? *What if I end up in a van down by the river?!*"

Can you see how quickly the *how* questions sent our fictional friend into a frenzy? *How* is a dangerous word to ask too early in the Pivot process. You do not have to know *the whole how* just yet, or even if what you want will be possible. I will provide guidance for the hows when it is time, primarily during the Pilot and Launch stages. At this point in the process, resist the urge to solve *how* before you know *what* your vision is.

Creating a compelling one-year vision can be intimidating because as soon as you identify something truly exciting that you want to pursue, your fear gremlins may rush through the door, sounding alarms that *you are an impostor* this and *you are doomed to fail* that.

Our impulse is to tuck our tail between our legs and turn away. Or stuff the dreams down and pretend we never had them in the first place. But the fears that ride in on the coattails of an invigorating vision are a *good* sign. They signal that you are approaching something meaty enough to challenge you, and that you are squarely in your stretch zone.

Avoid focusing too much on your fear, your dislike, what is missing, or what you *don't* want. Operating solely on an avoidance of fear or dislike creates a blind spot: you know what you are running *from* but cannot see what you are running *toward*. Fear does not put fuel in your tank. Your career will remain stalled until you examine what positive outcomes will motivate you into action and sustain you through the inevitable and unnerving dips in the Pivot process.

As one Cherokee legend goes, a man tells his grandson that we all have two wolves fighting inside of us: good and evil, or joy and fear. When the grandson asks which one lives, his elder replies, "The one we feed." Your one-year vision works the same way. You have enormous creative brainpower, so feed the outcome you seek, not the one you fear.

VISION CLOUDY? START SOMEWHERE.

People often come to me when they feel stuck and their vision feels too distant to describe, a far cry from where they are now. Or they might not know precisely what they want. Both are normal, and to be expected. But as I tell them, it is still important to start *somewhere*.

I never accept "I don't know" as an answer. Because every time (and I do mean *every* time) I follow up with: "Guess. Just take a stab at it, even if you don't know specifics," answers start pouring out. *I don't know* quickly dissolves after further inquiry.

Crafting a vision can start with a sweeping exploration, one as broad as how you want to *feel* one year from now. If you currently feel stuck, stagnant, or stressed, what is the alternative? If you are an impacter, it is likely that you want to feel more engaged, balanced, and healthy, and to know that you are making a positive difference in the world.

My sister-in-law, Gillian, graduated from law school and took the bar exam, but quickly realized her one-year vision did not include sitting at a desk every day working on legal briefs. Her one-year vision was to be engaged in a flexible work environment that would keep her physically active, surrounded by like-minded people, and provide stepping-stones toward a career that was conducive to starting a family and running a business with her husband.

After taking the bar exam, Gillian completed CorePower Yoga Teacher Training as a side project and reward to herself for finishing law school. Even though she hadn't planned to do much with it at the time, practicing yoga became an important element of her happiness formula.

A few months later, when she found out that she did pass the bar exam, Gillian decided to teach at a yoga studio rather than continue at the law firm where she was interning. She committed to learning the business side of yoga. Earning her yoga teaching certification, combined with her business and legal acumen, helped her pivot in a new direction that was more aligned with her vision. Gil was quickly promoted to a management role within the yoga studio, bolstered by her aptitude and unique background.

E Broad One-Year Vision Brainstorm

Coming up with a clear vision is like shaping a block of clay. Staring at a big square block can be intimidating, so it is best to start broad, then refine the details of your vision later. Your vision may sound like your values at first, then becomes differentiated as you specify the activities that your vision encompasses one year from now.

Here are some common broad one-year vision statements:

- Do work that makes me excited to get out of bed every day.
- Feel like I am making an impact; see the positive results of my work.
- Prioritize my health, get in a groove with daily routines.
- Make a career or business change while also aiming for financial security.
- Be surrounded by a community of like-minded peers and friends.
- Live and work in an invigorating environment.

After you come up with broad vision statements like the ones above, continue shaping what each item might look like one year from now. What kind of work are you doing? What impact are you having? How much are you earning? Where are you living? What are your health routines? Who are you surrounded by? How do you feel?

I encourage my clients to express a safe, nice-to-have version of their vision at first. But what I am really digging for is the excited disbelief of *"What?! I can ask for that?! Is that really even possible?!"* Ultimately, your one-year vision should be so riveting that the thought sends a rush of adrenaline through your body and gets your idea synapses firing.

E Define Success One Year from Now

Now that you have started a broad vision outline, apply the Give-Receive-Achieve framework below to further shape what success looks like in the coming year. This is a shortcut I developed to assess how you want to contribute, what you want to experience in return, and what specific results or milestones will indicate that you are on the right track.

Give: Impact on Others

- What impact do you want to have on your family and friends? On your local community? On the global community?

- What types of information and resources are you most excited to share with others?

- If you were invited to speak at TED, and you knew your talk would go viral and be seen by at least one million people, what message would you send?

Receive: What You Want to Experience

- What result will your contributions to friends, family, and society have on your own life?

- What major life experiences, work or personal, are most exciting to you? How do you want to feel on a daily basis while pursuing them? Who do you want to meet?

- Take a look at your bookshelf, Kindle, blog, or podcast subscriptions. What themes stand out? When you go into a bookstore, which section do you beeline toward, and what does that say about you?

Achieve: Specific Results

- What does success look like one or two years from now? What will be happening in your life and work?

- What are your metrics for measuring financial or professional success?

- What achievements will indicate that you are having the impact you seek?

- Imagine an award ceremony in your honor. What organization is giving the award, and for what are you being recognized?

E "Sliding Doors" Careers

As we move from a broad outline to one-year Give-Receive-Achieve aims, next is time to creatively explore what elements might still be missing.

In the movie *Sliding Doors*, the story of Gwyneth Paltrow's character plays out in two parallel universes based on whether or not she catches a certain London train. Imagine you get to live in an alternate reality, one parallel to the one you are living in now, one in which you get to pursue any type of work you want. What would you do?

Maybe you will never pursue your "Sliding Doors" career, letting it live only in your imagination as a path you could have taken if circumstances were different. Or maybe you try this career for a year or take a few related classes as a hobby.

The key is giving yourself permission to explore: If time, money, skills, or *judgment from others* were not an issue, what would you do for work? How would you spend your time? Which of your values could be more fully expressed? What do you daydream about?

I have seen people list Sliding Doors vocations like professional chef, magazine magnate, talk-show host, schoolteacher, bed-and-breakfast owner, and photographer, among many others. Even if they never intended to pursue these careers, the lists offered valuable insight into their vision. The lists might indicate they were interested in working with their hands, creating artistic experiences for others, sparking conversation, and working with people—probably not all in one role, but you never know! These attributes may not have been on their radar after completing the more straightforward exercises; coming from a creative angle sparks new ideas and reveals hidden interests.

Jot down a few notes about what entices you about each item on your Sliding Doors list, then identify any repeating themes that cut across all the roles you listed to reveal elements that are important for your vision as you move forward.

CLARIFY YOUR VISION STATEMENT

Now that you have done some expansive exploration, it is time to narrow down to a concise vision statement, a vivid call to action.

The clearer your vision, the easier it will be to decide what next steps to take and the stronger your instincts will become along the way. Remember, your vision does not need to address *how* to achieve anything, or *if* it is possible—at this point it shouldn't—but rather *what* success looks like, written in the present tense.

You are going to exit your comfort zone to pivot for a reason, so now it is time to state, as best you can, what that reason is. Challenge yourself. This may not come easily, but make your best guess, then adjust and fill in the blanks as you work through subsequent Pivot stages.

E Write a One-Year Vision Statement

Draw upon your values and the vision exercises you have completed so far to write a cohesive one-year vision statement, written as if it is already happening, that will guide your Pivot strategy and brainstorming.

Part one: Imagine that it is one year from today and you have achieved wild success. Describe in the present tense what you are doing, how you are feeling, and what you are proud of. Be as detailed and creative as you can. In 2012, my big, hairy, scary dream was to be a thought leader— an author and speaker—like Daniel Pink and Malcolm Gladwell. I wrote this one-year vision statement at the time:

I am contributing innovative ideas and frameworks to society by bringing disparate fields together in a unique way. I am earning a healthy living through speaking, writing, and coaching. I have more work than I can handle, which allows me to build a scalable business of workshops and courses. I feel engaged, inspired, and like I am helping people improve their lives in a meaningful way.

One of my coaching clients, Julien Pham, a physician and entrepreneur, identified his one-year vision as follows:

I am comfortable and confident in my hybrid role of being a physician and an entrepreneur. My start-up, RubiconMD, has acquired funding and is experiencing explosive growth, and I am leading a thriving team. I have a strong network of colleagues who have influence in both medicine and entrepreneurship, and a fine-tuned personal mission, something I can express with more clarity at an event like TED. I help inspire the new generation of aspiring clinician-entrepreneurs who learn from my wins and my losses, and try to contribute to making something better in society around technology and medicine, while getting feedback from others. My website, Startup Clinic, has launched, and serves as a virtual headquarters where physicians can learn about start-ups and connect with each other. I am happy, healthy, in a great relationship, and thinking of starting a family.

Part two: What parts of your vision are already present in your life, even a little bit? In what ways is this vision statement already true? Regarding what I wrote in 2012, I had already been focusing on writing, coaching, and speaking full time, with an aim to continue growing my speaking platform. I was involved in activities similar to those of the people I admired, though on a much smaller scale. I hadn't yet landed on my next big idea, but now, four years later, you are holding it in your hands.

Julien had already been playing dual roles as physician and entrepreneur for several years. He cofounded RubiconMD, and started hosting informal dinners with other physicians, which became the beginnings of Startup Clinic. Together we clarified his core philosophy for guiding other physicians and medical institutions—to simplify and amplify—and outlined a speech he could deliver when asked to speak at conferences.

As Julien put it when reflecting on this exercise, his vision did not seem out of reach when he viewed it as an existing work in progress. "I have done versions of what is in my one-year vision successfully in the past," he said. "Now it is just a matter of enhancing my skills in the present to build into where I want to be in the future." By the time this book went to press, Julien was signing the term sheet for RubiconMD to receive Series A funding, just six months after he wrote his vision statement.

E *Clarifying your one-year vision can also be done as a mind map on an ongoing basis. Write the current year in the center with spokes for different life areas—such as career, creative projects, money, social, health, learning, hobbies, and relationships—then brainstorm a handful of desired outcomes across each area. I do one of these at the start of every year instead of more traditional New Year's resolutions.*

SUMMARIZE KNOWNS AND UNKNOWNS

During my biggest dips of self-employment, one thing remained clear: New York City was my home. No matter how expensive, how noisy, how crowded, I knew it was where I belonged. That was a core "yes," or known variable. From there, it was up to me to get creative about how to support that decision with my business model, an unknown at the time in terms of exactly what form it should take.

When Brooke Snow reached a point of boredom and burnout with her online business, she started planning her pivot by getting clear on her knowns and unknowns. After launching five successful online photography courses over five years, Brooke realized that she wanted to teach subjects that were more personal, such as work-life balance and creativity. Her *known variables* and strengths were in teaching, curriculum development, and running online courses. Her *unknown variables* were how to set up the new business and what to do with the old one.

Brooke applied her strengths in course and community building to shift her focus into classes related to personal growth. She brought on a partner with a complementary skill set who helped rejuvenate her work, an unexpected boost. Soon after, she rebranded her website with a new tagline that was a better fit for her vision: "Living and documenting the thriving life."

Take a moment to summarize your knowns (your must-haves) and your unknowns (elements you are still uncertain about) in your one-year vision. List knowns and unknowns across categories, such as location, finances, projects, people, results, and lifestyle.

Summarize Knowns Versus Unknowns: Specific Outcomes One Year from Now			
	1) Knowns	2) Unknowns	3) Best Guess
Location			
Finances			
Projects			
People			
Results			
Lifestyle			

In clarifying your vision, you plugged your destination into a maps app. *Ping!* Pin placed. But what is your mode of transport? How can you get there most efficiently? What potholes, traffic jams, and road closures should you avoid? What shortcuts are available to you and only you?

CHAPTER 3: FUEL YOUR ENGINE

What Is Working? Where Do You Excel?

I'm no genius. I'm smart in spots—but I stay around those spots.

—Thomas Watson

MONICA MCCARTHY HAD BEEN AN ACTOR IN NEW YORK CITY FOR FIFTEEN YEARS when she decided she was ready for a more stable role, one that offered more creative control over her work. She started her own business doing video production and direction for entrepreneurs, but one year in she began to feel isolated. Monica realized she worked more effectively when partnering with others. As a result, she started looking for full-time jobs—her first time seeking office work since college.

Prior to kicking off her job search, Monica started hosting a monthly dinner salon called Cheshire Parlour. These events connected interesting people with each other around big ideas like freedom, time, and fortune—not the usual Saturday night networking and bar banter. This side project was a natural extension of her core strengths as a people connector and facilitator of meaningful conversations. Though Monica loved these monthly dinners, her funds available for hosting began to dwindle. It was a classic "pursue your passion" conundrum. This *was* her passion, but it was not providing sustainable income. She needed another outlet for her vision of working with purpose-driven people and organizations.

Monica applied for an office manager role at a company called Holstee, a lifestyle brand that creates products such as wall art, greeting cards, and office decor to help people live more mindfully. Their mission of creating products and experiences for an inspired life resonated with Monica. You might be familiar with their viral manifesto video "This Is Your Life," which quickly racked up nearly two million views and became a bestselling wall poster.

Though she was not exactly a fit for the office manager role, during the interview she and the founders got to talking, and she told them about her experiences with Cheshire Parlour. As it turned out, they had been thinking about hiring an event coordinator to host classes and dinners, but had not yet listed the position on Holstee's careers page.

Fast-forward a few weeks, and Monica landed a full-time consulting gig as Holstee's events impresaria, hosting dinners, launching a Learning Lab at their Brooklyn studio, and delivering manifesto-writing workshops all around the country. She loved working with a team in a collaborative office environment, while still being able to pursue her own ideas for programs within and outside of the company. Monica said of her time working with Holstee, "I learned so much more in one year there than I would have in a decade working by myself."

Monica's story illustrates how planting in what you are already good at prepares you for what's next. When she was not getting traction from acting, Monica drew on her knowledge of how to be effective in front of the camera to provide video production and creative direction for entrepreneurs. She then planted in her academic background in philosophy by connecting people and hosting the Cheshire Parlour dinners, building her own creative outlet even without knowing what it would eventually become. Because she was clear on her values and one-year vision, she was able to translate her community-building strengths into a custom role at Holstee—an example of putting her unique career portfolio to work.

Your *career portfolio* is the aggregate of your strengths, prior work experience, and existing connections. Just as investment portfolios can be diversified by asset class, such as stocks and bonds, your career portfolio includes a blend of assets that are already working in your favor. The exercises in this chapter will help you understand what your biggest inner resources are, and how you can apply them to accelerate the next stages of the Pivot process.

IDENTIFY YOUR STRENGTHS

First up: identify your strengths to determine which ones energize you most in your present-day work, and which ones you could direct even more attention toward. The most engaging work allows you to apply your best skills, interests, and unique "Zone of Genius."

Childhood Interests

Start homing in on your innate talents by looking at what activities you enjoyed as a kid; your career strengths have probably been expressing themselves in some way long before adulthood.

Joanna Bourke loved to cook growing up and had been interested in food her whole life, though she decided to pursue business studies when she went to university. That choice led her to many work opportunities and invaluable professional experience, but her passion for food remained. After eight years in a finance operations role in the United States, Joanna left to enroll in a three-month cookery school program back in her hometown of Dublin, Ireland, based on her vision of starting an events company someday. "My love of food never went away, but now I can apply my project management, analytical, and operations experience to pursuing a career in the food world," she said.

A few months after completing cookery school, Joanna launched her own company, The Chopping Board, which integrated her business experience with her childhood vocational aspirations.

During Jason Shen's move from content marketing to product management within the start-up he worked for, he stumbled across a piece of paper from childhood: his kindergarten teacher's end-of-year evaluation. She had written, "He especially enjoys computer work, games, and making things." Seeing this reminded Jason that the change he was seeking at work was not out of reach—it was a logical extension of activities he had always loved. "That reminded me that my desire to build stuff and use computers was clear from a young age," he said. "Wanting to be a product manager wasn't just something I had been brainwashed into by Silicon Valley or other external sources."

When I was ten years old I started a family newspaper, the *Monthly Dig-Up*, featuring technology tutorials, interviews, and family updates that I sent out faithfully every month for the next eight years. I also loved playing "business" and "school" with my younger brother, teaching him things I was learning and creating worksheets for him to fill out. Today I earn a living from activities that center around writing, technology, and teaching.

E Study Your Past for Patterns

Think about activities you most enjoyed growing up. Perhaps you will remember this entirely on your own, but this is also an opportunity to inquire among your family and childhood friends about your interests. Ask them: "What did I enjoy doing as a kid? What was most important to me? Any quirks about my personality that stood out to you, or that made me different from my sibling(s) or classmates?"

Given that the activities you enjoyed at six years old were probably different than at sixteen, even if they are related, list your favorite recreational and creative interests across the four age brackets below for a more fine-grained examination.

Childhood Interests			
Age 3–8	Age 9–13	Age 14–18	Age 19–21

Zone of Genius

Earlier we talked about the four Career Operating Modes, two of which are sweet spots for impacters: proactive and innovative. What separates the two? Innovative impacters are fully applying their unique talents to make a powerful contribution to the communities they care about. So how do you discover what your sweet spots are to ensure that you are doing the same?

Ask yourself: What am I insanely good at? When do I feel most "in the zone"? What natural talents have I refined into strengths over time? In *The Big Leap*, author Gay Hendricks says our work activities fall into one of four buckets: a zone of incompetence, competence, excellence, or genius. He describes each one as follows:

- **The Zone of Incompetence:** This is made up of all the activities you are not good at. Others can do them a lot better than you can.

- **The Zone of Competence:** You are competent at these activities, but others can do them just as well.

- **The Zone of Excellence:** These are activities you do extremely well, and from which you can make a good living. Hendricks says this zone can be a "seductive and even dangerous trap" as it often prevents us from fully "taking the leap into [our] Zone of Genius."

- **The Zone of Genius:** These are the activities you are uniquely suited to, that draw upon your special gifts and strengths. As Hendricks says, "Liberating and expressing your natural genius is your ultimate path to success and life satisfaction. . . . [It] beckons you with increasingly strong calls as you go through your life."

How do you know when you are working in your Zone of Genius? How do you find it in the first place? Laura Garnett is a peak performance strategist who focuses on two key factors to discover someone's Zone of Genius: innate talents and purpose.

Talent, as Laura defines it, is the unique way you solve problems. By identifying the types of challenges you are attracted to and how you tackle them, you can steer toward these areas for greater fulfillment and impact with your work.

Purpose, the second ingredient, relates to the motivation behind what you do. What is the impact you want the work you are doing to have, and for whom? Purpose is your personal mission statement. It goes deeper than your one-year vision, connecting all the work you do to an underlying theme. Some people's purpose is to raise a family; for others it is to create delightful experiences by hosting events. Many impacters find purpose in helping others in some way. To explore your purpose, Garnett suggests thinking about a core challenge you have faced in your life. What struggle have you overcome, either for a short period of time or as a recurring theme throughout your life? How might you be able to share what you have learned to help others in this area?

E Zone of Genius Observation

Observe the work you are currently doing: What is working best in terms of your day-to-day activities, job roles, daily routines, and social interactions? When are you working in your Zone of Excellence versus your Zone of Genius? What activities from your past were in your Zone of Genius that may be latent now?

Be an observer this week, noting when your work falls into a Zone of Competence, Excellence, or Genius. There may also be activities that have potential for your Zone of Genius that you are not objectively great at yet, but that serve as clues to what you can invest more time and energy into if they line up with your vision.

Another way to understand and describe your core strengths and interests is to take personality assessments such as Myers-Briggs, StrengthsFinder, and the Enneagram. You might also include more esoteric profiles such as astrology and numerology, which can illuminate innate talents and preferences. If you have taken any assessments in the past, now is a great time to revisit your results. Copy and paste all your reports into an Evernote notebook or Google Doc titled "Personality Assessments" for easy reference.

WORK-HISTORY HIGHLIGHTS

If your strengths and childhood interests are your inner fuel, then your past experiences—how you have applied those strengths and the resulting accomplishments—are your external accelerators.

Career experiences are important, but they are not sufficient for landing your next opportunity or client. Prospective bosses and business partners are looking for *marketable skills* that lead to *results*, giving you a *reputation* as a must-hire.

Let's explore these key experience elements that you bring to the table.

Work Experience

Your prior jobs may have more in common than you think. For example, working as a server in a restaurant and as a sales representative are not such dissimilar roles. Both involve building relationships quickly, working with a range of personality types, learning how to address and anticipate customers' needs, and getting comfortable with irregular pay.

Consider your last five to ten jobs or projects, even those that did not earn income:

- What were the key activities associated with each role?

- List between five and ten unifying themes among these jobs and projects.

- Now get more specific: What are the related skills, results, and industries on your list? Themes might include: departments (such as marketing), job responsibilities (such as people management or teaching), key projects (such as creating systems or brand strategy), or key activities (like financial modeling or coding).

Marketable Skills

A marketable skill is a specific service you provide at the intersection of talents, strengths, and education that a customer or company will pay you for.

Even better are two marketable skills that might seem unrelated, but that complement each other in a unique way. For example, if you are fluent in a foreign language and you have a background in accounting, you might be a prime candidate to work for the FBI.

- Identify the marketable skills you have already developed. What do people *currently* seek you out for?

- As in the FBI example, do you have two (or more) marketable skills that intersect in a unique way?
- Look for clues in the exercises earlier in the chapter. Often what you loved to do as a child and activities that fall into your Zone of Genius inform the marketable skills you are using today. Which of these interests are you not yet applying to their fullest potential?

Results

Results are the meaningful impact that you have had on people or projects. These can be qualitative and quantitative, whether improving existing systems or launching new initiatives. Qualitative results might relate to soft skills, such as leadership and teamwork, while quantitative results are often characterized by increasing effectiveness, efficiency, revenue, or reach, or a combination of all of the above.

- What specific results have you helped people or organizations achieve?
- What are your most significant work projects to date? What was important about each one?
- What professional accomplishments are you proudest of? Why?

Reputation

When you consistently help others achieve results, you develop a reputation as a must-hire. Reputation refers to how others see you, the strengths they recognize and seek you out for.

The most agile pivoters, whether entrepreneurs or employees, hardly have to look for work; they have a reputation that makes them easy to spot and desirable to hire. Clients pursue them, and are often willing to wait to work with them or even recruit them away from existing full-time positions. When seemingly bad things happen, their bounce-back time is quicker than average because they know who to call, their skills are in demand, and their reputation makes others feel fortunate to work with *them*.

- In what areas have you developed a strong reputation, personally or professionally?

- What skills are you best known for among friends and acquaintances?

- What types of assistance or advice do people ask you for most often? What do they end up walking away with, beyond what they initially asked for?

- What awards, accolades, and public praise have you received?

- What do you *want* to become a known expert in?

———

By emphasizing strengths in the Plant stage, you will see that you are not starting from scratch. Still, there is a big difference between dreaming about a pie-in-the-sky, theoretical pivot and making one happen in real life. The latter requires facing the reality of the world we live in: life costs money. How will you pivot without sending yourself into a panic?

CHAPTER 4: FUND YOUR RUNWAY

What Is Your Timeline? How Can You Earn Extra Income?

[M]oney is only a tool. It will take you wherever you wish, but it will not replace you as the driver.

—Ayn Rand, *Atlas Shrugged*

"I SPENT MY ENTIRE TWENTIES TELLING MYSELF I WAS GOING TO DO SOMETHING, then not doing it," Andrew Deffley said when I asked him what brought him to Manhattan for an acting audition. "This time I am following through. I quit my job two months ago and am giving myself six months to try to earn a living acting, which I have loved since I was a kid."

Andrew had been working at NFL Films as a production manager for eight years. He had a brand-name gig, but hit a wall when he turned thirty and felt there was more out there for him. Deep down, he had always harbored a vision of being in front of the camera as an actor, not hidden behind the scenes as an editor. Tired of succumbing to his fears, Andrew pivoted on his strengths and experience in video production and began taking acting classes and auditioning for roles, knowing that even if he failed, he would be happy he tried.

Andrew didn't just have passion, energy, and excitement. He also had a financial plan.

BUILD A SOLID FINANCIAL FOUNDATION

For a time, the online business zeitgeist was *"Quit your job! Work from a beach sipping coconuts! Outsource everything!"* However, once the adrenaline of the big leap wore off, reality quickly set in for many people who realized they were running on fumes in their energy levels and bank accounts.

Change is challenging enough to navigate without financial pressures. With them, it places a choke hold on your creativity and your options.

With rare exception, pivots require financial resources, or at least sound planning for a number of scenarios that may play out. The more you can clarify your resource needs and bolster your financial reserves, the more options you have for making your next move.

You might want to take a "pre-cation," time off before starting a new job. You might want to go back to school, or do long-term traveling. Maybe you just need time to slow down and reflect. By clarifying your financial needs through the exercises in this chapter, you can proceed to later Pivot stages with a sense of which risks you can afford to take and when.

Andrew knew he wanted to try his hand at acting as a career after an "aha moment" during his first acting class in 2010. Before launching into it full time, he planned for how he would support himself throughout his pivot. He didn't just quit his job and hope *the universe* would pay his bills. He saved up enough for a six-month break from his work with the NFL to test his hypothesis that acting would bring him professional happiness and enough income to support himself.

Even if he spent every penny of his financial runway, Andrew knew his experiment would be a success. No matter what outcome resulted, he would know that he had given it his best shot. If acting did not pan out in six months, he would keep auditioning, but he would add a more consistent side gig doing production-related work to tide him over financially between roles. This approach is significantly different from the starving artist model of, well, starving indefinitely while praying for a big break.

PIVOT FINANCE 101

This section covers common business and finance terms adapted for planning a pivot, whether you are starting or running your own business, working a "side hustle" in addition to a full-time job, or looking to pivot within your company.

A caveat: Although some worst-case scenario planning is helpful in case you get laid off or lose a big client, it is more sustainable to build a sound business model, capitalize on marketable skills, and find steady income than it is to just *sell-sell-sell* or scrimp and save until your bank account is barren. As former Google CEO Eric Schmidt once half jokingly, half seriously remarked during a company all-hands meeting, "The answer to all known problems is revenue."

Monthly nut: How much do you need to earn each month to cover your basic expenses? When I work with people approaching a career pivot, I ask for three numbers:

- Minimum needed: to cover rent, utilities, groceries, and basic expenses.
- Nice to have: to maintain something close to your current or desired lifestyle; might include shopping, meals out, hobbies, weekend trips, and the ability to fund long-term savings.
- Jump out of bed with glee: this number lets you do anything on your lifestyle wish list without hesitation, such as long-distance or long-term travel, large or luxury purchases, or having an abundance of resources for charitable donations or to support extended family.

Business strategist Nick Reese calculates the ideal *monthly nut* a person needs to pay living expenses (and taxes, if self-employed) as 3.4 times their monthly rent or mortgage. For parents, or for people living in expensive cities, the multiplier is 5. For bootstrappers willing to live frugally or "lean," the multiplier can be 2.5 times rent.

To calculate your *yearly nut*, multiply your monthly rent by 41. If you have debt, such as a mortgage, Reese suggests multiplying your monthly rent or mortgage payment by at least 50.

Crunch Your Numbers:

- What is the amount of your monthly nut, calculated using the formulas above?
- What is your yearly nut?
- What are your total *average* monthly expenses for the last twelve months? How does that figure stack up against your monthly nut?

Runway: How long will your savings support you if you do not earn any income? The rule of thumb for emergency funds used to be three to six months until recent years, when the average unemployment duration hit thirty-one weeks, or nearly eight months. When I left Google, my cash runway was equivalent to six months of living expenses, which is consistent with many other pivoters I spoke with. I had other assets, such as a condo, a car, and a 401(k), but did not count them as part of my runway since they were worst-case scenario cash-outs.

If you do not currently have any savings, your runway is likely too short to make any major moves that might require time without pay, at least without also taking on more risk. Part of your Pivot plan may include increasing how much you earn (something we will cover later) or how much you set aside from what you are currently earning, possibly delaying bigger moves and risks until you have more flex in your financial system.

Crunch Your Numbers:

- How much do you currently have in cash savings?
- How much do you have in other assets?
- How many months will your cash savings last if you are not earning any income (total savings divided by monthly nut)?

Burn rate: In Silicon Valley parlance, *burn rate* is defined as the rate at which an enterprise spends money, especially venture capital, in excess of income. In pivot terms, are you being financially prudent or spending like the Wolf of Wall Street? The higher your burn rate, the faster your runway will disappear. During a pivot, cutting back on nice-to-have lifestyle indulgences, such as meals out and shopping, will buy you more time to strategize and build your business or land your next gig.

Bridge income: The term *bridge loan* refers to short-term commercial real estate financing. A bridge loan is meant to be paid back quickly, bridging the timing gap while investors implement their plan to improve a property's performance before securing a long-term loan. *Bridge income* tides you over while making a change, but is not your desired primary long-term solution.

Although your savings *can* act as bridge income, this is not ideal for two reasons: savings are a finite resource, and the more you spend, the more you may stress out, impairing your ability to think creatively. Treat your savings as a backup account that you only dip into if your bridge income fails.

Bridge income creates stability as you test other income avenues. Figuring out a source of bridge income and steady cash flow, either part time or on the side, puts the power in your hands and will make you more confident and agile when you do make a change, or if change chooses you.

In identifying bridge income, we are going for consistent cash flow, not a Hail Mary, a long shot with much greater risk. Now is not the time to bet big on a passive income play to build a business that earns money while you sleep. Something like that is fine for a longer-term move, but only if you can offset it with more reliable income in the meantime, or are willing to burn through your savings runway to build it.

Trading time for money often gets a bad rap. However, if you exchange services based on existing skills to paying customers, you can buy time for implementing longer-term or higher-risk aspects of your pivot. For some, bridge income might come from a part-time job such as bartending, temping, or freelancing. My most stable, reliable source of income comes from one-on-one coaching, whereas keynote speaking and corporate training pays much larger sums but tends to be more sporadic, with a longer lead time and invoicing period.

No matter what your current employment status, if you were to suddenly find yourself self-employed and *had* to make it for a year, how could you add value to any market? If you had to implement the following three streams of income right now, what would they be?

- "So you can breathe" income: hourly wage, possibly projects below your skill level
- Mid-level: monthly retainer, steady cash flow, part-time work
- Big bets: high income potential; big contracts, clients, or job offers; income sources with longer lead times but greater reward

Side hustle: This term refers to modern-day moonlighting, earning income on the side while maintaining a full-time job. This is often not sustainable indefinitely, though some people will be perfectly happy with a light side hustle, like making and selling jewelry or doing freelance design work for friends, that brings them joy without having to quit their job. Even entrepreneurs can have side hustles, or creative sandboxes to play in outside of their main revenue-generating activities.

My mom's advice for me growing up was, "You should always know how to support yourself." As a result, I always make a point to know where my money is going, how to bring in a steady income, how to invest wisely, how to pay my bills, and what my backup plans are.

Since the day I started earning money consistently in college, I have always had a second source of income on the side. Whether it was getting paid to take lecture notes in college, babysitting, doing web development tutoring over the phone for small-business owners, coaching, or working on my first book, for the first ten years of my career before striking out on my own, I always had my main paycheck and my "hustle" check.

My version of freedom is being able to make choices in my best interest. I do not ever want to feel trapped in a job or relationship because I can't afford to leave due to lack of savings or earning ability, two areas I can directly influence.

Side hustles represent a calculated risk: you willingly invest some of your spare time (and maybe money) into a project that you are excited about, with the hope of making a greater proportion of your living off this someday, or to land your next full-time role. To take a side hustle full time, you need to identify the bridge income within it—the marketable skill, product, or service that will pay the bills most consistently.

One of my friends, Kit, loves fishing. When he finds a good spot in the lake, he refers to it as a "honey hole." The honey hole is the secret spot he can return to that is likely to yield a great catch. The best side hustles are your equivalent of a honey hole: you enjoy them, you are excited to return, you have discovered something unique to you, and they provide value in return.

There are four criteria to developing a strong side hustle:

1. **Cash (flow) cow:** If it does not create income, either now or in the future, your beloved side hustle is a hobby. The best side hustles will demonstrate a monetary return on your investment, if not now, then at some point in the not-too-distant future. How long are you willing to wait? I suggest experimenting with a side hustle that allows you to test revenue generation fairly quickly.

   At first, the income you earn from your side hustle is likely to be labor intensive. You will invest time and sweat equity for little pay. In his *Startup School* podcast series, Seth Godin calls this "front-loading." Better to do the hardest work up front, then reap the rewards later, he says, rather than be surprised down the road when you have much more at stake.

2. **Market reach:** Your side hustle should offer a solid amount of growth potential. If you love teaching underwater basket weaving, but there is no one interested in learning it, you will be quickly catapulted back into unprofitable hobby territory. Look for side hustles with a sizable

market to serve, yet not so broad or undifferentiated that you have difficulty resonating with ideal clients.

3. **Enjoyment:** A side hustle doing grunt work is valuable if it helps you pay the bills or save up for the next big trip you want to take. But a side hustle with even better potential is one that emphasizes your strengths and makes you excited to work on it, whether you have fifteen minutes to spend that day or five hours.

4. **Skill building:** Ideally, your side hustle will also help you learn or improve skills that may be needed in your field in the coming years. Think about what skills, if you were to develop them now while this is a side project, would serve you well if you took these activities full time. Some are universal and can benefit you in almost any role or business, such as sales, marketing, copywriting, technical coding or troubleshooting, and design.

Make-or-break marker: Let's say all hell breaks loose: you lose your job or your biggest client the same week your car breaks down, and your bank account is running on fumes. Still, you are not ready to give up on your vision. Or you are not clear yet on what's next, but deep down you feel that a breakthrough is right around the corner if you can hold out a bit longer. You may not be done with your pivot, but you need to pay your bills, and the fire under your rear end is getting uncomfortably hot. If you hit rock middle, you will know objectively that it is time to rethink things . . . before you have to hit FUBAR rock bottom. A *Pivot paradox* caveat: Sometimes rock bottom is the beginning of a breakthrough, and tough as it feels in the moment, it forces a new way of thinking, acting, and reacting.

Regardless, plan your worst-case scenario from the outset. In what order are you going to cash out your assets? What is your make-or-break marker to change strategy if things are not going as planned?

When I left my job to start my own business, I decided that if I was still not earning enough income to pay my bills after six months, but I was not yet ready to take a full-time job again, I would (in order):

1. Cash out my savings account ($20K)
2. Sell Red Velvet, my Prius ($15K)
3. Sell my stocks ($10K)
4. Dip into my 401(k)—my make-or-break threshold for when I would start to look for full-time work again
5. Sell my condo in California
6. DONEZO! All assets are gone. (Note to self when I made this list: *Do not get to this point! Change strategy at #4 or earlier.*)

Pen to Paper

- What would you do, in order, to address your worst-case financial scenario if you were not meeting your monthly nut, or after spending your savings runway?
- What existing assets could you draw from?
- How could you shore up those assets with bridge income or a side hustle?

Pivot Paradox: Scarcity Versus *The Secret*

Maintaining equilibrium in your money mindset while pivoting can be a complicated dance, particularly since our financial habits are often tied to deeper emotions and operating principles. Find a way to inquire into your financial fear without letting it paralyze you. Ignoring it may send you into scarcity mode, which is not conducive to long-term planning.

According to Sendhil Mullainathan and Eldar Shafir, the authors of *Scarcity: Why Having Too Little Means So Much*, scarcity is not just a physical constraint, it is also a mindset—one that makes us less insightful, less forward thinking, and less controlled. "When scarcity captures our attention, it changes how we think—whether it is at the level of milliseconds, hours, days, or weeks. By staying at the top of our minds, it affects what we notice, how we weigh our choices, how we deliberate, and ultimately what we decide and how we behave."

At the same time, there is a danger in some self-help teachings (à la *The Secret*) that imply merely thinking positive thoughts is enough to manifest a parking spot or a red Ferrari. Going all in on hope, without taking practical steps in tandem, will not pay the bills.

Get crystal clear on how much money you need to live, your income sources, and your emergency plan. At the same time, cultivate an abundance mindset. Life is not a zero-sum game; there is enough opportunity out there for each of us to thrive and be successful. For example, if you are a website designer, even though there are thousands of designers in the world, including inexpensive options for people looking to outsource overseas, you can still differentiate yourself by the quality of your work and find ideal clients who are looking for the premium services you offer.

INCOME-ANXIETY SEESAW AWARENESS

When it comes to money and pivoting, imagine a seesaw with anxiety on one end and income on the other. The *income-anxiety seesaw* is a checkpoint to determine when you need to correct course.

As you increase your cash flow consistency, your overall income, or your savings, anxiety about making a change will decrease. Your anxiety may not disappear completely, but you will start to trust that your basic needs are addressed.

However, as your income or savings start to decrease, your anxiety may climb. This threshold varies, but for almost everyone too much anxiety creates tunnel vision. You may stop thinking clearly and creatively, start losing sleep, and sacrifice in other areas that are important to you, such as health and quality time with friends and family.

When this starts happening, put the bigger experiments of your pivot on hold while you buckle down and get your income figured out. Very often this will involve creating a source of bridge income or taking a transitional role that will support you along your pivot path, even if it is not the exact result you are aiming for in your one- to two-year vision.

———

After running through the calculations in this chapter, you will be clearer on your financial constraints, monthly income requirements, backup plans, and bridge income. You will know how to gauge when your income seesaw tips from ease into anxiety, and how to even it back out.

You might not know precisely what your pivot will cost in terms of time, energy, and money, or exactly what it is yet, but you will be proceeding confidently from a strong financial foundation. You bought yourself breathing room, now what will you do with it?

Plant: Online Resources

Visit PivotMethod.com/plant for additional tools, templates, and book recommendations for this stage.

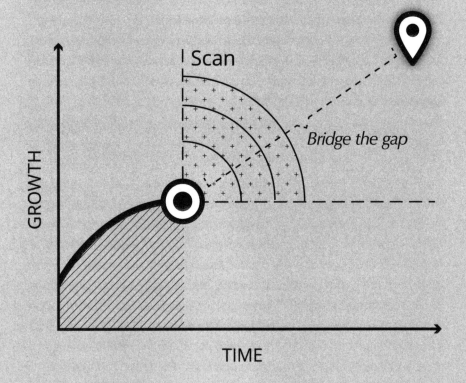

STAGE TWO

SCAN

Explore Options

PLANT

SCAN

PILOT

LAUNCH

LEAD

SCAN OVERVIEW

THE PLANT STAGE PROVIDES A FRAMEWORK FOR WHERE YOU ARE NOW AND where you generally want to end up. Now, in the Scan stage, you will start looking for people, skills, and opportunities to help you get there.

The aim of this stage is structured exploration, which involves research, plugging knowledge and skill gaps, having conversations, and clarifying what types of opportunities interest you most. You will harness serendipity by expanding your network and exposure, while being mindful not to scan so much that you fall into analysis paralysis or compare and despair.

Consider Amazon's "Recommended for you" and "Customers also bought" algorithms. They match product suggestions to what you have previously demonstrated interest in. This is analogous to connecting your scanning activities to the values and strengths you identified during the Plant stage.

The downside of Amazon's matching algorithms is that suggestions can become myopic, so rooted in what you have enjoyed in the past that you don't go sideways to discover new, unrelated books or products that might surprise you.

The Scan stage requires that you look at both—new opportunities anchored in your existing strengths *and* ways you might expand beyond your comfort zone, revealing blind spots or hidden pockets of potential.

The most effective pivoters use the Scan phase to collect ideas and become "discoverable" to interesting new opportunities, even if they do not yet know exactly what will result. These are people who create opportunity, not just find it—so much so that new work and opportunities are often *scanning for them.*

This stage will help you scan efficiently—separating signal from noise—so you do not flood yourself with unnecessary information. Instead, bolstered by the Plant exercises, you will be like a pig searching for truffles in mud: operating with finely tuned senses to find exactly what you need.

It is easy when scanning to default to a self-focused mode of, *What can I get?* but scanning should also be about asking, *What can I give? Who can I serve? What problems need solving?*

CHAPTER 5: BOLSTER YOUR BENCH

Who Do You Already Know? Who Can Provide Advice? What Can You Give in Return?

He will have friends from whom he may seek counsel on matters great and small, whom he may consult every day about himself, from whom he may hear truth without insult, praise without flattery, and after whose likeness he may fashion himself.

—Lucius Seneca

NETWORKING. IS THERE ANY TERM THAT GIVES MORE PEOPLE HIVES WHEN IT comes to career change? One study revealed that the word itself actually makes people feel dirty.

You have probably heard phrases like "Connections are currency" and "Your network is your net worth"—clichés repeated so often that they are easy to cast aside. Yet it remains true that authentically connecting with others is a far superior opportunity-building strategy than "spray-and-pray" outreach or résumé blasting across online marketplaces.

Nearly everyone I interviewed for this book mentioned that, in addition to excelling in their current roles, career opportunities came from two key places:

- Their existing network, friends of friends, and colleagues
- Reputation-building activities, such as writing or speaking on subjects that they have expertise in

Both of these factors hinge on creating two-way conversations with people you already know and those you have yet to meet. I remember speaking with an executive, Sam, at a conference. After my keynote, he approached me to share the story of his most recent pivot. He had worked at one job for twelve years before taking the risky move of leaving to work at a start-up. Nine months later he was laid off.

Shell-shocked and worried about supporting his wife and children, he started placing calls to his network the same day he was fired, *on the commute home.* Within two weeks, Sam was starting at another job. The speed of this transition was based upon several factors:

- Sam had developed a strong reputation as a chief information officer. He was at a high level in his career and could easily be slotted for a new role based on his leadership abilities.

- He had a "warm" network that was willing and ready to support him when needed. The conference we met at, the HMG Summit for CIOs, had been a central venue for keeping in touch with his peers throughout the years.

- He did not hesitate to jump into action. He reduced his "woe is me" mode (to a pulp) and proactively reached out to people who could help him.

I am not here to tell you to eat your networking spinach. Rather, this chapter covers specific tactics you can use to authentically put yourself out there and develop a robust support system for connecting with people in a way that excites, not drains, you.

The strongest people strategies involve a blend of the following:

- **Warm connections:** Mutually beneficial relationships you nurture over time, from which you both derive a sense of fulfillment and even exchange from your interactions.

- **Reputation capital:** Expanding your sphere of influence by mastering your current role; establishing yourself as an expert; developing a name as someone with a unique skill set at the top of your field.

- **Thought leadership and platform:** Publicly expressing your ideas; giving potential clients or companies an idea of what you stand for; making it clear who should seek work with you, who you enjoy working with, and how you can add value.

EXPAND YOUR SPHERE OF INFLUENCE

Shawn Henry worked his way up from an FBI file clerkship at twenty years old to a leadership role as the "number three guy" at the bureau—the executive assistant director—by the time he retired. Shawn pivoted thirteen times within the FBI over twenty-six years, each time expanding what he calls his *sphere of influence.*

Rather than stick to the traditional job ladder for his role, rising in the ranks as a bureau chief, he moved into emerging fields based on his strengths and interests. Shawn maintained a short-term vision each time; he focused on mastering the skills required for the role he was in and the impact he could make, incrementally increasing his level of responsibility and his ability to influence a greater portion of the bureau. By the end of his tenure, Shawn had become a key figure in creating international cybersecurity protocol.

Shawn encourages others to be cognizant of what their sphere of influence is, whether as a janitor or the president. "By examining your sphere of influence, you have the ability to quantify what you are doing every day," he said. "There are very specific times in my career when I remember engaging with people where I know my being there had an impact. Whether quietly working behind the scenes or standing in front of the camera, I looked for opportunities to affect people, policies, and processes."

That sphere of influence does not just magically appear—you have to actively pursue those opportunities. "People always say it's a small world. That doesn't just happen," Shawn said. "The world becomes smaller when you increase your circle and *make* that happen. It's a huge world for someone sitting on the couch watching TV every night."

BUILD A NETWORK OF COLLECTIVE BRAINPOWER

Change does not happen in isolation. Even something that feels solitary, like training for a marathon, becomes much easier with friends and family checking in from time to time to hold you accountable and cheer you on throughout training and the big day.

As Adam Grant revealed in his book *Give and Take: Why Helping Others Drives Our Success*, there are three types of people: givers, takers, and matchers. Those who are most successful in their careers are *givers* who help others freely, without expectations, and thereby establish goodwill, reputations, and relationships that enhance their success.

Impacters, though driven strongly by their own learning and curiosity, are givers at heart. For all of the categories below, consider yourself not just high net growth but high net giving, and you will reap rewards on both sides of the coin.

One-Off Mentors and Shadowing

Standard career advice says make sure you find a mentor. However, in practice this can be intimidating. *Who? Where? How? Will people say yes to a mentoring relationship if I reach out?* Rather than pressuring yourself to find one Holy Grail Mentor, start by setting up one-on-one conversations with people you admire, people doing work that interests you, and peers who might also be able to provide sound advice (and vice versa).

Given that you may not have the specifics of your pivot figured out yet, start with wide-ranging outreach. Approach those you are intrigued by, and make a point to include people who are doing work that seems only tangentially related to what you are currently doing or might want to pursue.

A *one-off mentor* is someone you admire who has achieved something you aspire to, or who knows more about an area of interest than you. Rather than awkwardly asking a semi-stranger, "Will you be my mentor?" or trying to start a long-term relationship with someone you hardly know, approach one-off mentors for short, targeted, fifteen- to twenty-minute interviews instead.

If your initial conversation goes well—you hit it off and you value their advice—you can always ask to follow up at a later time with updates or questions. Even if that person does not end up providing specific counsel on your next pivot, you never know where the relationship might lead, or how you could be helpful to each other later down the road.

People often tell me they are nervous about reaching out to someone out of fear of rejection. Keep in mind that the worst someone can say is no. A no is almost never personal to you. The person you approached may be focused on other things at the moment; prefer a different format than the one you suggested (i.e., a phone call instead of lunch); or, in some cases, giving specific advice is how they earn a living, so they may direct you to existing programs they offer. Chalk up every no as another successful outreach effort and keep moving. Many will say yes if they can, remembering everyone who helped them along the way.

Allow one-off mentorships to evolve naturally if both parties are interested in developing the relationship further. In some cases, the person you speak with may even offer to stay in touch, as one of my longtime mentors Susan Biali did with me nearly ten years ago. During our first call, she said she would love to support me on an ongoing basis, and asked if it would be helpful to set up a monthly check-in. I am deeply grateful for her counsel and our idea exchanges throughout my career, and for her believing in me from such an early age and stage in my business.

In other cases, you may be the proactive one in following up after having these one-off conversations. No need to harass or bombard; just start with sending a thank-you note afterward, then check in a few weeks or months later with an update on action you have taken related to your conversation.

Find people in roles that interest you, whom you could ask about their daily experiences, perhaps even by shadowing them for a day or more. This will help determine whether the realities of their work match how things appear from the outside. Does the reality of this role fit your strengths and interests?

That was my brother Tom's approach with his first mentor, an accomplished real estate investor. After he graduated from UCLA, where he played football as a defensive end, Tom began attending football alumni tailgate events to network with real estate professionals, a group that was living his one-year vision. Tom asked one booster he admired if he could help manage his portfolio of commercial properties and apartment buildings without pay for a few months, in return for getting an inside look at his operations.

By starting with a shadowing arrangement, there was little risk to Tom's potential mentor other than teaching time, and it helped complete a significant amount of work. Tom performed well and ended up parlaying that arrangement into a full-time role managing his mentor's properties for two years. Bolstered by the base of experience he acquired from this apprenticeship, Tom then pivoted into commercial real estate brokerage and started investing in multifamily units for his own portfolio.

E One-Off Mentor Outreach

1. **Make three wish lists of people you admire:** These are people with whom you want to develop deeper relationships. Consider:

   - Strongest Ties: People you already know; connection is already warm; the person is likely to be responsive and willing to help.

   - 50/50: People you know loosely or through one or two degrees of separation; you could be introduced through your network; the person *might* respond to an e-mail or call request.

   - Long Shots: People you do not know, and with whom direct connection would be difficult; "big fish" who, if they said yes, you would be ridiculously excited to speak with. To quote *Dumb and Dumber*, "So you're sayin' there's a chance!"

2. **E-mail three people from the lists above:** Ask if you can speak with them for twenty minutes, or even send one short question via e-mail to start. Mention why you admire them, and why their specific advice would be helpful for you. The key here is making it easy for recipients to say yes.

3. **Be curious:** On your call or in your e-mail, ask open-ended questions, and let the other person do most of the talking. Ask what they would advise you to do in your situation, what they would have done differently if they could do things over, what the drivers were to their

success. You can ask if there are any key resources that were particularly helpful, and if there is anyone else you should speak with.

4. **Respect the time parameters you set:** Do not go past your scheduled time. This will make them much more likely to be willing to set up a second meeting in the future.

5. **Thank you, Part 1:** Send a note describing what specific advice resonated, and the impact the conversation had on you.

6. **Thank you, Part 2:** Do something with their advice! Take action. Report back with a progress update on specific steps you took as a result of your talk.

Board of Advisors

As one-off mentoring relationships progress, you will develop deeper relationships with a handful of people that you can consult regularly and exchange ideas and feedback with, ideally to benefit them as well. In doing so, they can become members of your *board of advisors*. This is your brain trust, your mentor clan, your strategic "been there, done that" crew who offers lessons from their triumphs and missteps (both of which are invaluable sources of road-tested wisdom).

Although I have been fortunate to have several advisory board members proactively offer to support a particular pursuit, their participation usually came after I initiated the relationships by reaching out to introduce myself. I also make a point to place equal effort on my own reputation-building activities, so that when I do approach people, they will hopefully find me interesting to speak with as well.

You might assemble an informal board of advisors that you consult with questions without explicitly inviting them to be part of your team. Or you can do as Rebecca Rapple did with me and send a formal invitation. After I agreed to be on her personal advisory board, Rebecca sent a spiral-bound packet of her goals for the year in every area—a twenty-page life and business plan.

Sometimes your advisory board members will know each other and interact with each other, but most often they will not. That is okay; your board does not have to convene all at once. Still, they are a short list of five trusted people that you can turn to for advice when you get stuck.

Similarly, you may not have direct relationships with each of your advisory board members. You can still follow their progress, learn by observing what they are up to, and look to them as an inspiring part of your vision. Think of people you admire: perhaps you have no contact with them, but their actions and career approaches still serve as guiding lights. For example, many people swear by "the Church of Oprah," whose talk show reached ten million daily viewers at its peak. These advisory board members from afar can be inspirational and aspirational, as you learn from their path by staying current on what they are doing. Just remember to also keep your eyes on your own paper and not get *too* caught up in others' definitions of, or pathways to, success.

Drafting

If you have seen the Tour de France, you know about *drafting*: riders clumping behind the lead bike, not passing on purpose, so they can benefit from reduced headwind and effort. They are mimicking a technique used by many bird species. The lead biker or bird is doing the hardest work, while the others flock closely behind to reduce their drag and the energy needed to achieve the same speed.

Career drafting can be a mutually beneficial technique, though it should not devolve into stalking, stealing, plagiarizing, or leeching. Think of someone further along in their career, either in your industry or the one you may want to be in, who is doing what you are hoping to achieve, and ask if you can help with any overflow he or she does not have the time or desire to tackle.

This is not about being lazy. By drafting behind someone who has already cleared a way forward, you can learn from their approach and benefit from overflow they cannot handle. You will pay it forward someday by helping others draft behind you.

I was in a lead position when coaching other solopreneurs, people running their own one-person businesses. As I shifted toward working with executives and entrepreneurs, I referred anyone who reached out for postgrad coaching to several of my clients whose primary goal was working with young professionals. It was rewarding to pass these opportunities along to other coaches who were thrilled to have the work.

On the flip side, I drafted behind other professionals when I was building my speaking business. I told other speakers in my career niche that I loved working with organizations and speaking at conferences, and was happy to travel to do so. Several speakers were glad to refer me for gigs that did not appeal to them, or that they did not have time to take on, particularly those with small children at home.

The people you want to surround yourself with will endorse the adage that "a rising tide lifts all boats." Andrew Deffley, from Chapter 4, drafted behind an actor who had ten years more experience by forming a genuine friendship with him. They kept in touch after crossing paths on various sets, and when the veteran actor landed a gig on a new web TV series, he recommended Andrew for one of the supporting roles. Based on this introduction and the strength of his audition, Andrew got the job.

Drafting can take several forms:

- **Apprenticeship:** Working for potentially little compensation in exchange for total access and mentoring about how the lead runs their business or career.

- **Overflow:** When the lead has incoming work demand that they cannot fulfill, *if* you are skilled in your trade but not yet generating the same flow of incoming interest, the lead can recommend you in their place.

- **Books and podcasts:** You do not have to know experts "in real life" to learn from and draft behind them. Books represent years of knowledge, research, and mistakes that you don't have to make. The first thing I do when someone hands me a book is crack it open, stick my face in it, and inhale its new book smell. *Ahhh, the glory of all that wisdom in one condensed package!* The author poured years of his or her life experience and expertise into one guide, all for the cost of a few lattes. You can also draft by listening to TED Talks and podcasts, especially if you are an audio learner or want to experience another dimension of an expert's work.

Friendtors

You have heard the adage that you are the average of the five people you spend the most time with. I say the more the merrier; but at a minimum, if you do not have friends that inspire you and help you expand, it is time to add new ones. There is no room for toxic people ever, but certainly not when you are making a major change. Pivots have a way of forcing these relationships to the surface so they can be dissolved or reconfigured with clearer boundaries.

Friendtors, on the other hand, are the amazing people we are fortunate to call friends, who can also wear the mentor hat professionally by providing domain-specific advice. You may have friendtors in your local area already; if not, start seeking like-minded people in online communities or meetup groups focused on your interest areas. Your closest friendtors may also be part of your board of advisors who you turn to when facing big decisions.

One of the most helpful actions that pulled me out of unproductive navel-gazing during a business pivot was setting up phone calls, coffee dates, and walk-and-talks with peers in my industry who had figured out solutions to major sticking points I was facing. Because we were developing mutually beneficial friendships, we met more regularly than we would have had the chance to with more formal "big fish" mentors.

These friendtor conversations provided many benefits: they got me out of the house and my own head, helped me connect with others, gave me real-time feedback and solutions to my specific issues, and uncovered new opportunities and ideas that I would not get from merely reading books and listening to podcasts.

I did *not* approach these conversations as "can I pick your brain" sessions—that phrase is a personal pet peeve—*who wants their brain picked?!* Instead, I saw these meetings as an opportunity to provide mutual value. I set an intention to enter those interactions with positivity, feedback, helpful suggestions, resources, encouragement, and connections for the other person, too.

Connecting with friendtors can become a habit just like working out, without feeling like a nausea-inducing form of networking. Set a goal to meet with one or two interesting peers every week. Make reaching out a regular part of your routine, whether forming new connections or revisiting with people you have met in the past. If you do not live in the same city to meet with a friendtor in person, it works just as well to set up a "calfee." Yes, that is an amalgam of call and coffee—hat tip to my brother for that one!

Another way I catch up with friendtors is by organizing gatherings, events I refer to as "catchalls" because they allow me to catch up with many friendtors at once, and create value by introducing them to each other. Every summer I host Potluck Picnics in Prospect Park, and I encourage invitees to bring others. This allows us to casually connect with old friends and make new ones, all over low-key conversation and delicious food.

Luke Schrotberger turned to his friendtors when he wanted to pivot within his company, where he had worked for nearly ten years, from consulting on projects for defense manufacturing to a group that worked on oil and gas in Alaska. He started by reaching out to close friends inside and outside the company. Luke spoke with one friend who started around the same time he did and was now in a leadership role in Alaska and could provide honest insight and perspective. It was this conversation that ultimately helped him land the job and pivot internally.

Two years later Luke decided he wanted to pivot once again, this time to start his own company, since it seemed there were no more growth opportunities for him with his current employer. Two weeks after he announced to his boss that he was leaving, that same colleague who brought him to Alaska during his last transition made an offer for him to move to Australia to start a new division. Luke's friendtor outreach provided critical insights during his first pivot, and a job offer at the next.

Mastermind Groups

In addition to casual friendtor relationships, I have also found great value in more formalized peer *mastermind groups*. For many years now, I have set recurring weekly or biweekly calls with one or two friends who are doing similar work or who share similar goals. These mastermind groups provide consistent accountability, encouragement, and brainstorm buddies.

I recommend finding people who are at your level, with whom you can have an even exchange of ideas, feedback, experiences, and introductions to others. Even if you are not in the same industry or do not share the same goals, these groups can provide a great source of accountability and support if you set those as the central aim.

I met Lora Koenig when she signed up for one of my courses, a ten-week program for generating momentum for a big goal. In that course, I assigned each person to a small mastermind group for weekly accountability check-ins. When Lora joined the program, she was in debt, unhappy with her job, longing to see the world, and wishing she "could just escape from life and start fresh." Lora said, "I felt restless and miserable, that if something didn't happen soon, I would be stuck in an unhappy life forever."

That hopeless feeling made the trouble of change worth it, and sparked her to take three Scan steps at once: apply for the Peace Corps, sign up for a conference for creative types, and enroll in my course. Within six months of completing the course, Lora was accepted into the Peace Corps and pivoted from working in product management to agricultural development in rural Ethiopia.

"The peers I met really helped support me during this time, especially when I felt like I was crazy," Lora said. "While people I knew at my job and in my city would say they didn't understand why I wanted a change, my online peers were saying, 'It's okay to feel like this,' and 'It's *your* life.'" For Lora and so many others I have worked with, finding a group of like-minded people online helped her feel less alone, less crazy, and more courageous.

My friend Adam and I hold a 30/30/30 call for 90 minutes, approximately every three weeks: one-third for catch-up, one-third for brainstorming for his business, and one-third for brainstorming on mine. Whenever my friend Elisa and I need extra motivation and accountability during busy times, we start an e-mail thread for the month, then reply at the end of each day with a list of work completed and what we plan to tackle the following day.

When my friend Alexis Grant and I were writing books at the same time, we set up a shared daily writing tracker. It was motivating to see each other's entries and cheer each other on. A few months later we created a similar spreadsheet and invited people to join us for a challenge of writing 50,000 words in one month during the popular National Novel Writing Month held every November. We named ours NaNoBlogMo to fit our blogging aim, and nearly a hundred people joined. Aided by the power of group accountability, we wrote a combined 556,000 words, with four people hitting the 50,000-word target.

Knowing that my peers would see a goose egg if I didn't write motivated me to get a little bit done each day. It was the first time in my life, and eight years of blogging, that I had written consistently every day, even when I did not feel "struck with inspiration," something I had often waited for in the past.

A few things to keep in mind when setting up a mastermind group:

- Choose one or two other people whose skills and goals complement each other.

- Set up a recurring day and time for your calls. I prefer forty-five minutes every other week, though some mastermind groups do ninety minutes or more.

- Start each call by each doing a check-in: talk about a high, low, and something you learned since you last spoke. And share any big wins to help celebrate each other's successes!

- Take turns with a focused brainstorm: succinctly describe one challenge each person is facing, minimizing backstory, and brainstorm with the group for ten to fifteen minutes. Rotate as time allows.

- When closing, have each person identify one or two next steps to take before the next call.

- On a monthly or quarterly basis, set higher-level goals and reflect on the previous period.

Bartering

If you are short on cash, or even if not, and you have a unique skill to trade for another expert's services, *bartering* can be a way to get professional help while keeping expenses down. In a study of a thousand freelancers, 83 percent said they refer work to fellow freelancers, 52 percent team up on projects, and 37 percent trade services by bartering. Bartering agreements work best when there is a start and end date, and clear deliverables on both sides.

I have bartered successfully by trading my business strategy coaching with other coaches, a lawyer, a massage therapist, and a website designer. I even created a website in exchange for having a fee to a yoga retreat in Italy waived. All my barter buddies are good friends to this day, partly because we have been able to come through in the clutch for each other by exchanging expertise over many years, and throughout many ebbs and flows in our lives and businesses.

Bartering works best when you can benefit from a skill the other has and vice versa. This can be tricky; it is not always easy to find two people whose skills directly match up with each other, at the time when both are looking for help, and also have the time, energy, and financial flexibility to take on unpaid work.

Keep in mind that you want to identify a fair exchange rate; given that money will not be changing hands, it is important to determine what would satisfy both sides. Things can get weird (and fast) if the exchange starts to tip unevenly in one direction, or even if one person starts to feel like it does. For this reason, consider whether bartering really is best.

If you are building a business, you might want to pay someone neutral—someone you do not have a personal relationship with—so that you do not feel reserved when giving feedback or bumping up against inevitable creative disagreements. Barters should not be confused with actual business partnerships, which require greater commitment and do involve money or equity.

CAREER KARMA: SEEK RECIPROCAL SUCCESS

On several occasions, I have had potential clients approach me a bit hesitantly since they wanted to do work similar to mine. *Would I still be willing to work with them if we are technically competing for the same type of client?* "I don't worry about that for a second," I reply, often to their surprise. I am delighted to send them referrals, even to people who could just as easily work with me, because I fundamentally believe there is enough for all of us.

This is what I call *career karma*. When I give freely, I reinforce the idea that plenty is on the way back. Plant enough seeds of generosity, without expectation, and it comes back tenfold, often in ways you will not see coming.

Lisa Danylchuk, a San Francisco–based psychotherapist, calls this *reciprocal transformation*. "The principle of reciprocal transformation says that one person's growth is another's," she says. "Learn to see the other person's awesomeness or good fortune as a reflection of your own possibility."

Sharing resources and celebrating others is a start, but not sufficient for reciprocal success.

Your ability to help others starts with you. You must fill your own cup first by asking for help along the way. Don't just give until you are empty. Going it alone is tough. It is lonely, and most of all, it is frustrating.

I learned this the hard way. I once nicknamed my inner whip cracker "the self-sufficient warrior." It represented the protective shell I built for myself early in my career and relationships. If I did things alone, I did not have to rely on anyone, and no one could let me down. I could handle and control my own happiness and success *thankyouverymuch*.

Except that it didn't work. The more I protected myself, the further away people got. The more I tried to go it alone, the more burned out I became.

Conversely, when I got so low that I had no choice but to ask for help, the exact next steps I needed came to me. People entered my life at just the right time. I started to trust the wisdom that the events in my life had to offer, the perfectly timed unfolding of lessons that seemed handpicked just for me, no matter how challenging in the moment. I recommitted to the full cycle of giving *and* receiving.

————

The best network-building strategy is not about making a landgrab for favors and business cards. It is about developing mutually beneficial, resonant relationships that do not feel like work; ones that bring you energy, ideas, and connections and vice versa.

People are a linchpin of your Pivot strategy . . . but it is not time to call in favors just yet. What will motivate others to connect you with opportunities before you even have to ask?

CHAPTER 6: BRIDGE THE GAPS

What Skills and Expertise Will Take You to the Next Level?

I hope that in this year to come, you make mistakes. Because if you are making mistakes, then you are making new things, trying new things, learning, living, pushing yourself, changing yourself, changing your world.

—Neil Gaiman

TECHNOLOGICAL INNOVATION IS HAPPENING AT SUCH AN EXPONENTIAL RATE that none of us can predict exactly what skills will be needed to complement technology in the future versus those that may be rendered obsolete. Therefore, it is not sufficient to simply figure out what skills you need and master them.

As the adage goes, "Give a man a fish, feed him for a day. Teach a man to fish, feed him for a lifetime." We must now adjust the second directive to: "Teach a man to *teach himself* how to fish, feed him for a lifetime." The most agile pivoters improve upon the learning process itself so they can adjust quickly as new technologies are introduced.

You *can* accelerate how quickly you spot skills that are needed, and how rapidly you learn them. While the Plant stage helped you identify strengths already under your belt, this chapter will teach you how to effectively scan for new marketable skills. You will learn to discern what areas are worth an investment of further learning and research.

MIND THE GAP

Once you are firmly anchored in your strengths from the Plant stage, it is time to start closing the gap between where you are now and where you want to end up, as outlined in your one-year vision. It is likely that you will need to increase your skills or knowledge to plug these gaps and further refine your vision.

Before you start binge ordering how-to books on Amazon, set a learning strategy by identifying what you *don't* know. This can be a bit of a catch-22, as part of the Scan phase involves revealing blind spots. This is the foundation of learning and growth: pushing yourself past your current limits and levels of awareness.

E Revisit the vision exercises from the Plant stage. Identify areas where you want to increase your skills, expertise, reputation, and network. Consider:

- What are you wildly curious about?
- What could you do to further develop in those areas? Where can you go to learn these skills on your own?
- Who can you shadow or train with as you improve?
- Take a moment to also examine what *isn't* currently working in your career setup: what skills would help you move on or correct course?

LEARN HOW TO LEARN

Once you have some ideas about new skills to pursue, there is a sea of resources to help you acquire them while experimenting with other Pivot elements. Part of scanning—and pivoting—effectively involves learning how to learn. Books like Josh Waitzkin's *The Art of Learning*, Tim Ferriss's *The 4-Hour Chef*, and Josh Kaufman's *The First 20 Hours* provide instruction and shortcuts on how to learn just about anything in a fraction of the time you might assume is necessary.

There are also dozens of low-cost online learning platforms—including

Skillshare, Khan Academy, Codecademy, General Assembly, Udemy, Coursera, Udacity, and more—that you can join to acquire new skills. And thanks to Massive Open Online Courses (MOOCs), we now have access to courses and professors from all over the world via universities that open their doors to thousands of online students each semester.

The progression of building a new skill follows four stages, or levels of learning. This is known as the conscious competence model, developed by Noel Burch at Gordon Training International. Familiarizing yourself with this model will help you push through the inevitable dips and discouragement that accompany the learning process.

Levels of Learning

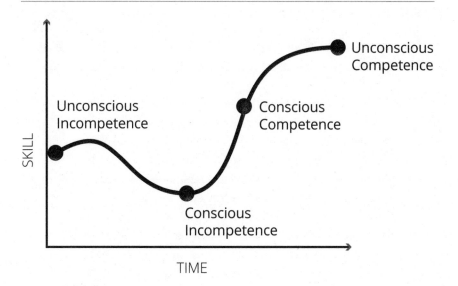

Levels of Learning

- **Unconscious incompetence:** You don't know what you don't know; ignorance is bliss. You are not yet aware of the skill, or what is required to master it.

- **Conscious incompetence:** The dip. As you start practicing, you become aware of how much you have to learn. You might feel incompetent, frustrated, or discouraged as you realize you need more time or practice to excel.

- **Conscious competence:** You have started to master the new skill, but you still have to actively think about whether you are doing it right. Similar to the first days after getting your driver's license, you are capable, but vigilant attention is required.

- **Unconscious competence:** You do not have to actively think about the skill any longer. Applying it comes naturally; as a result, meeting your objectives becomes attainable and enjoyable. Momentum builds.

Harness Momentum from Hobbies

It is helpful to have a hobby or skill you can cultivate during a pivot, something that has nothing to do with your career. When I first moved to New York, I set a personal goal to start practicing handstands in the middle of the room during yoga class. This was so scary to me that in the first handstand workshop I attended, I did not attempt to go upside down even once in the packed two-hour class.

The next year, I set a goal of nailing just one handstand in the middle of the room, holding it for a few seconds, and coming down by choice. For the hundreds (if not thousands) of repetitions I did that year, I accomplished this once or twice, more by fluke than anything.

The year after that, I made a point to practice every day in the park, where no one I knew was watching and where the grass would soften my falls. Slowly, my skills improved. I was no longer afraid to try in class, and by the end of the year I was sticking my handstands in the middle of the room most of the time. I felt like a kid turning myself upside down every day, and loved the sense of play, delightful distraction, focus, incremental achievement, and confidence that pursuing this practice brought.

A hobby can boost your outlook during a pivot in several ways:

- When you are fried from wrestling with big questions, it can be helpful to set thorny issues aside and distract yourself with an engaging hobby. The time away often sparks new insights when you return to your big questions later.

- There is a special confidence that comes from building a new skill very slowly over time. It is fun to see even tiny amounts of progress, and this gives you something to celebrate even on your most challenging days of cracking complex pivot questions.
- Building new skills changes our brain wiring, increasing neuron connections and myelin production. This improves performance, particularly the more we practice.
- Hobbies teach the skill of failure. The learning process inherently involves sucking at first, and in many cases you can't learn the skill without screwing up 100 times, until you finally nail it on try 101.
- Hobbies encourage you to get out of your comfort zone, and you may even end up serendipitously meeting people who are helpful to your pivot in surprising ways.
- If you have a hobby that involves being physically active, so much the better. You will get all the happy chemicals from exercise, and the endorphin reward of succeeding as your skills develop.

Albert Einstein called this *combinatory play*, and would often discover innovative ideas during his violin breaks. This practice was so important to his process that he famously said, "Combinatory play seems to be the essential feature in productive thought."

LIMIT LINEAR THINKING

When asked about his strategy for writing stand-up comedy, Chris Rock said, "Forget being a comedian, just act like a reporter. What's the question that hasn't been asked?" The same applies to scanning: in this stage, you act like a journalist, inquiring into new areas with expansive, open-ended questions to determine what to learn, who to talk to, and what opportunities to pursue.

Asking open-ended questions does not always come naturally. One common Pivot pitfall occurs when people skip the question-asking step altogether, instead selling themselves short with a laundry list of precursory qualifications. They wait too long for more training, more experience, or more certifications, instead of building from their current strengths.

You know you are falling into this *someday trap* if you are putting linear conditions on a desired outcome, such as "*When* I earn $150,000 a year, *then* I can travel more," or "*If* I get an MBA, *then* I can start my own business." Some of us fall into perfectionistic thinking as a delay tactic: "*When* my website is completely buttoned up, *then* I can launch." Others turn to defeatist thinking: "If I *only* have a hundred subscribers, what is the point?"

If you have ever taken an improvisation class, you learned a fundamental building block of improv, the "Yes, and" technique. This technique means that anything your improv partner says goes. Between the two of you, you can combine crazy, unrelated concepts if you build on what the other is saying. In fact, that is the only effective way to keep the story moving.

The same goes for your biggest pivot questions. Although some reflection is good, as is some future planning, the real gold lies in the middle—your present reality. Only by adding to your current reality, asking combinatory questions from seemingly contradictory statements, do you move the conversation with yourself forward.

Frame your linear beliefs as combinatory questions: How can I pursue what I love *and* keep my job? Or, how can I leave *and* maintain a strong sense of financial security?

Another way to circumvent faulty if-then logic is to ask what the "then" state would really get you. If you had a master's degree, then what? If you had more money, what would that enable you to do? These "then what" questions point toward the real goal, where we can start to ask much better questions, such as:

- How can I test my ideas with a small audience?

- How can I make progress toward my pivot even without my next gig or client lined up?

- How can I bolster my health, happiness, and hobbies given my available free time?

- What is *already* present in my life and work that I am grateful for?

I have also seen many people afraid to make a career change lean on worst-case scenario questions, usually a variation on: *What if I fail and hit rock bottom emotionally and financially?* I certainly had this thought when I considered taking my coaching and consulting business full time.

Once I became aware that I was letting fear consume my thinking, I started a thought-replacement exercise. Every time fear-based scenarios popped into my mind, I countered with a more productive question: "But what if I earn twice as much in half the time?" This allowed me to turn my attention toward building a business that would achieve that more motivating aim.

E Fix Faulty Linear Logic

List your three biggest Pivot concerns, then rewrite them as "Yes, and" statements. Next, rewrite those statements as "how" questions.

Here is an example, starting with the fear-based concern. "I want to start my own business, but I am afraid of not earning enough money to be financially secure."

Restating this as a "Yes, and" statement, it would become: "I want to start my own business *and* be financially successful."

The third step, rephrased as an expansive question, would be: "How can I start my own business and earn enough to maintain my current lifestyle?" An even more direct version is "What business model would most fit my strengths and provide a healthy living?" You could get more specific still: "What type of business would earn at least $150,000 per year, while supporting a lifestyle that expresses my core values of freedom and vitality?"

Reflect over the course of a week and see what develops. From time to time, I write open-ended questions at the top of a sheet of paper or Post-it Note on the back of my front door, where I know I will see it every day, then add ideas and potential solutions throughout the week or month.

Drop the Bucket on Unanswered Questions

My dad and I developed a game called "Drop the Bucket." Imagine that there is a bucket in your brain where you place an unanswered question. If you *drop the bucket* into the well of your brain, like a wishing well, when it is ready it will rise with the answer—maybe in an hour, maybe when you are in the shower, or maybe a week or month later.

According to Steven Kotler, author of *The Rise of Superman: Decoding the Science of Ultimate Human Performance*, "The secret is to take yourself to the edge of frustration, then stop. Go until your brain can't take it anymore, then change the subject. Take your mind off the problem." In doing this, our brain switches from conscious to subconscious processing, and answers seem to pop up out of nowhere.

When you are looking for answers or ideas, frame them as open-ended questions, then drop the bucket. They *will* come up eventually; the bucket always returns. Asking the right question is the hard part; once it is out there and you review it periodically over the course of days or weeks, your mind will begin to wrap around it and give you some answers.

What are your unanswered questions at the moment? As my dad says, "Put those 85 billion brain neurons to work!"

INVESTIGATIVE LISTENING

In a video interview for Jonathan Fields's *Good Life Project*, renowned vulnerability expert Brené Brown shared her approach to research and discovery. Brown follows a social science method called grounded theory, a system for discovering theories or hypotheses by looking at a data set first, then coding it to determine themes later. This process is reversed from most traditional research methodologies that say one should state a question or hypothesis first, then prove or disprove it with data.

Brown explains that with grounded theory, you first observe the "lived experience" and use that to make conclusions, which may or may not clash with existing theories. "It is all about resonance and fit—do the concepts that you are coming up with resonate with the studied population?" Brown explained. "Do people see themselves in the lives and stories that you are creating with your data?"

According to Brown, *trust* and *emergence* are two of the most important axioms of grounded theory. "Trust in whatever emerges from the data, trust in people's lived experiences, and their perceptions of those experiences," she said.

How does this relate to a pivot? Oftentimes you will need to put your ear to the ground *first*, then look for themes and clues. This is the purpose of the Scan stage: to have a two-way conversation with many different groups— your peers, mentors, clients, colleagues, companies, friends, and family, anyone who can help you discover new themes, strengths, and opportunities.

Marques Anderson did exactly that when he pivoted from playing football in the NFL to starting his own global nonprofit, the World Education Foundation. Since its conception in 2010, the WE Foundation has worked with an international network of experts, interns, and volunteers, assisting in project structure and implementation in four key developmental areas: health, education, infrastructure, and sports.

Rather than dictate what should happen among his volunteers, partners, and the communities he serves, Marques takes the perspective of "servant leader" instead. In his travels to over fifty-one countries, he makes a point of immersing himself in the local community and culture. Whether he is going to birthday parties, having tea or dinner at someone's house, or going for a walk with a local community leader, Marques listens with engaged curiosity more than he talks.

"I realized very early on that I needed to let the people guide me rather than me trying to guide the people," Marques said. "It is very important to me to get those stories from on the ground, where it is not me sitting in an ivory tower telling people what to do and what is best for them. Instead, I let them tell me what is best, then serve as a facilitator to bring those opportunities to them," he said.

I racked my brain for months about what business model would be most sustainable for me during the pivot I described in the introduction. Over and over I asked myself, "What is a scalable business model?" without a good answer, until one day I realized I was approaching the problem the wrong way. I needed to use my version of grounded theory to focus on *others'* needs, not my business: put my ear to the ground *first*, then create something valuable based on what my new community at JennyBlake.me would find most helpful.

This can be a humbling experience. It means you are admitting that you do not know. It means returning to a "beginner's mind," as the Buddhist saying goes, releasing attachment to preconceived ideas and being open to whatever responses emerge.

A few weeks after this realization, I sent a quick two-question survey to my blog readers asking how I could be most helpful. I asked, "What is your biggest challenge at the moment?" and "What can I create for you this year?"

You can do the same thing without an audience by asking people in areas that interest you what their biggest challenges are. Companies hire employees, contractors, and consultants because they have a problem they want to solve.

The survey submissions I received were incredibly helpful. Some people were in the midst of a career pivot, others were looking for specific business tools and tactics, and others were addressing the balance and burnout side of the equation. Some challenges and requests were on my radar, but others were not, and the survey responses helped shape the projects I was considering.

Suddenly I was benefiting from the power of hundreds of minds, not just one. I could find themes and patterns, then mix in my own intuitive sense about what people might find helpful, without trying to do all the heavy lifting myself.

With the data I gathered, I ended up creating a private online community called Momentum, where impacters could exchange ideas, tools, and connections to further their creative goals—aided by my templates, courses, live workshops, and support. I created a section within it called Brilliance Barter that operates on a take-a-penny, leave-a-penny philosophy for giving and receiving feedback, where I evaluated several key elements of this book.

This process was consistent with what Brown and Fields discussed in their *Good Life Project* conversation. "You can create a product and then find the people and the market to sell your product to, or you can get to know a community, listen to the current conversation, and cater to what they actually need," Brown said, adding that the best researchers and entrepreneurs "are open to the market proving them wrong, listening to what the market says is right, and then deciding whether they want to create that or not. This ultimately requires a lot of discomfort and vulnerability."

One caveat: *just* listening won't propel you into innovative mode. As Henry Ford said of getting into the automobile business, "If I had asked people what they wanted, they would have said faster horses."

E Investigative Pivot Listening

1. **Identify your ideal audience:** the people or companies that you would like to learn more about.

2. **Formulate a few key questions to ask this population:** Examples that work well across the board are:

   - What are your current challenges?

   - Where are you heading? What do you want to create or do next?

   - What does success look like? How will you know when you get there?

3. **Deploy your listening tool or research method:** It may be casting a wide net by creating a survey that you send to friends, coworkers, or your community, or it may be starting in a more intimate way by setting up conversations, or a combination of both. In the design-thinking community, these conversations are called *empathy interviews*, and refer to finding out as much as possible about potential customers' experiences with a given topic or environment, even if you do not ask directly about your product or services.

4. **Gather data and parse key themes:** Whether you send a survey or meet with people face-to-face, collect all your notes in one place. What are the common threads among the responses? What are the biggest challenges for the people you care about? How might these tie in with the strengths and interests you identified in the Plant stage?

5. **Identify small next steps:** Based on your active listening, what next steps could you take? Are you ready to start prototyping, or piloting, a potential solution, or do you want to conduct another round of research? You might do both simultaneously—keeping up with active listening even while taking steps forward, which tends to be the most successful route by enabling the two-way conversation to continue.

Pivot Paradox: Why Ignorance Is Bliss

Some of the smartest, most self-aware people I know also report sometimes feeling the most unsure or insecure. This is the Downing effect at work. The Downing effect, also known as *illusory superiority*, says that the more intelligent someone is, the lower they rate themselves on the intelligence scale. The *lower* someone's IQ, the higher they rate themselves. Ignorance truly is self-assessment bliss.

On its face, self-doubt might appear to be a bad thing for impacters, but there are positive implications underneath it:

- You are constantly pushing yourself outside of your comfort zone, seeking knowledge from new and diverse fields for use in your own industry.
- You are aware that the more you learn, the more you realize you don't know.
- You aim to surround yourself with people who challenge you. You don't want to be the smartest one in the room, at least not most of the time. You look for symbiotic relationships where all parties bring something helpful and unique.
- You are not afraid to break from the status quo, from society's "white picket fence" ideal of success. For this reason, you may feel

out of place in traditional situations. It takes courage to bust deeply embedded cultural norms.

In his 1951 book, *The Wisdom of Insecurity*, Alan Watts implored readers to accept that there is no such thing as safety or security, and in fact, most of the joys of human life are lovable because they are changing. "Music is a delight because of its rhythm and flow. Yet the moment you arrest the flow and prolong a note or chord beyond its time, the rhythm is destroyed," he wrote. "Because life is likewise a flowing process, change and death are its necessary parts. To work for their exclusion is to work against life."

Fear, insecurity, and uncertainty are the price we pay for a conscious, fully awake, fully alive life. Rather than making yourself wrong for feeling fear and insecurity on the winding roads of change, honor them as the signs of a courageous life.

BE DISCERNING ABOUT YOUR LEARNING

Even with the pace of change, all hope of strategically positioning yourself for success in our economy is not lost. Instead, focus your energy on *how* you spot skills that are needed, particularly those rooted in your existing strengths.

In their book *The Second Machine Age: Work, Progress, and Prosperity in a Time of Brilliant Technologies*, authors Erik Brynjolfsson and Andrew McAfee make the point that the fundamental metrics of our economy have changed, saying, "More and more what we care about in the second machine age are ideas, not things . . . interactions, not transactions."

According to Brynjolfsson and McAfee, there are some guidelines to keep in mind regarding what skills and opportunities to pursue to *complement* technology, rather than compete against it. We will see the most success and upward mobility among people who demonstrate:

- **Strategic thinking, ideation, curiosity, and combinatorial innovation:** Humans are still much more creative than machines when it comes to inventing new products or making improvements to existing products or processes. We also have the unique ability to ask powerful questions that can lead to new solutions by combining complementary or seemingly unrelated components to create something new.

- **The ability to become "superstars" through reputation, platform, and leverage:** If you can develop a reputation as being the best at something within your target market, then build a platform to disseminate your expertise or related products, you position yourself for positively disproportionate gains. *Leverage* refers to being able to parlay your reputation and platform into greater exposure, and therefore opportunities (we will talk more about this in the next chapter).

- **The ability to work alongside technology:** A midlevel computer can beat a human at chess, but teams of humans working *alongside* computers triumph over machines.

Even still, this may not always be the case. As Geoff Colvin writes in *Humans Are Underrated: What High Achievers Know That Brilliant Machines Never Will*, it is futile to ask what computers will never be able to do, since the answer is most likely nothing.

Instead, we should focus on the unique value people can provide as we shift from our role as *knowledge* workers into *relationship* workers. Colvin suggests that the guiding question then becomes, "What are the activities that we humans, driven by our deepest nature or by the realities of daily life, will simply insist be performed by other humans, regardless of what computers can do?" He adds, "To look into someone's eyes—that turns out to be, metaphorically and quite often literally, the key to high-value work in the coming economy."

———

This part of scanning is about asking expansive questions, observing what arises, discovering holes in the market, and pinpointing potential skills to develop. But the Scan stage is not complete just yet. The flip side of asking and listening is building a reputation engine that hustles on your behalf through-out your pivot and far beyond.

If a tree falls in the forest and no one is around to hear it, does it make a sound? If you have a one-year vision and the skills to get there but no one is around to help line up opportunities or benefit from your expertise, can you really make the progress you desire?

CHAPTER 7: MAKE YOURSELF DISCOVERABLE

How Can You Add Unique Value and Build Visibility?

Chance is always powerful. Let your hook be always cast; in the pool where you least expect it, there will be a fish.

—Ovid, *Heroides*

BLUETOOTH IS THE MAGIC TECHNOLOGY THAT PAIRS TWO DEVICES WITHOUT ANY cables. Connecting two Bluetooth-enabled devices, such as your phone to your car or wireless speakers, requires making them both "discoverable." When a Bluetooth-enabled device is discoverable, other devices can detect, pair, or connect to it.

Pairing up in the career sense works the same way. You will have an easier time navigating between career moves or clients if you are discoverable, which means putting your ideas out into the world through your own platform, or piggybacking on an existing one. Both require that you stand for something and commit to sharing your unique ideas and expertise.

So far in the Scan stage we discussed whom to connect with, and what types of skills would be most beneficial to develop. Now it is time to zoom in on specific opportunities and platform-building activities to round out your Pivot portfolio. This third Scan step is about investing your searching time wisely and getting your story straight: making your desired direction known to others, and developing a strategy that enables opportunities to find you by increasing your visibility and reputation.

DEFINE YOUR PROJECT-BASED PURPOSE

In the Plant stage, we explored the idea of purpose, a driving theme that propels your entire body of work. If you are compelled by a force that calls you toward a specific type of work or group of people, that can provide great clarity when pivoting. But what if you still don't know what your purpose is? Maybe you skipped that section because it seemed too abstract.

For some, the pressure to define a purpose or mission statement is stifling and causes much unnecessary angst. In many cases, particularly mid-pivot, trying to get *too* specific with one Be-All, End-All Purpose causes more anxiety than anything else. So ditch it. Focus on shorter-term aims instead.

If your one-year vision is the *what*, or the desired destination of your next career pursuit, your *project-based purpose* is the *why*. In a world of shorter-term work, defining your *why* with project-based purpose will help you better sift potential opportunities while scanning, without the pressure to guide your entire life by one magical, all-encompassing statement.

Defining personal projects, and by extension your project-based purpose, is not a trivial exercise; it turns out this process is central to our overall sense of happiness. Cambridge University professor Dr. Brian R. Little, author of *Me, Myself, and Us: The Science of Personality and the Art of Well-Being*, believes that when asked, "How are you?" our answer hinges on how we feel about our personal projects. He writes, "Well-being is enhanced if your projects are meaningful, manageable, and effectively connected with others."

Nerissa Gaspay is a San Francisco–based preschool teacher for children with disabilities, including cerebral palsy, Down syndrome, rare genetic disorders, and epilepsy. She has a project-based purpose to bring more play into her classroom after seeing how much it accelerates her students' development. One of her experiments to meet this project-based purpose is starting each day with an obstacle course. Although more traditional teachers may wonder about its merits, Nerissa's kids love it, and she has already seen tremendous progress as a result. Her longer-term purpose is to help parents better understand and communicate with their children with disabilities, and to develop new methods for helping her students learn and acclimate to their surroundings.

Julien Pham, the physician-entrepreneur you met in Chapter 2, has a project-based purpose for his website, Startup Clinic: to connect physicians with each other so they can transfer knowledge, share innovative ideas, and help bring medicine into the twenty-first century by encouraging the institutions they work for to think like start-up companies. As someone who was born in Vietnam and raised in Paris, and grew up with a doctor dad and business-founder mom, Julien's longer-term purpose is to connect cultures to improve communication—between medicine and technology, and between physicians and patients.

As you scan for projects that might suit you, look for the underlying project-based purpose. Why take on that work? What do you want to accomplish? Who do you hope to impact, and in what way? If someone were to send you a glowing thank-you note related to this project one year from now, what would it say?

If you are still having trouble coming up with a purpose for your next phase, simply ask: how can I be most helpful to the most people? And this doesn't have to mean the masses. "Most" right now might be your nuclear or extended family. Or shift from thinking to doing by volunteering at local organizations that are always grateful for extra hands, such as homeless shelters, food kitchens, meal delivery services, animal hospitals, and homes for the elderly.

The one thing that has brought me peace in my most unclear career moments is rededicating myself to serving others. *That's it.* It doesn't have to be more complicated than that.

PLATFORM AND LEVERAGE

Becoming an expert and developing a strong reputation is helpful, but it will not take you very far if the people you want to work with do not know who you are or where to find you.

Developing a public-facing *platform*, a corner of the world from which you can share your ideas and expertise with a community you cultivate, greatly amplifies your *leverage* during and after a pivot. Like the pole-vaulter who uses a pole to catapult over the high bar, your platform gives you leverage to find new and previously unseen opportunities.

When I left Google, I had big plans for launching my book and online courses. But to pay the bills while working on those elements, I did one-on-one career coaching, which was 20 percent of what I had been doing in my role at Google. This ended up sustaining me as my most reliable source of income for five years. It provided reasonably predictable cash flow, I could throttle it up and down relatively easily, and I could do it from anywhere. When I decided to work from Bali and Thailand for two months in 2013, I was worried no one would want to work with me because of the unpredictability of Internet access or having to make our calls over Skype across time zones. But surprisingly I got the most clients in the history of my business. That was enabled largely by the platform of readers with whom I had built trust in the years leading up to my travels, negating potential distance issues.

Developing a community takes time, and strong ties will be more helpful than large stats. Whether 50, 500, or 5,000 people, it is not the size of your platform but the level of engagement that matters. This inner circle will become your best advocates, supporters, connectors, and someday, perhaps, customers and clients. Kevin Kelly, founding executive editor of *Wired* magazine, suggests aiming for "1,000 True Fans," or people who will purchase "anything and everything you produce."

Building a community and becoming a thought leader should not be about a selfish aim for fame. As Dorie Clark, author of *Stand Out: How to Find Your Breakthrough Idea and Build a Following Around It*, wrote, "It's about solving real problems and making a difference in a way that creates value for yourself and others. It's a willingness to be brave, open up, and share yourself. It's a willingness to risk having your ideas shot down, because you genuinely believe they can help others."

Not everyone has to become an entrepreneur, blogger, or "personal brand." Nowadays, with social media, many people feel that they must "live their lives at the same time they brand the shit out of it," as my friend Stacy Sims puts it. Branding, and becoming a thought leader in some area of expertise, is not going to be every impacter's passion, nor does it have to be. But becoming an *expert* in your desired field—not just technically the best, but recognized and publicly known for it by generously sharing that expertise with others—will become your most powerful generator of new opportunities.

Instead of feeling like you must constantly pound down doors to get hired, others will swing those doors open for you.

Julie Clow, author of *The Work Revolution*, was a senior vice president in HR at a hedge fund while writing and publishing her book. As her growth within the company began to wane, she received a message through LinkedIn asking her if she wanted to interview for a job that exceeded her wildest dreams: senior vice president of global people development for Chanel. If she got the job, she would split her time between Paris and New York, with great perks to boot.

Julie was perfectly positioned to be poached for a new role because of the platform building she had done: continually achieving great results at her company, writing a book based on her expertise in organizational behavior and company culture, taking on a board position with a prestigious global learning and development organization, and cohosting a Work Revolution conference. Julie developed a strong reputation in her field and a platform that she could leverage into an even better-fit job.

Julie does not maintain a public-facing platform for the purposes of running her own business; she loves working within large, innovative companies and transforming their people and leadership programs. She enjoys writing, and applies that skill to publishing high-quality content just often enough to keep her engaged in conversations within her industry. In addition to bringing her career fulfillment, contributing to large media platforms helps her expand her leadership influence and remain discoverable.

Photographer Daniel Kelleghan also has a platform that makes him discoverable to others, allowing him to seize opportunity when it shows up. After six months photographing products for Groupon in Chicago, Dan quit to pursue his own photography business full time, traveling to shoot fashion and architecture, while bridging his income with corporate clients. He worked diligently at posting high-quality, artistic photos on Instagram to build a following.

Over the first three years of building his Instagram platform, Dan amassed a little over 7,000 followers. Then, because of the unique quality of his photographs, Instagram featured him on its suggested user list for two weeks, showcasing Dan's account to new users worldwide. By the end of the second week, his following skyrocketed to over 100,000 people. Hotels and clothing brands started reaching out to offer goods in exchange for Dan's sharing photos of their products with his audience.

Now Dan stays for free in many places by proactively offering sponsorship opportunities to companies in cities he will be traveling to. New clients such as Audi and Warby Parker are finding him rather than the other way around. Dan became the fifth-highest-followed Chicago Instagrammer after his initial boost, propelling his platform even further. On one hand, this may seem like a random lucky break. But Dan has been committed to producing high-quality work for years, knowing that if something like this were to happen, he would be ready to capitalize on that luck.

E Platform Options: Ways to Leverage Expertise

Unlike Julie and Dan, you may not want to build a platform on a foundation of ideas or creative expression. You might want to teach, interpret others' data, or build software that replaces you altogether. Below is a wide range of high-leverage platform ideas to consider. Just for kicks, brainstorm three avenues you could pursue within each, no matter how far-fetched:

- **Expert as teacher:** Teaching large groups of people, either in person or through online channels. For example: creating software tutorials or teaching guitar by posting videos on YouTube or online course platforms.

- **Coach or consultant:** You or a team you teach use your expertise to guide others. For example: running time management workshops like David Allen, creator of the classic productivity system *Getting Things Done*, or working as a professional organizer like Marie Kondo, author of the runaway hit *The Life-Changing Magic of Tidying Up*.

- **Subject matter expert (SME):** Sharing ideas, solutions, and best practices on what you know about a specific area; forecasting or interpreting trends in your industry; disseminating knowledge and projections beyond the classroom. For example: in addition to teaching computer science at Georgetown University, Cal Newport shares "study hacks" for career success in his blog and books.

- **Software as a service (SaaS):** Create software or systems that improve efficiency or automate a specific market need. For example: online scheduling tools like Calendly and ScheduleOnce make booking meetings a snap; an accountability tracking service like AskMeEvery.com sends a question you have written, such as "Did you work out today?" to your inbox at a specified time, while tracking your yes or no responses in a dashboard to show progress.

- **Combinatorial innovation and curating:** Make sense of the massive amounts of information across several interest areas by curating and consolidating content. For example: NextDraft.com creator Dave Pell opens over a hundred browser tabs each morning and synthesizes the ten most important news themes for the day, with articles neatly (and humorously) summarized in a NextDraft mobile app.

- **Specialized community building and connecting people:** Bring like-minded people together to enhance your network and theirs, connect in an interesting setting, and align around a mission or big idea. For example: Nick Grey founded Museum Hack "for people who don't like museums." Nick and his team lead groups through New York City, San Francisco, and Washington, D.C., museums in "highly interactive, subversive, fun, non-traditional museum tours."

- **Brokering between buyers and sellers by creating a marketplace, facilitating comparison shopping:** Systematizing the buying and selling process, or finding ways to reduce fees in traditional industries by connecting buyers and sellers. For example: Airbnb for finding a place to stay, or Upwork for finding creative freelancers.

- **Aggregating and analyzing data, conducting original research:** With increasingly more data available on everything from how many steps we take, to our heart rate, to mapping our genome, people will need help making sense of this data, "separating the signal from the noise," as political pollster Nate Silver does. Some say that "data is the new oil" in our digital economy, and must be refined in order to add value.

REVEL IN THE WORK OTHERS REJECT

After four years at her PR firm, Amy Schoenberger, who you met in the introduction, started feeling uninspired. She knew that it was time to make a change; however, she loved her company, the culture, and the people, and she did not want to leave. Amy ended up creating a new role for herself at the firm by finding opportunity in a strange place: by seeking out, taking on, and excelling at the work that no one else wanted to do.

In 2009, PR strategy recommendations increasingly included social media and blogger outreach. While many of her coworkers saw social media as annoying and beneath them, Amy decided to dig into the field. She learned everything she could, following the industry as it was evolving, and quickly became the firm's in-house social media expert. Soon she was consulting with most of the firm's clients. She parlayed this work into a new role as director of digital entertainment, a position she created from scratch by demonstrating the impact of her work on the organization.

While I was working on this book, Amy was approached by a former manager and mentor to join her at a new company. This opportunity developed because of her excellent results and reputation. Amy became vice president of social strategy at M Booth.

Amy's advice is to follow a counterintuitive approach to opportunity. "If you don't know what you want to do next and you are feeling stuck, do the work no one else wants to do," she advises. "It may lead you to a surprising and rewarding answer about what you like, what you are good at, and where you can differentiate from everyone else in your industry, especially in a cluttered field."

LEAPFROG: WORK BACKWARD FROM TWO MOVES AHEAD

If you are still having trouble culling opportunities or clarifying a project-based purpose that is aligned with your vision, consider the *leapfrog approach*.

Many people actually *do* have an idea of what they want two "moves" from now, even if they do not have a clear understanding of what they want in the moment. Imagine a frog hopping on lily pads. Oftentimes people can identify the lily pad that is two leaps away; they just can't see the one right in front of them that should come next in order to reach their further goal. The leapfrog approach will help you scan for opportunity two moves out, then work backward to find a transitional in-between pivot.

When I applied to Google for a role on the AdWords training team in 2005, part of what attracted me to the position was that I knew deep down I wanted to be an author and professional speaker someday. At the time, public speaking was so nerve-racking that I wore turtlenecks when giving big presentations to cover the splotchy red marks that would show up on my neck and chest. I knew that taking a job where speaking in front of others was a daily requirement would serve as good immersion therapy—and it did. In this case, my desired role to be an author and professional speaker was two leaps ahead, and the job I took at Google helped me progress toward my longer-term lily pad.

Graduate school is another example of an intermediate pivot that narrows the gap between the current state and the desired leapfrog move, one that is two steps ahead. Although it does require a significant investment of time, money, and opportunity cost, graduate school can provide many benefits, including networking, skill building, time to explore in a structured environment, expertise in your desired field, and in some cases, required professional licenses.

Adam Chaloeicheep, who you met in the introduction, climbed up the ranks quickly as a creative director in a branding agency. But at twenty-six years old, he felt completely burned out. So he sold all his belongings and moved to Thailand to study in a Buddhist monastery, wiping the slate clean. When he returned home, Adam knew he wanted to expand beyond just graphic design. He envisioned himself in high-level brand strategy roles as a chief experience officer, or CXO, the translator between CEOs' business goals and their product design teams.

However, Adam hit wall after wall when he applied for these types of jobs. Even when his résumé and pitch book made it to executives' desks and he interviewed, no job offer materialized. This was a sign that he was shooting too far ahead of his experience, at least in terms of what was visible to others from his résumé and public-facing platform. The latter didn't exist at the time, as he did not have a website or professional online presence beyond his LinkedIn profile.

In parallel to this search, Adam started exploring options for graduate school. He knew that he was a *good* graphic designer, but would never be "the best." Adam asked himself, "How am I going to grow into something I want to be, in a CXO-type role, if I don't feel completely confident in being able to apply those ideas to add value to companies?"

After debating whether to attend graduate school for a few years, Adam decided that it would indeed be his best next step. It would improve his business acumen, bolster his résumé and network, and buy time to pivot his own fledgling freelance business. Adam applied to Parsons Business of Design program, accepted a scholarship, and moved to New York City with just $5,000 of his savings remaining. Within one year, thanks to the structure, connections, and mentoring he received in graduate school, Adam started his own brand strategy firm, hired a team of fellow students, and quickly surpassed mid-six-figure revenue—all prior to graduation.

Adam made the business school trade-offs worth it by tying school projects directly to his business, experimenting in practice, not just in the classroom.

"It was hard to swallow moving all the way from California to New York with barely any money in the bank and taking on the expense of two years of tuition," he said. "So I just told myself that if I am going to do this, I am going to do it so that I can apply things in the real world as soon as possible." Throughout school, and in his wider life, he maintains an impacter mindset for experiments like these: "Care deeply, but have no expectations."

Now Adam does serve as a chief experience officer, his vision two moves out, by running his own brand strategy company. Graduate school was the lever that enabled him to achieve his goal.

The leapfrog approach has three key benefits: it helps build transitional skills and experience, allows you to explore what you enjoy more deeply, and enables you to form key relationships in the area you want to pivot to, even before you have your following steps lined up.

LET OTHERS KNOW YOU ARE LOOKING

Until this point, much of the Pivot prep work is solitary—identifying your values, vision, strengths, interests, and allies. Although you identified people to connect with earlier in the Scan stage, you have not yet applied the full reach of your network's resources.

Now it is time to clearly state what you are scanning for and how people you know can help. Even if people you contact do not have an open opportunity right away, they can put their feelers up in case something related to your desired direction surfaces.

Casey Pennington started to feel stuck two years after graduating college, despite having "done everything right her whole life." She said, "I made straight A's in school, got into a top business university, snagged an internship and subsequently a full-time offer from a large corporation. I thought I was set for life. Fast-forward two years and the thought of spending my entire career navigating bureaucracy and politics was causing me increasing dread each day. I knew something needed to change."

Casey first identified what she wanted, the known variables of her one-year vision, as a work environment that provided learning, challenge, autonomy, flexibility, relationship building, and the time and money to have the life she wanted outside of her career. Working for herself was appealing, but Casey knew she was not ready to venture out on her own just yet. When she decided to pivot within her company from accounting to IT, she first let her managers know. Then she leaned on her strengths by transitioning to an accounting role on another team with an upcoming software implementation project.

She scanned further by talking to anyone she could find with experience in software development and learning as much as she could about current systems to prepare herself for a future role. When the first software project she landed was delayed, an unexpected opportunity came up to help on a related temporary assignment.

"Because I had laid the groundwork to let my managers know I was interested, they recommended me for the project and I got it," Casey said. "I had been making my interest in moving to IT known for a while, even though this offer seemed to come out of the blue."

I have heard many stories like Casey's. Once people get clear on what type of opportunity they are looking for and make it known to their network, prospects materialize in surprising ways. Although they may not have actively sought out those exact opportunities, spreading the word generated momentum behind the scenes, even when they did not realize it was happening.

I call this the universe rolling out the red carpet. When you are heading in a direction that resonates, every step you take prompts another fortuitous rolling out in front of your feet. Each courageous move uncovers new people and opportunities, encouraging you to keep going and reminding you that you are on the right track.

When you are ready to put the word out, send an e-mail to your closest friends, family, and trusted professional contacts with the following sections:

- An introduction succinctly stating the pivot you hope to make: what you are doing now and where you want to go (one to two sentences max).

- Your background: three to five brief bullet points on your strengths and experiences.

- The ideal company or clients you are looking for: a few bullets on types of work, location, and how you can make an impact.

- Call to action: how recipients can be most helpful; for example, by forwarding the e-mail, and keeping their eyes and ears open as opportunities come up.

Even if you do not know exactly what you are looking for, opening the process up to your trusted contacts can generate fruitful next steps. When Carlos Miceli made the difficult decision to step away from the three-year-old company he cofounded in Argentina, he sent an e-mail to his network with a Google Doc linked at the bottom called "Carlos's State of Affairs," which he described as a "private and more vulnerable LinkedIn profile."

In the note, he expressed his knowns and unknowns. He stated what he was looking for, and how his network could help or collaborate with him.

"This is looking like a bridge year for my long-term vision," Carlos wrote. "I'm not worried about *what* the next big project will be, or if I should join someone else's 'rocket' instead of launching my own—I am more interested in figuring out *with whom*, and *where*."

The document outlined Carlos's preferences and current ideas on potential directions for his next career move, skills he wanted to improve, content he was interested in, and ways his network could help. At the end of his e-mail, he also made it clear that he was happy to provide advice, ideas, connections, and resources in return.

Pivot Paradox: When the Grass Really Is Greener

"The grass is always greener on the other side." Too often this is used as a phrase to keep people in line. "Don't bother being upset! The grass is always greener!" The message is to settle, to be happy with what you've got. If you have a job, don't bother looking elsewhere. Don't listen to your gut; take it on blind faith that no matter what you do or where you go, you will always have this itchy, unsettled feeling. Let the wave of peeking through the fence come and go, then sit back down and stay put.

It is important to be present in our own lives, to be grateful for what we do have, and to understand that any next move will have drawbacks and rough days. We should resist chasing what is shiny or seems easy, or basing our happiness on impermanent things. Relationships, jobs, and daily life inevitably become challenging at times, but we find our most rewarding growth experiences on the other side of discomfort.

That said, there are times when the grass *is* greener! I once read a book about entrepreneurship that, at every chapter, seemed meant to deter me from actually leaving my job. This book provided a "realistic" view of how difficult it would be, and spoke at length about how many businesses fail. By the end, it was clear that the author's advice would have been to ditch my greener grass fantasy and continue trucking along at my dependable corporate job.

But what the book did not account for is the invigorating feeling of giving it a shot. Of having all day, every day, to apply my best creative energy to my own business and success. I am glad I had a realistic view of the challenges I might experience over the first few years in business, but I am much more thankful that I did not take her advice.

The grass really is greener for me, based on my values and vision, on the other side. I still work with big technology companies, including Google; I just prefer to set my schedule and strategy for doing that. For me, any brown grass patches are worth it. Sure, I face challenges, but I am sitting on the right plot of land, and will continue improving my grass-growing abilities over time.

While your day-to-day experiences might vary, it is important to listen when your gut is telling you that there is a greener plot of grass that is a better fit than where you are now. Ultimately, you will not know until you gather more real-world data; don't just spin out on speculation.

That is what the next Pivot stage, Pilot, helps you do: step on one patch of grass at a time to determine if, in fact, you like it any better. The more patches you test, the more indicative they will be of the whole.

However, a Pivot paradox caveat: these patch tests cannot capture the entire experience. To switch metaphors for a moment, it is akin to the difference between a piece of cake and an entire bakery: one piece of cake will give you an accurate assessment of how the whole cake tastes, but trying a piece of cake will not be a complete indicator of how everything else in the bakery tastes. One side hustle earning $200 each week will show you if you enjoy that side hustle, not what it is like to try to earn a living from it full time.

———

Some people become dizzy during the Scan stage of a pivot because they are scanning without a plan, falling prey to too much searching and overthinking: *What is out there? Who can I talk to? What is next? WHO AM I?!*

If you find yourself aimless or frustrated while scanning, return to the Plant stage. Reconnect with your vision, values, strengths, and what *is* working.

From there, determine what exploration would be a logical extension from those known variables.

Channel Sherlock Holmes: every conversation and piece of new information is a clue. *How* you react to what you are discovering is as important as *what* you are learning; notice how different options make you feel. It is likely that your Scan phase will be as much about eliminating solutions you do *not* like as it will be about picking up new ideas that you want to pursue.

Searching, scanning, and narrowing can only take you so far. How do you take smart action when you do land on several strong idea leads? If you are at a pivot fork in the road, which path should you pursue?

Scan: Online Resources

Visit PivotMethod.com/scan for additional tools, templates, and book recommendations for this stage.

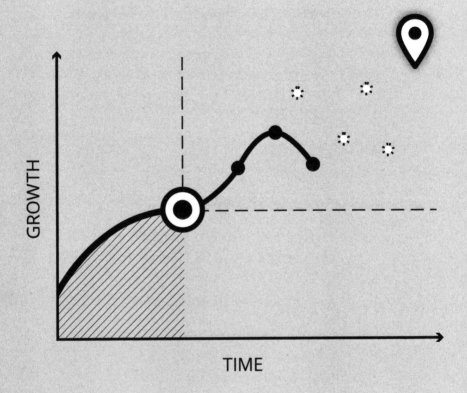

STAGE THREE

PILOT

Test What's Next

PLANT

SCAN

PILOT

LAUNCH

LEAD

PILOT OVERVIEW

A TELEVISION PILOT IS A TEST EPISODE USED TO SELL A SHOW CONCEPT TO A network. Before the network purchases the entire series, they watch a sample and sometimes show it to an audience to gauge interest and estimate its financial viability. Television pilots get their name from the pilot light, a small flame that is used as an ignition source for a larger burner, like the central heating unit of a house or a hot-air balloon.

For our purposes, the primary goal of the Pilot phase is ignition and validation: generating ideas, testing those ideas, then taking small, smart risks to eventually inform bigger decisions about what's next.

After identifying potential opportunities and ideas in the Scan stage, you will likely have several hypotheses about what to pursue. Instead of betting big on any one, it is best if you can pilot—reduce risk by conducting small tests—then expand upon what is working to launch in the most promising direction.

Newton's first law states that an object in motion tends to stay in motion, while an object at rest remains at rest unless acted upon by an external force. Piloting is critical because it gets your momentum snowball started. Small pilots will help you get unstuck, without the pressure of having to figure out *all* the answers up front.

Pivot is a state of mind, and the most agile impacters make a habit of continually learning and piloting. As a general rule, maintain an open, curious mindset, testing one hypothesis at a time, ideally several.

I can sense what some of you may be thinking: *This sounds exhausting! Must I always be looking for the Next Big Thing?*

Not necessarily. Pilots can be as simple as tweaks to your morning routine. They can be personally rewarding, such as spending time living in another country. Or they can be as ambitious as experimenting with a community-wide, nationwide, or global program within your company or business.

Assumptions Versus Hypotheses

In his book *The Voice of Knowledge*, don Miguel Ruiz says, "Making assumptions and then taking them personally is the beginning of hell in this world." We are likely to hit roadblocks when making assumptions about what *should* happen, rather than approaching our ideas with unattached curiosity. Piloting helps form open-ended hypotheses so we can test assumptions and make informed decisions about next steps.

Prepare to be wrong during the Pilot process. At times it may feel like you have taken two steps forward, immediately followed by two steps back. One reaction to this process might be, "I am an idiot and my ideas suck." It is up to you to shift that to, "Awesome. There's another one I can throw back into the refinery of my brain."

Oftentimes that failure or missed mark provides the next important clue. Recall Thomas Edison's famous quote, "If I find 10,000 ways something won't work, I haven't failed. I am not discouraged, because every wrong attempt discarded is often a step forward."

CHAPTER 8: GET SCRAPPY

What Small Experiments Can You Run?
What Real-World Data Can You Collect?

If you have built castles in the air, your work need not be lost; that is where they should be. Now put the foundations under them.

—Henry David Thoreau, *Walden*

IN *THE LEAN STARTUP,* ERIC RIES POPULARIZED THE CONCEPT OF THE MVP, OR minimum viable product. By his definition, the MVP "helps entrepreneurs start the process of learning as quickly as possible. It is not necessarily the smallest product imaginable, though; it is simply the fastest way to get through the Build-Measure-Learn feedback loop with the minimum amount of effort." When it comes to product development, the message is not to delay a launch by months or years so you can craft every last immaculate detail behind the scenes. Instead, form an educated guess and test it sooner rather than later with your target audience.

During my time at Google we referred to this as "being scrappy." We knew the conditions or output of our work would not be perfect, but it was important to release anyway, to "launch and iterate." Just get something out, then test it, get feedback, revise, and do it over again. Holding a mindset of *launch and iterate* encouraged us to get minimum viable products out to the company, then have our peers test the programs, letting their feedback guide future versions. Getting a program out, even a scrappy, imperfect, 70 percent version, was better than waiting for 100 percent perfection. That ideal state may never happen, and by that point users' needs would likely have shifted.

For many of my clients who are starting their own businesses, a minimum viable product might mean launching a website with a free, prepackaged theme long before hiring a website designer to design something fancier and fully customized. The latter is not the biggest priority for a new business whose primary goal is generating income. They *can* get new clients without a website at all; the original MVP is spreading the word via existing networks, and for that, e-mail and phone calls can do the trick.

Pamela Slim, author of *Escape from Cubicle Nation* and *Body of Work*, is a longtime mentor of mine and universal "auntie" to thousands of people in her community who benefit from her extensive career and business advice. Pam ran an experiment with her audience when she created a workshop called Indispensable Community, a program that would teach community-building skills for entrepreneurs. She set clear parameters for what her pilot would entail, and tested the idea by asking her readers what places they would like her to deliver the live course.

Over a hundred people responded. Pam narrowed the recommendations down to twenty-three cities, and put together a four-month, cross-country tour across the United States and Canada. She partnered with sponsors that served the small-business market, ultimately reaching over a thousand entrepreneurs. Based on the success of this pilot, she doubled down by making it a core part of her business strategy moving forward. Pam's tour pilot indicated support for her desire to shift from over ten years of online platform building based on career and business content toward programs related to her skill and experience with community building and leadership.

After her tour, Pam displayed her philosophy proudly and prominently on her website's landing page: "Community feeds personal, professional and economic growth." This experience spurred her next pilot: creating a scalable community-building program that would help others "realize their deepest mission and solve big problems in the world."

AIM FIRST FOR QUANTITY, NOT QUALITY

There are many ways to pilot your hypotheses about what's next, ranging from low risk to high risk; from observer to hands on; and from short execution time and investment to longer and more involved in terms of time, energy, and resources.

Below are common pilots I have observed. I encourage you to think about at least one way that you could apply each of them to your current situation:

- Taking on advisory board positions with other companies.

- Hosting friends for a meal around interesting topics, or for conducting grounded theory–type research.

- Conducting informal client or employee focus groups, then creating a prototype solution based on their needs.

- Trying out 10 or 20 percent projects at work in addition to core responsibilities.

- Volunteering for a team or interest group related to your one-year vision.

- Creating an informal pop-up group or program, such as a book club.

- Experimenting with a new service offering by taking on one new client in that area.

- Tweaking the cost or format (or both) of your existing services.

- Sharing a sampling of new ideas on social media to see what topics resonate; providing more in-depth exploration on the ones that do.

- Seeking out an internship or apprenticeship with a company or individual you might like to work with. (Writer Melani Dizon calls these "returnships" for mid-career professionals.)

- Enrolling in experiential work-study programs, such as those offered by Vocation Vacations and PivotPlanet.

- Advertising a few different services on a contractor marketplace to see what areas have most demand.

WHAT MAKES A STRONG PILOT?

When considering a pilot, aim to hit the following criteria:

- **Tie experiments to the Plant stage:** How many touch points does it have to your strengths, career portfolio, and one-year vision?

- **Start small:** How can you pilot in a low-cost way in terms of money, energy, and time?

- **Tip the risk scales in your favor:** What small experiments would have the most potential upside with limited downside?

Let's take a closer look at each of these.

Tie Experiments to Your Strengths

If you are at a career fork in the road, you need to strategically determine which of several paths is most likely to lead in a successful direction. What would be the best investment of your time and energy?

Recall what you discovered in the Plant stage. The best pilots are connected to your:

- **Values:** What is most important to you.

- **Vision:** What you are most excited about.

- **Career portfolio:** Your marketable skills, past experiences, results, and reputation; what is already working best.

- **Finances:** What fits with your budget and runway, and has future income potential and long-term viability.

- **Existing network:** The mentors, friends, mastermind groups, professional groups, clients, and current or former colleagues who can offer insight and support.

A good pilot is connected to one of the above; a *great* pilot ties directly into all five.

Choosing an experiment that is not anchored in your strengths, past experiences, or desired future state is likely to send you on a wild-goose chase. Some people trick themselves into thinking these types of experiments are a good idea—either because they *should* attempt them to adhere to social norms or because they have seen something work for others. Neither gives you a hook unless you actually have innate talent or interest in the same skills required to be successful on that path.

Christian Roberts and Bill Connolly are improv comedians who formed a monthly comedy showcase in New York City called Angry Landlord. On their third show, they hit a major dip: only eight people showed up. They were embarrassed about having to pay the theater money to make up for the losses, and disappointed that they let down the other comedians they invited to perform with them that night.

Christian and Bill went back to the drawing board and revisited what *had* been working for them: networking with other comedians who had also developed followings, and reinvesting in their own brand building and social media channels. They set up a Facebook page to expand their platform and become discoverable, and started experimenting with social media advertising when they had open seats to fill.

Beyond piloting *within* Angry Landlord—trying new formats to attract an audience—the showcase itself is a pilot anchored in their strengths and interests. Angry Landlord is a side project, as both of the founders have other full-time jobs. Bill works at a visual marketing company, where he also teaches improv workshops to business audiences, based on his first book, *Funny Business*. Christian is pursuing a career in acting while working as a server. Both are applying and developing their strengths—their love of people, writing, and making others laugh—even when not working on Angry Landlord.

The next Angry Landlord pilots will focus on expanding to a bigger venue, posting short sketch videos on YouTube, and continuing to network, collaborate with, and invite other comedians to perform with them. It is a constant evolution. After the empty audience experience, by returning to the anchors of what excites them most and what works best with their audiences, Christian and Bill have sold out almost every show since.

Start Small with Lean Pilots

In keeping with Eric Ries's MVP (minimum viable product) concept, I recommend taking a lean approach to piloting bigger career changes. A lean pilot is one that does not cost a tremendous amount of time, money, or energy. They are small tests to help you determine if you enjoy this area, have the skills to succeed and differentiate yourself within it, and have the potential to earn income (or any other top priority value). How can you experiment with 10 to 20 percent of your free time, without having to bet the farm on your next direction?

Lean Versus High-Risk Pilots

Here are a few examples:

Lean/Low Pressure	Not Lean/High Pressure
Employed at a company	
Taking on a small 10 percent project at work in addition to your core responsibilities to test your idea and opportunity for expansion.	Waiting to get involved until it can become your full-time role; waiting for a promotion instead of suggesting stretch projects.
Side hustle	
Starting a blog that you can tend to with one to two hours of focused attention per week.	Quitting your job to start a business . . . from scratch.
Self-employed	
Pitching a new product or delivery format to a prospective client.	Letting go of all your current clients while you "manifest" new ones.

My friend Ryan White—not his real name (you will see why in a moment)—is an agile business consultant for Fortune 100 companies. Ryan had an interest in creating a Beginner's Bondage course for couples interested in safe "knot play." The book and movie *Fifty Shades of Grey* propagated myths that he wanted to clear up after years of teaching private workshops.

Rather than quit his job and bank everything on this course—including his reputation—he set up a series of pilots. He created a free guide under the pseudonym Ryan White, and a landing page that would allow him to advertise the program with Google AdWords to see if there was genuine interest in this topic. He did not sink tens of thousands of dollars into creating a complex website, a full brand identity, and an entire book or video series. Instead, he piloted by creating a simple guide in a few months, one that he could build from if time and consumer interest allowed.

In an e-mail to friends, Ryan laid out his process: first he would set up a landing page that collected e-mail addresses in exchange for a free PDF of "Tips and Tools for Beginner's Bondage." The PDF included a call to action that would drive traffic to a Facebook group. If things went well with the free PDF and Facebook group, he would write a longer e-book to self-publish and offer on Amazon. If that succeeded, he would create an online course expanding on the e-book.

Look for Pilots with Asymmetric Upside

In *Antifragile*, Nassim Nicholas Taleb talks about the principle of "optionality," asymmetric opportunities that provide much more to potentially gain than lose.

Look for career pilots that have high potential upside with limited downside. Taking out a second mortgage on your home to pursue a business idea is a very risky endeavor: it may expose you to a great deal of debt, high interest rates, or bankruptcy if your idea does not succeed. On the other hand, taking a small chunk of your savings to pilot a prototype—to see whether there is interest and whether you enjoy it—does not expose you to risk in such a vulnerable way.

Ryan White's bondage course pilots had *asymmetric* upside. If he decided not to pursue it as a side business, he would lose only a small amount of money and time. Conversely, each pilot, if successful, would encourage him to move on to the next stage and take on incrementally greater risk, investing more money and time in proportion to any gains.

Conducting a series of small pilots paid off, though not in the way Ryan expected. He realized that this was an aspect of himself that he wanted to integrate more fully and share more publicly, but not as his full-time occupation. As Ryan put it, "It wasn't the market's no, it was my own." He wanted to continue investing in his career as an agile business consultant, not become an Internet marketer for his bondage course.

Rather than stay behind the scenes, Ryan realized that his true value would be in owning his quirks and writing about this side of himself *alongside* his business acumen. Though nerve-racking at first, this authenticity would bring him an even greater sense of freedom, and could inspire others to share their stories and full personalities more publicly as well.

Ryan has since dropped the pseudonym. His real name is Bob Gower, and he continues running pilots in writing, by sharing his story more publicly, and in his main job as an agile organizational consultant.

Pivot Paradox: Embrace the Slow Build

Sometimes you will want to pilot quickly, acquiring information and feedback as soon as possible, in a lean and scrappy manner. At other times, you may take a more deliberate approach to piloting, aiming not to make change happen within the year, but rather as a long-term strategy for developing your career portfolio. In the former scenario, you may sacrifice quality by moving too quickly, trying to force ideas and income streams to ripen before they are ready.

Theodor Geisel was a cartoonist who earned a living during the Great Depression as a writer and illustrator for newspapers, magazines, and advertising agencies. He dabbled in comic strips, poetry, and propaganda films to pay the bills. In 1936, Geisel wrote his first book of poetry, inspired by his travels; however, publishers rejected the manuscript many times. On his way home to burn it, he ran into a friend who helped him get the book published. When he was forty-nine years old, his first and only feature film was released. It was said to be a critical and financial failure, discouraging him from attempting another movie and prompting his return to simpler, more humorous stories.

In 1954, in response to a children's illiteracy report in *Life* magazine, Geisel's publisher asked him to produce a short book using just 250 of the report's words. Geisel complied and, at fifty, wrote and published the short poetry-like book. The title is one you might be familiar with: *The Cat in the Hat*, published under his college pen name, Dr. Seuss.

Dr. Seuss, like most professionals, was not an overnight success. He worked hard at his creative projects and always had several irons in the fire. He piloted by working across a variety of genres, investing more time into what was working and dropping what wasn't. From his days at the college newspaper drawing comics, to his poetry, to his interest in cartoons and humor, Dr. Seuss evolved his voice and found his audience over time. He worked in advertising to pay the bills while keeping his creative spark alive.

No matter what his day job, Geisel took time to explore projects that were interesting to him. He took smart risks. He continued exploring meaningful work long before he hit commercial success, and long after. I see this story not as encouragement to aim for one tiny peak at the top of a pyramid of success, but rather to enjoy the process of winding around the insides of the pyramid, appreciating every corridor and hidden room.

My late grandfather Harold had a similar but different form of slow-build piloting. His career pivot spanned thirty carefully planned years. He started at the ABC television network in 1949 doing hand-drawn lettering, including those for *Batman* (*Pow! Shazam!*) and titles for the Oscars and the Emmy Awards shows. Meanwhile, on the side, he set his sights on building a more sustainable income source that would support his family in later years. His first move was to buy and rehab a house—making him one of the early house flippers, before it became a trendy reality TV genre.

He parlayed the house into a six-unit apartment building that he moved his family into. Then he sold it and applied the profits to a larger building, until at one point he was managing a building with twenty-four units. At fifty-eight, when he was ready to leave his job as ABC's creative director after thirty-five years at the company, he had a second income stream ready and waiting. Once his second income surpassed his steady income, he had the freedom and confidence to leave ABC at any time.

My grandpa worked until his last days, far beyond retirement, even though he changed the risk profile over time, transitioning into second mortgages instead of buying and rehabbing buildings. His side hustles also allowed him to travel freely with my grandmother for many years, from China to India to Africa to Alaska and to many interesting places in between. He lived frugally and worked thoughtfully, never leaving one income source until the next was ready to take its place.

INCREMENTAL PILOTS WITHIN ORGANIZATIONS

Seth Marbin started at Google in 2006 doing search quality evaluation, which meant reviewing several hundred of the worst-quality websites every day to make sure they did not show up in search results. Needless to say, the job was not a direct connection to what Seth felt was his higher calling.

In 2007, Stacy Sullivan, Google's chief culture officer, put out a call for team-building ideas, as Google had just doubled in size from 7,000 to 14,000 employees. Seth proposed a companywide service day to help employees connect to each other and their local communities. He had experienced the power of volunteering to break down social barriers during his time in Ameri-Corps, and was inspired by Timberland's Serve-a-palooza, in which the company shut down all operations for one day to perform service projects.

In his spare time Seth recruited a small team (not yet officially sanctioned as one of Google's well-known 20 percent projects), and together they launched a companywide initiative called GoogleServe. Under this program, all employees could take one day off to volunteer over the course of a designated week. In their first year, the GoogleServe team engaged 3,000 participants across forty-five offices. Over two years, they doubled that number to 6,000 in seventy offices, and the program became recognized as a cornerstone of Google's community involvement. By 2015, GoogleServe had ballooned to 14,000 participants.

Though it would have been a massive pilot success at that, this was not the end of Seth's pivot. After three years of leading GoogleServe as a side project, Seth pitched then moved into a full-time role focused on Google's philanthropy efforts, an internal pivot encouraged by his manager at the time. He is now a program manager on the GooglersGive team, working with a group of ten people focused on year-round employee volunteering and giving programs.

Seth's trajectory demonstrates several important piloting principles:

- Starting with a small test to determine viability and interest.

- Piloting without any attachment to this being his full-time job, though he had the vision that one day that might be possible.

- Demonstrating increasing adoption and success each year; integrating GoogleServe with his core role after proving its value to the organization.

- Not waiting until an official role opened up to begin, though he did get agreement from his manager that he could work on this initiative as a part-time project.

- Creating a shared vision for the company, for employees, and for himself about what would be possible by doing projects in this area.

Seth chose a pilot—then repeated it each year in a bigger way—that led to a fourfold win for the parties involved: Seth got to spend time doing work in line with his values, strengths, and vision; Googlers were thrilled to take time off to volunteer and serve their communities; on a company level, Google advanced its social impact efforts; and thousands of community projects around the world received much needed hands-on resources and support.

REDUCE RISK WITH REDUNDANCY

In engineering, *redundancy* is defined as the inclusion of extra components that are not strictly necessary for normal functioning, but are included in case of component failure. Although it is not always possible to have complete career redundancy in terms of timing a move, it can help to aim for at least some overlap.

By piloting new ideas simultaneously, in addition to your current source of career stability, you gain important information before betting big on a new direction. Best to avoid panic about your next paycheck in the midst of major change, whether transitioning to a new client base if working for yourself, or to finding a new job if working for someone else.

Pilots can help you build backup systems and test ideas in a low-risk manner so that you are positioned to make your change when you need to. Marisol Dahl, communications director for my business, built her business slowly, learning and piloting little by little. She created career redundancy while in college to maximize available opportunities after graduation.

I met Marisol when she was a junior at Yale. She and her friend Davis Nguyen invited me to speak on campus for Yale's Master's Tea series. During my visit I mentioned that I was looking for a community manager for my *Life After College* platform. We piloted by setting up an internship at first. That worked so well that the following quarter Marisol moved to a paid position, in which I continued to increase her responsibility over time. She was a quick study, detail oriented, and completed every task on time with high quality. In six months, she helped me completely transform my business. In turn, I taught her all the systems and tools I used to run my operations. Within a year, we were in lockstep, each enriching the other's career ecosystem.

During Marisol's senior year, I started referring her to friends as a content and community manager. As her schoolwork lightened in her final semester, Marisol took on clients one at a time, raising her rates a little bit each time, piloting her strategy and systems for bringing on additional work. As she developed trust with each client, they also expanded her responsibilities, increasing her hours and project complexity.

By the time Marisol graduated, she had full-time job offers lined up *and* more potential clients than she could handle. By building redundancy and piloting self-employment while she was in school—each new client a pilot in itself—the choice of what to do after graduation was completely in her hands. She was in a win-win situation: because her résumé was already so stacked with interesting work in social media and online marketing, she could either take a great job with a company or go full time with her own. After taking a few months to explore, she chose the latter.

While many graduates were lamenting their lack of opportunities,

Marisol had become a magnet for them by expanding her expertise and existing network, and doing an outstanding job generating results for her clients. She knew that even if she did take a full-time job after graduation, she could have income and fulfillment redundancy by continuing to run her own business on the side.

After getting passed over for promotion on that fateful day in Iraq, Kyle Durand, from the introduction, spent the next ten years building a portfolio of businesses related to his strengths in law and accounting, while still working for the military part time in the reserves as an international human rights lawyer in combat zones. It was this redundancy that smoothed his definitive transition from the armed forces when he fully retired from the military after twenty-seven years of service. Kyle noted that the second major shift felt much easier than the first. "This one doesn't feel like a big deal because I already went through the really tough work ten years ago," he said.

On the redundancy of the last ten years, Kyle also pointed out how his diversified portfolio approach has also served him well within his current business activities. "It has been a damn good thing, because other businesses that I have started have fallen off-line," he said. "The redundant tracks have kept me going. At various times in the last ten years, one of my businesses has been on life support. If that was my only source of livelihood, I would have been dying, too."

Even in the military, Kyle made a point to gain skills, experience, and education that would transfer into the civilian sector. "When I was young I saw people who were getting out and had no idea what they were going to do, and not many transferrable skills. I never wanted to be in that position," he said. "That's why I kept changing course in the military and pursuing advanced degrees in law and accounting. Unlike most people who go into the military and do one career path, I had several."

Pivot Paradox: The Fauxspiration Foe

Got a tornado of great ideas and good intentions swirling around in your mind, but having a little trouble translating them to the real world? You might be afflicted with *fauxspiration* if:

- You read dozens of articles and blog posts to *get inspired!* . . . but feel too drained or discouraged to take action afterward.
- You read dozens of books to learn a new craft . . . without practicing the craft.
- You browse the websites of people you admire to figure out how to do what they are doing . . . only to be accosted by the comparison monster, who tells you that you are an unoriginal hack and everything worth doing has already been done.
- You get stuck in analysis paralysis in the name of research or draft mode, which might just be the big bad wolves of procrastination.

Impacters all fall into this trap from time to time, because it comes from a good place—the part of us hungry to learn, grow, share, and make a difference; the part of us that thrives on human interaction and community and wants to live vicariously at times through others' creativity and courage. It also originates from the part of us tempted to seek endless information to avoid the sting of regret that might come from making a wrong move.

But piloting is *not* reading, thinking, curating, organizing, outlining, filing, shuffling, e-mailing, hoping, making coffee, drinking coffee, or drinking another cup of coffee. Some of these may very well be part of the creative process, but they do not count for *output*.

During her pivot from nonprofit work to a career in public speaking, Gigi Bisong pulled herself back from information-seeking mode when she realized that, although her scanning seemed helpful, it was making her feel more stuck and it did not equate to real-world insight.

"I was signing up for every online conference I could find and realized I was even more confused after all the researching," she said. Her mentor compared this to reading about how to ride a bike, instead of hopping on the bike, falling down, and repeating until she could ride smoothly. Gigi shifted from scanning to piloting by volunteering to speak at smaller events to get real-time feedback, and started trusting her own wisdom for answers about next steps.

TRAVEL PILOTS TO SHAKE UP STAGNANT THINKING

If you are not generating the traction you seek from piloting, travel can be a tremendous way to spice things up.

Immersing ourselves in new cultures allows us to break free from current routines and obligations as we open up to the unknown. Travel teaches us to push past our fears, find courage to explore our inner and outer world, and forces us to turn off autopilot. As a result, we naturally become more present as we navigate unknown roads, meet new people, sample exotic foods, and awkwardly fumble through foreign languages.

The adventure and spontaneity of being away from home can foster creativity and a surge of new ideas. The solitude and quiet time provides space for introspection and direction setting. If you choose a destination with a lower cost of living, these trips can create financial breathing room and a longer pivot runway. Meeting others around the world injects friendship and fun. Travel can bring us back to a sense of gratitude and appreciation, opening our eyes to the larger global community by observing cultures vastly different from our own.

I hear the saying "It is about the journey not the destination" ringing in my mind, but sometimes during major changes, it *is* about the destination. A fresh location can provide exactly the creative catalyst we need.

Many people say they want to travel, even long term, but the accompanying uncertainty can be overwhelming, as can the costs. There are logistical elements of travel: get or renew a passport, save money for the trip, buy a flight, book accommodations.

Other considerations are more subjective: *Where should I go? For how* long? Who should I go with? How will I take time off work? Or will this be a working trip?

Sometimes we also face a litany of fears: Can I do this by myself? What if something bad happens? What if I don't enjoy where I end up? How will I find my way around? How will I communicate with others who speak a different language?

The Pilot process works just as well for travel as it does for career change.

Elisa Doucette had never been outside of the United States when she accepted a job with a company of expats, Tropical MBA, as communications director. She got her first passport and a one-way ticket to Bali, and started consulting for them as she traveled throughout Southeast Asia. Her pilot was the length of her first contract, six months, but she quickly proved herself indispensable and loved the lifestyle, so she extended her stay at each six-month checkpoint. Elisa worked with Tropical MBA for three years in this manner before diving back into her writing and editing business, Craft Your Content, full time.

Before my longer trip to Bali and Thailand in 2013, I conducted my own travel pilot by taking one month off from my business to travel to both countries in 2012. Buying the ticket for that trip was the most intimidating step. Once that was done, the rest fell into place, even how I would work with my coaching clients while on the road. I enjoyed my two-day stay in Ubud, Bali, so much that I returned to that exact spot the following year for a full month, then again two years later for another month to work on this book. Each trip gave me more courage for the next. Contrary to some of my biggest fears approaching each one, business and productivity actually improved—in fact, significantly so.

Travel pilots are different from vacations in that they stretch you out of your comfort zone. The stretch zone might be how long you travel, where you go, or your intentions for the trip. Perhaps there is a class you want to take abroad, or an industry you want to explore further as a potential next career move or location.

Travel pilots allow you to experiment with long-term or long-distance travel without committing to a giant leap, such as moving to a foreign country outright, though sometimes that can be just the shocking cold-water plunge your system needs.

———

The Pilot stage is about action—putting your ideas into practice to gather data and make informed decisions about what to pursue. But for some people, opportunities always seem to find them. What are they doing differently?

Consider the adage "A bird in the hand is worth two in the bush." A Pivot mindset is "A bird in the hand, with a second one camped at *the bird feeder I built*, is worth a flock in the bush." How can you build your own bird feeder? Which of your pilots, if you invested in it further, is most likely to bring opportunities *to you*?

CHAPTER 9: PAUSE, REVIEW, REPEAT

What Worked? What Didn't?
What Could You Do Differently?

Expect nothing. Live frugally
On surprise.

—Alice Walker

SLEEK AND QUIRKY VINTAGE CARS THAT WOULD MAKE ANY COLLECTOR DROOL.
Coffee close-ups so intricately shot that you can practically smell the espresso grounds and taste foam on your lips. Comedians conversing casually in diners, candidly discussing fame, humor, family, neurosis, and hard work.

Jerry Seinfeld pivoted from stand-up and *Seinfeld* to producing a web series called *Comedians in Cars Getting Coffee*—and the show is as addictive as his caffeine costar. Sure, it is fun to see two celebrities in their natural habitat, shooting the breeze for twenty minutes. But more contagious is how this show represents the total embodiment of a person's unique talents. Seinfeld found a way to follow his interests—his love of cars, comedy, coffee, and diners—while innovating within the TV industry and creating a viable business model around his experiment. The result is a joy to watch.

Comedians in Cars is not a 180-degree turn from his sitcom, but rather more of a 90-degree shift. *Seinfeld* episodes often depicted friends meeting in restaurants discussing day-to-day pet peeves in what was described as "a show about nothing." *Comedians in Cars* follows similar lines, in that

Seinfeld's predilections combine to form what he describes as "an anti-show about a nonevent." In one memorable episode President Barack Obama jokes, "I always wanted to be in a show about nothing and here I am." Seinfeld replies, "There is nothing—nothing more nothing than this."

In a *Fast Company* interview on what inspired him to experiment with a web series instead of a traditional TV show, Seinfeld said, "It just seems like the Internet is screaming at artists to be creative. It's like an art-supply store: You walk in, and there's paper and cameras and paint and pencils. It's like someone throwing down the gauntlet."

Seinfeld piloted the *Comedians* web series with the first season, then refined the style and production value over time as he gained audience traction and paid sponsorship. At the time of this writing, *Comedians* had wrapped its seventh season.

Seinfeld made a point to ensure that his pilots led quickly to viable income. Though he probably does not need the money, in evaluating this next career move he said it was important to generate enough profit to make the show worthwhile for him and his guests. In an interview with David Letterman, he said, "I wanted it to work as a business. To create a [web TV] show that made money hasn't really been done. That was part of the puzzle I wanted to solve."

Just like the TV pilot, a career pilot is an experiment that is meant to be evaluated, and quickly. Drop your attachment to the outcome and stay curious: What can I learn here? How might this inform my next move? How can I expand my original vision?

Once you have completed a pilot, or even several concurrently, the next step is to evaluate what worked and what didn't. What would you do differently? What has potential for greater opportunity? After that, you will identify another round of experiments and repeat the Pilot process.

Piloting is not a one-and-done proposition. It is likely that you will run several pilots until you figure out what sticks. What smaller bets might you want to expand upon? Each time you go through this process, you will learn about yourself and refine ideas about who you want to work with and what you want to work on.

PAUSE AND REVIEW

After conducting a pilot, ask yourself these key questions, the *three E's:*

- **Enjoyment:** Do I like doing it? Is it engaging? Am I excited to return to it?

- **Expertise:** Am I good at it? If not, can I increase my skills in this area? Am I excited to do so? Is this a natural extension of my strengths?

- **Expansion:** Is there more opportunity to expand in this market? Can I earn a living doing this?

Piloting removes the pressure of having to find *the* perfect next move, and instead fuels creativity and dynamic in-the-moment planning. Piloting should be fun. If it isn't, you may be overshooting; break your experiments down into smaller steps that move them from your panic zone to your stretch zone. If you are not excited about piloting something, ditch it or revise it and move on.

Thomas Frank pivoted from blogging about tips for college graduates to becoming a video production expert on YouTube through purposeful pilots. He ran small experiments, evaluating them at every step, as he built his reputation and expanded his platform:

- The first video was an experiment to expand his blog. Thomas settled for bad lighting (resorting to desk lamps after building a custom light that almost caught fire), filmed without a script, and posted with very little editing.

- Next he tried mixing academic topics with video games. In one video, "Is College Worth It? Use the Tony Hawk Method," Thomas included skateboarding moves from *Tony Hawk's Pro Skater* as a metaphor for the viewer to decide if and when to apply to college. Thomas believes these early efforts at "combining geek references with academic content" helped him stand out by creating a unique video signature.

- Another pilot was creating an entertaining six-minute summary video of a popular one-hour lecture on YouTube. That video has become the third most popular on his channel, with over a hundred thousand views, which indicated that Thomas should create more like it.

While building his YouTube following, Thomas pursued parallel opportunities to develop his platform across diverse media, including podcasting and writing a book for college students called *10 Steps to Earning Awesome Grades*. The book turned out to be a major catalyst that spiked his e-mail list from 2,000 to 27,000 people and brought in a handful of speaking inquiries.

During this time, Thomas also pitched himself as the new cohost for a podcast called *Listen Money Matters*, another pilot. In one episode, he talked about his goal of retiring by forty. A writer for *U.S. News & World Report* heard the episode and interviewed him, leading to an appearance on national TV at the Fox Business studio in Manhattan, a peak career moment.

Thomas has become a pro at piloting by improving bit by bit, building key relationships, and creating redundancy by testing new ideas simultaneously within his platform. In evaluating the three E's, it was clear that he enjoyed creating videos and podcasts, he was able to learn quickly and increase his production skills, and the market was responding favorably—demonstrated by reader e-mails, outside inquiries, and a steadily growing base that soon surpassed a hundred thousand subscribers.

TAKE INCREMENTALLY BIGGER RISKS

Even while following the Pivot Method at a high level, you can return to the first two stages as a way to evaluate a particular pilot:

- **Plant:** What worked well that you can repeat?
- **Scan:** What additional information might you need? Is there anyone else who would be helpful to connect with?
- **Pilot:** What might be a variation on the initial test that you can try next?

After gathering data, you will be more prepared to take greater risks, even if you are still intimidated by the scope of the opportunity. You will soon reach a point at which the clearest next step requires a bigger launch, covered in the final Pivot stage.

As she pivoted from accounting to IT within her company, Casey Pennington was also piloting with a side hustle. She ran a small experiment by interning for an entrepreneur as his virtual assistant, working on his tasks during nights and weekends. Although she enjoyed the work, she gained important insight leading her to correct course.

"I thought I wanted to work full time for one entrepreneur as his behind-the-scenes operations support," she said. "But after networking and speaking with other entrepreneurs and interning for a while, I realized that small businesses are so unpredictable and change focus so often that I didn't feel like I could rely on one employer for job security."

Casey's pilot clarified her long-term vision and desire to work for herself. "I realized that becoming a systems expert and consulting with many businesses would be more secure," she said. "I could rely on multiple sources of income, and this approach would be a better fit with my love of learning and my love of new challenges."

Next she returned to scanning by signing up for an online business course, and started talking to entrepreneurs to learn about their biggest challenges.

Casey's subsequent pilots were to add additional clients instead of taking direction from only one. This moved her closer to her goal of running her own full-time consulting practice. In doing so, she further refined her systems and reduced risk by learning more about what working with several clients is really like.

When Casey decided to make the leap to full-time self-employment the following year, she knew that uncertainty would still lie ahead, but that she had increased her expertise and risk tolerance by piloting and making adjustments along the way.

E 30-Day Decision Tracker

Spin, spin, spin. Second-guess, scrutinize, analyze, journal, ponder, meditate, marinate. WHERE IS THE ANSWER AND WHY ISN'T IT HERE YET?!

Whenever I find myself trying to overintellectualize something I am stuck on, talking through the same issues with friends in an endless loop, or otherwise evaluating a next move without making any progress toward clarity, I know it is time to step back. The mental spinning is merely a chew toy for my mind, one that keeps me busy, but offers no nutrition.

At this point, there are two courses of action to take—or a combination of both:

- **Get quiet:** Relax, meditate, tune in to your intuition. If there is no clarity, sit with the discomfort and have faith that the right next action will arise. Surrender to the uncertainty. Trust that things will work out, and look for learning in the meantime.

- **Get curious:** See the situation like a scientist. Look for experiments to run. Gather more data. Ask different, more refined questions. Observe your thoughts over a period of time.

If you are having trouble evaluating a pilot or a decision, and that confusion is preventing you from moving forward, try tracking that focus area for thirty days.

Rate how you feel about the pilot or decision every day on a scale of 1 to 5. At the same time, write down short, daily notes to add a qualitative observation component to the tracking exercise. Oftentimes just the increased awareness from being an observer during this time inspires new, small actions within each day.

At the end of the observation period, review the data. What trends emerge?

As my friend Jenny Ferry says, "Stay curious. Situations are either resolving or dissolving." The same can be said for anything you feel stuck on. Stay curious and open to the direction the situation is taking, rather than forcing a solution or weighing it down with expectations. In doing so, you can objectively observe whether it is *resolving* or *dissolving*, and what next steps to take as a result.

————

Piloting should not happen in a vacuum. The evaluation step is a critical one for getting feedback, reviewing your observations, and asking for input from others. That way, when you do launch, it will not be blindly. Every pilot is an opportunity, a small test to determine if you actually enjoy the *doing* of what might be required for your one-year vision. Pilots expand your knowledge and skills, and help you close the gap between where you are now and where you want to go.

The simplest way to evaluate a pilot is to revisit the hotter/colder game: Was it *hot* and on the right track, *lukewarm* and not quite right, or *cold* and a misguided flop? Did the pilot energize you, yield positive results, and encourage you to keep going in that direction? Or did it cause frustration and difficulty as you hit one roadblock after another, not yielding the return on investment you desired?

If your evaluation indicator is warm, what next pilot could you run, this time with slightly higher stakes or wider reach? If your evaluation indicator is cold, or not yet achieving the results you seek in terms of enjoyment and impact, return to the Plant stage to see how you can hook back into your strengths or vision. You may also need to spend more time scanning by asking others for feedback, finding accountability buddies, and learning new skills.

You can be quite content in the Pilot stage for months (if not years), so long as the experiments are aligned with your broader career vision. However, some pilots are so positively charged that they become massive magnets drawing you closer, leaving you powerless to resist.

You will know when you have stumbled onto something promising. But how do you know when to promote a pilot from your farm team to the big leagues? When is it time to go all in?

Pilot: Online Resources

Visit PivotMethod.com/pilot for additional tools, templates, and book recommendations for this stage.

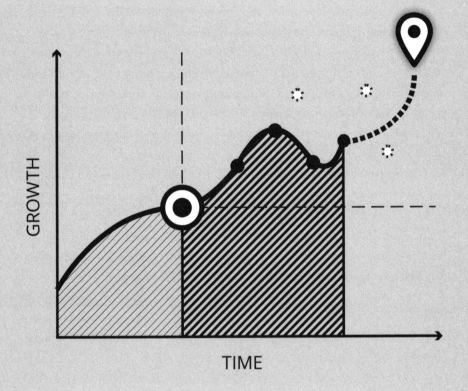

STAGE FOUR

LAUNCH

All In

PLANT

SCAN

PILOT

LAUNCH

LEAD

LAUNCH OVERVIEW

WHILE PILOTING INVOLVES A SERIES OF CONTINUAL, SMALL EXPERIMENTS THAT provide information about your next move, the Launch stage is when you make the big decision that completes your pivot. These decisions do not have a guaranteed successful outcome, though you will have reduced risk throughout the Pilot stage.

How do you evaluate these final steps to avoid launching too soon or too late? Remember: if you wait *too* long to pivot, change will choose you. How can you make smart career decisions in the face of remaining uncertainty and fear? What if you make the wrong choice and things do not go as planned? In this stage you will address remaining uncertainties and determine when to launch and what benchmarks to hit so you can transition with confidence.

Tricia Krohn landed her dream job in the financial industry, only to find that it was not what she had expected. She was a self-described "corporate ladder climber" throughout her twenties and thirties. Eventually she reached her optimal position, which she describes as "*the* job, the position, the ranking I craved." She soon realized how unhappy she was, even though she had reached her highest career aspiration. Tricia couldn't picture staying there until retirement.

By working through her own version of the Pivot stages, Tricia felt increasingly free to make a change, and became clear on her decision: return to school to become an English teacher, while bridging her income by working as a restaurant server and substitute teacher.

As it turns out, she could not have planned her exit from banking more perfectly. The market tanked two weeks later. She had pulled her 401(k) out within days of losing half its value. Tricia said the most challenging part of her launch was making the decision. "My life has been a dream since quitting," she says. "I still have ups and downs but I am not unhappy with life, I always have something to look forward to."

This is a sentiment I hear often from impacters. Even with bumps on the new road, the majority never look back or regret their Launch decision. But how can you be so sure?

CHAPTER 10: BUILD FIRST, COURAGE SECOND

When Will You Make the Big Move?
What Are Your Linchpin Decision Criteria?

I have only one purpose: to make man free, to urge him towards free-dom, to help him to break away from all limitations, for that alone will give him eternal happiness, will give him the unconditional re-alization of the self.

—J. Krishnamurti, *Total Freedom*

WHETHER MOVING TEAMS WITHIN A COMPANY, CHANGING COMPANIES, START-ing a business, or shifting or shuttering one, launches involve a healthy dose of faith, smart risks, and adrenaline. Ultimately, you will know it is time to launch when you are ready to risk failure—knowing that you had the courage to go for it—for the possibility of success, challenge, and personal growth. Or, as Joseph Campbell put it, for "the rapture of being alive."

Do not expect courage to rain down from the sky before you make a move. It comes from taking action. Courage will not arrive in full *before* your launch; it will appear afterward, when the confidence from making a life-changing decision settles in. Because of how true this is in my life, one of my mottos is "Build first, courage second." The more courageous action you take connected with your vision and values, the more confident you will feel along the way.

By following the Pivot Method, you have reduced your risk, planned in-telligently for a number of potential outcomes, and narrowed options for what to do next and when. This chapter covers criteria you can review to reach a decision about your Launch threshold and timing. Although you may not be able to predict a precise Launch *outcome*, you can put as much into your own hands as possible to steer in that direction.

IDENTIFY YOUR LAUNCH TIMING CRITERIA

One of the biggest questions that troubles people during a pivot is "How do I know when it is time to launch?" The answer will be different for everyone, but there are general indicators for how you will know when to promote one of your pilots to a full-blown launch.

First, clarify your Launch timing criteria as objectively as possible. This will allow you to observe your pilots and detect when you are making true progress toward a bigger decision. You will have a clearer idea for when to launch based on reaching certain thresholds, and will know when you need to adjust if your experiments are not going as planned.

Below is an overview of common Launch decision-making criteria, including financial benchmarks, date-based timing, progress milestones, gut instinct, and choices that hinge on other people.

Note the factors that matter most to you, then rank that list in order of importance: critical "must-haves" for your decision, "nice to haves," and "don't matter." You might also identify a range for each, from minimum needed to ideal. If you have a strong reaction against one of the best practices I suggest, fantastic! That will provide key information about what you want instead.

Financial Benchmarks

- **Money saved (Pivot runway):** Ideally, you should have at least six months of savings to see you through a launch. Make sure that leaving your current job or clients will not send you into your panic zone due to financial stress. Ensure that you have enough financial runway to buy time to generate momentum in your new direction.

- **Money earned (When my side hustle earns X dollars or more):** Although your side hustle earnings may not yet equal your salary, analyze their likelihood of generating cash flow. Can they realistically provide you with recurring income? If not, it is probably a riskier gamble and should remain a side hustle.

- **Stay until OBO (Or Better Offer):** Only change if a more enticing offer appears.

- **Specific size compensation:** When considering competing offers, does the new offer match or exceed your current financial package? What is your minimum threshold for accepting another offer? What is your *ideal* offer? If a new offer provides exciting growth opportunity but lower pay, is that trade-off worth it to you? Can it provide other benefits such as more vacation time, flexible hours, or remote workdays to make up for the lower salary?

- **Financial incentive tied to a date (When I get my bonus, or when this deal goes through):** Although you will want to consider if you are leaving unrealized gains on the table (something I cover in more detail at the end of this chapter), if you have a bonus coming that you have worked hard to earn all year, it behooves you to stay to receive it. However, be wary of ever-escalating incentives presented just often enough to get you to stay, but mask that you are unhappy and ready for something new. Some impacters have recently started a family, have vesting stock options, are paying or saving for kids' education, or are nearing retirement, so they choose to stay for years longer than they might have earlier in their careers. As long as you know *why* you are staying, and what is most important to you, you can see your current employer or biggest client as a partner in your larger goal, not a hindrance. The point is not to get stuck in misery quicksand—unhappy, but not willing to forgo the incentives and make a change. If you stay, know why and adjust your attitude accordingly.

- **Outside funding approved (When I get a bank or family loan, or venture capital or angel funding):** I encourage you to consider whether you really *need* funding or a loan to proceed, or whether it is a form of procrastination or if-then linear thinking. If you were forced to bootstrap with just a thousand dollars, what would you do?

Tom Meitner was in a job he was overqualified for—answering customer service e-mails—and working the second shift. His wife, Amanda, worked at the same company, on the first shift. Newly married, they rarely saw each other or ate dinner together. They vowed to change the situation, no matter how precarious it felt financially.

Getting clear on their financial benchmarks and deadlines were the determining factors that led Tom from piloting to launching. He describes the moment he made the decision to start his own business: "One night, I walked in the door at 10:30 P.M., just getting home from work. My wife, Amanda, looked me straight in the eye as I greeted her and said, 'What would it take for you to replace this income and go off on your own?'"

Tom told Amanda what he would have to do: make a list of three hundred companies that might hire him to do copywriting, then send e-mails and make phone calls until he had at least $2,500 a month in steady work coming in, which he estimated would take one month.

Within three weeks, Tom landed three clients at a baseline income of $3,000. Although it was doing search engine optimization work, not the type of copywriting he was most excited about, Tom raised his rates and shifted the nature of his work to direct-response copywriting with every subsequent client. He transitioned from struggling employee to freelance copywriter making six figures a year and working from home most days.

Now, in addition to copywriting, Tom is piloting a side hustle that he hopes will be his primary source of income someday: an online magazine for men to help "new grads and new dads take control of their lives."

Date-Based Timing

- **Complete and launch X project at work:** If you are on a team and have been working on a big project, it is important to see it through, for yourself as part of your results capital, and for the team you committed to, so that you do not burn bridges by leaving others in the lurch. That said, sometimes projects take years to complete; it may not make sense to stay too far beyond the point you are ready to leave, which could also impact the team negatively if you are already mentally checked out. In that case, identify the work milestones that you *can* complete, and clearly document your role and any unfinished business to ease the transition for others.

- **Take X months to explore, or take a sabbatical:** It is inefficient for your mind to circle the same question repeatedly each day during your exploration phase. If you are scanning, scan. If you are piloting, pilot. Do not simultaneously examine, every day, whether it is time to launch or not. I often help my clients take the pressure off by saying, "You are not even allowed to *think* about a decision for the next two weeks. Give yourself that time off, then we can revisit it together." Buy yourself time to breathe by setting a future date when you will revisit the do-or-don't-launch question.

- **Make a Launch decision by X date:** Having a firm "zero-hour" deadline can be freeing, and an important way to inspire action, knowing that you may never feel fully ready. There are several aspects to a big change: making the decision, communicating it, and carrying it out. Reduce overwhelm by separating these three elements. Giving yourself a deadline to *decide*, without yet worrying about *how* you will communicate it or *when*, can make the decision itself easier.

- **Make the move by X date or leave no later than X:** Once your mind is made up, it is time to take action. Set a deadline for when you will launch.

Date-based timing is usually paired with other factors, particularly financial. Many pivoters first decide what other criteria impact their decision; then by giving themselves a deadline they become clear on when to make it happen.

After a decade of climbing the ranks in a large technology company, Brian Jones, who you met in the introduction, decided to leave the organization, whether or not he had another offer in hand. He had enough savings to take at least one year off, if that is what he decided to do. He would either enjoy time to explore a range of interests, or, if he found another position during the time off that was a great fit, he would be happy taking that route, too. Once he was clear on his decision to leave, no matter which of the two paths worked out, he gave himself a deadline to resign after the holidays.

Progress Milestones

- **Build X prototype in my business:** Complete a project milestone that is a critical precursor to launch.
- **Land X new clients:** Indicates that the new direction is viable and income generating.
- **Planning readiness:** Have all the steps in place and know the ideal outcomes and make-or-break markers in worst-case scenarios.
- **Platform reaches a certain size:** Will lead to more opportunities and connections.

These items add a layer of depth and specificity to the financial and date-based criteria. One of the biggest safety nets when launching is the size of your platform and the reach of your reputation. The more robust and public your profile, either within your company or outside of it (or both), the more likely that opportunities will find you. You might consider waiting to launch until your platform reaches a certain size, or until you already have a certain volume of incoming leads. This can take the form of calls from recruiters if you are looking to switch companies, or client inquiries for those who are self-employed or want to be.

I encourage you to consider whether the items in this section carry enough weight to influence your decision, or whether they are delay tactics. Sometimes they represent a means to an end, but not the end itself. For example: What would the business prototype help you achieve or understand? Does the number of new clients really matter, or is it the monthly income target you are aiming to hit? Do you have to have a better offer in place first, or will making a decision now open up new opportunities? Will you ever feel fully ready in your planning, or are you getting mired in minutiae? The questions in this section *may* represent must-have criteria for you, but be real with yourself about where they fall on the scale from scrappy and lean to perfectionist procrastination.

Jennie Nash went from being a self-described mid-list writer to book coach with a booming business. She was teaching writing part time at the UCLA Extension Writers' Program and students were constantly asking her if she did one-on-one consulting. Because she wasn't sure what she could offer, she turned them away. Then one day a colleague praised her for her strategic, process-oriented approach and asked for her help on a book project. Something clicked. Suddenly Jennie saw how she could add value for aspiring authors.

After the success of that first project, she changed the title on her website from "Author Jennie Nash" to "Jennie Nash, Book Coach." Although this was a small pilot, it had important implications. "It was a way of giving myself permission to do something new," Jennie said.

She took a class in small-business strategy, a scanning move, and learned how to price her services to attract the right clients and hit her income targets. Armed with a clear vision for her new business and the tools to make it happen, Jennie began saying yes to incoming clients, and her success snowballed.

Upon reflection, Jennie expressed a sentiment similar to many people on the other side of their pivot: "It turns out that everything I have done in my life prepared me for what I am now doing. I just had no idea it was happening."

Even more interesting, and also quite common, it was her biggest disappointment that led her in this new direction. "The failure of my so-called Big Book freed me," Jennie says. "It was a horrible time, but it allowed me to stop and look around at what *was* rather than what might one day be." For Jennie, it was the demand for her expertise that informed her decision, not the other way around.

Instinct/Intuition

- **Gut feeling:** "I'm ready" or "I will know when I am ready."
- **Maxed out:** "I am miserable." "Any change is better than this." "It is no longer healthy for me to stay."

- **Gave the current gig my all:** "I know I tried everything I could."
- **Willing to go all out:** "I am ready to give this next thing everything I've got, no matter what happens." "To try and risk failure is more important than not trying at all."

What struck me as particularly interesting in the interviews I conducted was how many people said that, in the end, their decision came down to physical cues. They would get a gut feeling (often the first physical indicator that something needed to give), or if they didn't heed those warnings, their health declined until their body started screaming to make a change.

At a certain point, many people "just knew" it was time, either because their health was deteriorating and stress levels were skyrocketing or because the new direction beckoned them to the exciting edge of their stretch zone and no longer induced panic. Their Launch decision was so connected with their vision that they were willing to risk failure. As you get more skilled at maintaining a Pivot mindset, you will not need to wait until your body cries out for help to make the necessary changes.

Peter Carr was twenty-five years old and thought he had landed his dream job in sports video production. However, when he got there, the job and working conditions were far from ideal; he was working over eighty hours a week, and quickly realized it was not a sustainable lifestyle, nor could he see a happy future there. "I knew I was at a pivot point because I was miserable, and my body was telling me what my mind didn't want to accept: that it was time for a change and time for me to take a risk," he said.

Peter looked around at his coworkers and saw that they were stressed and overworked and did not have time for their families. At that point he decided that if he were to put in the long hours, he would rather be working for himself building a company that would help others, or find more aligned full-time work.

"Without having a terrible experience in what I dreamed of doing since I was a child, I would not have taken the risk to pivot my career," he said.

Peter's physical cues—seeing how coworkers' lifestyles conflicted with his values, and listening to his gut instincts—sparked his move. This pivot also motivated a complete turnaround in his fitness and work habits. In the following year, he traveled to more than thirty-seven cities and ran over thirty races, honoring his values of travel and living a healthy lifestyle, and meeting his one-year vision of completing an Ironman 70.3 competition.

In Others' Hands

- **"Gatekeeper" industry approval or offer:** You get a book deal, music contract, or grant funding.

- **Acceptance in an application-only program:** You have been accepted by a graduate school, the Peace Corps, Teach for America, or a start-up incubator or accelerator.

- **Partner earns X or completes Y:** Your partner gets promoted at work, finishes graduate school, or finds another job.

- **Awaiting full agreement or support from partner and/or other family members.**

Some big decisions lie outside of our immediate control, particularly if we are waiting to hear back from a job interview, a graduate school application, or any other program with limited acceptance. If you are waiting, stay actively engaged in earlier Pivot exercises.

Consider:

- What is my backup plan? If I do not get the offer or acceptance letter, what would I pursue? Scan for and explore options as you wait for a response.

- What pilots can I run while waiting that will continue to move me forward, or address these same values and vision elements?

- What is my waiting deadline, after which point I will pursue other options? How will I know when I have waited too long?

In the event that your original plan does not pan out, consider that rejection is often a blessing in disguise, prompting an even more creative approach forward.

Tara Decoda was a hairstylist living in New York City. After cosmetology school, she assisted at a number of high-end salons before applying to work at Glamsquad, an on-demand beauty services company. Glamsquad rejected her application twice, which was confusing because Tara always received rave reviews from her clients.

A few months after the rejections, she put her own twist on the motto "If you can't beat 'em, join 'em." Tara declared with conviction, "If you can't *join* 'em, *beat* 'em," and launched her own company, Blow On The Go. Soon after, she added a line of natural, handmade hair products called Bare Mane as an extension of her main business. After nearly two years of running Blow On The Go, she pivoted the business once more, to focus on lash extensions.

On what excites her most about Plush Lash, the new direction, Tara said, "I wanted to rebrand myself as a beauty aficionado and not just a hairstylist, so that I can share my overall beauty industry expertise through more than one avenue. Establishing myself as an expert across various trades in the field allows this." Tara continues to shape her services in a way that resonates with her values and the client experience she believes busy women are looking for. Her talent for doing a bang-up job keeps people coming back, with word-of-mouth marketing working in her favor.

Of all the criteria in this section, the one that seems to cause the most stress is waiting for full agreement from family members. The fact is, you may never get it, or it may come only *after* you launch. Determine whose approval is critical to your decision, and whose is nice to have, even if disappointing not to receive. For example, if you are married, making a decision might require consensus with your partner, which is different from making a decision to please your parents or to do what "they" (society at large) would approve.

My mom and I did not see eye to eye on my decision to leave Google when I did. We still don't! Although I can understand her point of view and wholeheartedly respect her advice and career choices, I also know that my process and Launch timing decision was the right one for me, despite our differing opinions.

Our family and closest friends are those who have the greatest emotional interest in our safety and survival. It is likely that their threshold for risk for you will be lower than your own, or that they may pepper you with "what ifs" that sound strikingly similar to your existing fears. Determine which of these fears you can and want to address, and which ones you are prepared to leave in the smart risk category that can only be reduced through action.

Pivot Paradox: Make Short-Term Trade-offs if Necessary

"Maybe you are being too picky." Perhaps you have heard this at one point in your career (or dating life). I do not believe this is the case most of the time. We are often not being picky or creative enough! With one exception: you may have become too picky if you are standing still in the midst of a pivot and growing increasingly despondent about it. At this point, it is possible that you may need to choose among several of your top criteria, even if they seem to compete with other important values. Choose and build steadily from a place of stability, even if it seems subpar at first.

Sometimes you need to take a job you are not crazy about for your own sanity, to gather new information and buy time. Counterintuitive though it may seem, that may be your best next move.

Now, before the Personal Development Police start protesting that "Anything is possible!" and you have to "Dream big!" I will say that there are absolutely careers that can meet your most important, even if seemingly opposed, criteria. But sometimes in order to get unstuck you need to find a bridge solution that requires trade-offs while searching for the pivot that will match most or all of your values.

PIVOT HEXAGON

On the subject of trade-offs, my dad, an architect, shared an industry maxim with me. For any project, a client can optimize for two of three core variables: time, cost, and quality. If the client wants their house done quickly and with the highest quality, it will cost more. If they need the job done yesterday and at a low cost, it suffers in quality. If they want the house low cost and high quality, it will take more time. There is an official name for this: the Project Management Triangle.

The Project Management Triangle trade-off shows up for impacters in what I call a *Pivot hexagon*. There are three reciprocal pairs of values people express frequently in the midst of career change, and they sometimes conflict with each other. Three of these values represent our desire for security, and three represent our desire for freedom.

Impacters are often aiming for one of each pair more than the other, even though all may feel important on some level:

- **Security**—minimizing fear, risk, and uncertainty; seeking outside protection, backup, consistency, or approval *versus*

- **Freedom**—financial freedom, ability to choose one's own projects, where one wants to work, and with whom.

- **Money**—steady cash flow, earning potential; amount and consistency of income *versus*

- **Time flexibility**—how much time someone wants or needs to make a move; the flexibility to choose how to spend one's time each day and overall work schedule.

- **Structure**—routine, predictability, set schedule and environment *versus*

- **Adventure**—excitement, creativity, travel, variety, meeting new people.

Pivot Hexagon

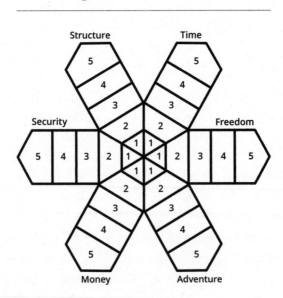

Until you land on a next move that takes you closer to your desired threshold for all six criteria, you may want to consider bridge options that meet at least a few values in your Pivot hexagon, even if they involve trade-offs. For example:

- A coffee barista job brings some security, structure, and money, but may take away from time and freedom. Adventure is up for grabs; you might end up liking it, and meet many new people.

- A leadership role within your company might bring growth, impact, and security, but not as much freedom or time flexibility.

- A job at a hot new start-up might bring you (potential) money and adventure, but lack security and take away from time, if the expectation is that you work around the clock.

- Starting your own business could bring freedom, time flexibility (though not always; as the business owner, your brain is never really off the clock), and maybe more money—but you may forgo financial security, at least in the early days.

- Returning to graduate school could bring adventure in terms of growth and connections, and some amount of freedom and security, but it requires money and time.

E Pivot Hexagon Assessment

You can measure your values on the Pivot hexagon in two ways:

- First, take an overall assessment of how important each of these six values is to you in general, where 0 is "not at all important" and 5 is "critical to my well-being." If any of the hexagon values I listed do not resonate, swap them out for your most important decision criteria.

- Next, if you are considering two or more potential opportunities, give each its own hexagon and rank how well each option fits the six values, where 5 is "meets this need completely" and 0 is "does not satisfy this need at all." How does each opportunity stack up against the hexagon and with your personal values?

KNOW WHEN TO HOLD VERSUS FOLD

One of the most challenging aspects of pivoting is knowing when to launch, especially when it means leaving a good option behind for something with the *potential* to be great, but that has no guarantee. As Kenny Rogers sings in his hit "The Gambler," "You've got to know when to hold 'em, know when to fold 'em."

We all know at least one person who is always on to their next big idea before seeing the current one through. They are famous for skipping out the minute things get hard, or ditching the last big idea for a fresher one, poking holes in all the reasons that once made the first one great. No *one* choice to shut down a project or switch directions is necessarily a bad one, but the cumulative effect is that they never give themselves time to ride out the dips and reach a point of momentum or critical mass in terms of results, reputation, or platform.

This operating mode is what SkilledUp cofounder Brad Zomick calls Career Roomba Syndrome. Roombas are the robotic vacuum cleaners that scan floors on their own, switching directions whenever they hit an obstacle. Brad defines Career Roomba Syndrome as "an occupational affliction that is characterized by a string of different job roles, some related, some starkly different than the last. The afflicted lacks passion for these jobs, and each time the 'patient' hits a dead end at a job, they back up and redirect their career path, but more often than not, the new path is not determined by any clear strategy."

If you shut things down before they have a chance to create value for yourself and others, you will remain stuck in the same cycle of feeling like you are starting from scratch without a clear strategy or rationale to back it up. How can you prevent this, while leaving room to make the tough choice of changing something that is not working despite your best efforts?

If you leave too soon, you risk leaving *unrealized gains* behind; too late, and you risk experiencing *diminishing returns* on your time and effort. Let's take a look at both of these Pivot pitfalls.

Unrealized Gains

If you are successful in your current position—which you probably are as an impacter—it is likely that you have unrealized gains on the table. In investing terms, *unrealized gains* refers to profit that exists on paper, but that has not been cashed in, such as a winning stock that has not yet been sold. In a career sense, unrealized gains typically fall into three categories:

- **Financial incentives:** A large commission, bonus, or stock options vesting.

- **Results and reputation:** Completing a project or receiving an upcoming promotion.

- **Growth:** Gaining skills and experience that will be helpful for long-term career goals.

Your unrealized gains could be an upcoming promotion, contributing to a large-scale project, working toward an annual bonus, or in the case of a commission-only job, negotiating several large deals over many months that would provide a hefty lump sum if and when they come to fruition.

Some employers dangle "carrots" in front of employees to encourage them to stay. If the incentives are valuable and you benefit from collecting them steadily over time, this is not an issue, it is a perk. It is when they become a far-off promise that delays your gut decision that they become more of a distraction and temptation than a payoff worth waiting for.

If I had left Google when I first entertained the idea, it would have been a huge mistake in terms of unrealized gains, but not solely for financial reasons. I was on the cusp of leaving three years in, when I ran into my coworker Becky Cotton in the parking lot. She asked how I was doing, and I told her I was discouraged from doing work that was not a fit, and I no longer felt engaged with my role.

When Becky told me about an opening on the newly formed career development team that she had joined, I applied for the one open role remaining. I was able to pivot internally, rejuvenating my Google career for another two years, and contribute to the company in even more significant ways. If I transitioned to self-employment too soon, I would have forfeited unrealized gains in results and experience across two areas I was increasingly passionate about: career coaching and manager training, both now central to my business.

Diminishing Returns

You will have to decide for yourself if you risk leaving crucial unrealized gains behind. On the other hand, sometimes we obsess over these potential gains out of fear or emotional attachment to what feels safe. We clutch at security while ignoring the fact that, like the boiling frog, our surrounding environment is no longer hospitable.

In economics, the *law of diminishing returns* asserts that past a certain point in production, adding more resources will no longer yield favorable results. In fact, every added effort or input yields increasingly lower returns.

Melissa Anzman left a job as senior manager of HR communications at a medical device company to launch her own business, Launch Yourself, aimed at helping clients launch books, brands, and career changes. Six months in, she realized she needed a source of bridge income while she got her business off the ground, so she started part-time contract work with a career transition company, coaching people who were laid off to find their next job. At fifteen hours per week, the outplacement company became her largest and most consistent client.

Although it was a great fit for the first six months, soon after that it became tedious, and Melissa's efforts no longer yielded a worthwhile payoff. Still, she stayed, out of fear of losing her biggest source of income.

"I stayed for way too long because I was nervous about losing that safety net," Melissa said. "From there on, I was not learning, and the work felt dreadful. I was really miserable. After coaching so many of the same clients with the same issues, it's not coaching anymore. It felt like rinse and repeat, and was no longer challenging or interesting."

Even with these realizations, it took Melissa a long time—in her words, *way* too long—to leave. She stayed for another two years. The last straw was when she had to turn down a client for her own business, the one she had left her well-paying job to launch. "I left corporate America making six figures for a reason, and here I was getting paid hourly for fifteen hours a week for the same grind, and turning down my ideal clients," she said. "It was unacceptable to me."

In year one of self-employment, the career transition company was Melissa's life preserver. She credits the part-time work as saving her business at a critical time when she felt scared and had little income coming in. However, by year two, it had become an albatross.

"Every call became a struggle, every e-mail was a drain," Melissa said. "I was doing all this to float Launch Yourself to begin with, and I ended up being so burned out that I didn't touch my business for months."

The silver lining of Melissa's diminishing returns was that after leaving the outplacement firm and taking a few months off to reflect, she completely shifted how she approached her business. Instead of focusing all her efforts on one-on-one clients, she sought corporate clients more in line with her HR experience. "I committed to working only with the right type of client, doing the right type of work." she said. "My burnout experience helped me focus on how important that was for me."

As you evaluate your pilots and Launch criteria, note when you may be passing the point of diminishing returns on your time, money, and effort. If unrealized gains suggest leaving too soon, how do you know when you are resigning from a job or a project too late? The following exercise will help you examine both.

E When to Hold or Fold

1. **Notice where you hang out on the spectrum of unrealized gains versus diminishing returns:** In work and relationships, since there may be parallels.

   - Do you stay far longer than you should, second-guessing yourself?
   - Is your response usually just right, balanced on the spectrum without swinging to extremes in either direction?

- Or are you more impulsive? Do you tend to quit too soon, often wondering if you should have given something a second chance?

In their book *Attached*, authors Dr. Amir Levine and Rachel S. F. Heller say that most of us fall into one of three relationship types: anxious, secure, or avoidant. Think about this as it relates to work. Are you secure in your position and the value you bring? Or are you constantly anxious that you are not doing enough or that you should make a change? Or are you avoidant, never sticking around long enough to find out, quitting a job, project, or client at the early signs of trouble or dissatisfaction?

2. **Separate must-haves from nice-to-haves:** Within the unrealized gains categories—financial, results, reputation, or personal growth—differentiate between short-term gains of three to six months and long-term unrealized gains of one year or more. First, eliminate those that would not substantially impact your Launch decision. Next, note any items that would be deal breakers, things you would not leave without completing. Finally, reflect:

   - How long are these must-have gains worth staying for?

   - What might you be forfeiting in the meantime, the longer you stay?

   - At what point do the potential gains of a new direction outweigh your potential losses?

3. **Zoom out:** Sometimes people struggle with smaller pilots because they have not yet envisaged the bigger Pivot umbrella that creates room for them all. If you find yourself conflicted between starting many separate projects, ask:

   - What do they all have in common?

   - What is the larger goal or theme that ties them all together?

   - How do they fit with the values and vision you identified earlier?

4. **Push past project plateaus:** In his book *Making Ideas Happen*, Scott Belsky writes that our addiction to new ideas often cuts project

journeys short. "The easiest and most seductive escape from the project plateau is the most dangerous one: a new idea," he says. "The end result? A plateau filled with the skeletons of abandoned ideas." To combat this, Belsky says that you must "develop the capacity to endure, and even thrive, as you traverse the project plateau."

Before you fold too quickly or declare it time for another pivot, consider:

- Are you hitting a natural plateau or is this a true sign that you should not continue?

- What is important about pressing onward, even without the shine of newness?

- Is there something about your approach that you can shift?

- Can you ask for help to make it through this motivation dip more quickly?

Pivot Paradox: Don't Push the River

The average life span of human cells is seven years. Skin cells regenerate every two weeks, and the cells lining our gut turn over every five days. Our bodies cycle through circadian rhythms—physical, mental, and behavioral changes—within each twenty-four-hour day. We hear about the seven-year itch for relationships. Now there's the two- to four-year itch for careers, and the eight-second itch of our attention spans. That's right, the average attention span is now eight seconds, one second *less* than that of a goldfish.

So why is it that change, and going through low or slow seasons in our work, can feel so disorienting? Because our culture is one that values doing, producing, and achieving.

"Don't push the river" is a Zen saying that reminds me not to force the rhythms of my life. Society glamorizes "go-getters" and people who "take the bull by the horns," but some larger life questions require the fullness of time to marinate. Again, if answers about next steps were easy, we would be doing them. Pivots require effort and cannot be

forced. Time is an unknown element, and big changes cannot be mus-
cled with brute strength simply to meet high expectations.

Besides, who is to say you know what precise timing is best? Periods
of uncertainty are their own indicator of "no" or "not yet." One day, you
will wake up and you will know that it is time to launch. Until then, be as
impartial an observer as you can.

In my own life, "unanswered prayers" have often made complete
sense in hindsight, no matter how challenging at the time. Unexpected
outcomes accelerate our growth. Trusting this truth requires not having all the answers up front, and maintaining a dose of faith throughout
seasons of change.

YOUR GUT HAS A BRAIN

Have you ever had a gut instinct that rocked you to the core? When you are
in a job or a relationship, and are suddenly overcome by a physical sense that
it is time to make a change?

This inner voice often starts as a quiet whisper, and can be confusing and
disorienting if we do not yet know what to do with it. But if you do not listen
to the whisper, get ready: it will likely deliver a very uncomfortable WHACK
instead. *Wake up!* our gut yells. *Listen to me!*

Maybe you feel your gut instincts as a pit or churning in your belly, a
lump in your throat, or a heavy feeling in your chest. *But what does it mean?*
If you go straight to problem solving with your mind, you might miss the real
message.

Our gut has a brain. Or more accurately, it *is* a brain, even though our
gut does not have the verbal sophistication that our head-brain does. Our gut
works on hunches—a hypothesis that something is not right or that there is
an opportunity ahead. It is up to us to suss out what that knock on the door
of our consciousness really means, and what to do about it. We must use our
heart- and head-brains to interpret the meaning of the message, then figure
out how to take deliberate action.

Gut instincts can be intimidating. We may know it is time to act—to leave the job or the relationship, to move to a new city, to have a hard conversation, or to face a truth within ourselves—and yet the action itself takes tremendous courage. Often our first reaction is refusal. *Noooooo.* No. It can't be *that.* I'm not ready for *that.* I can't possibly do *that.* I don't have the strength to face *that* head on.

These insights challenge us because our gut is the defender of our boundaries and core identity, both critical to our health and happiness. Your gut-brain is a fascinating, often untapped intelligence resource.

According to Grant Soosalu and Marvin Oka, authors of *mBraining: Using Your Multiple Brains to Do Cool Stuff,* the gut contains over 500 million neurons, equivalent in size and complexity to a cat's brain, and is the source of 90 percent of our body's serotonin production. The gut-brain is primal, forming in the womb before the heart- and head-brains. It deals with core identity-based motivations such as safety and protection. The majority of nervous messaging occurs from your gut to your brain, not the other way around: 90 percent of vagal nerve fibers communicate the state of our system to the head-brain, with only 10 percent providing communication in the other direction. Perhaps most surprising, the gut-brain exhibits plasticity, and can learn and form memories.

In other words, your gut *will* communicate with you when big decisions are on the line if you pay attention to it, and it will sound alarms when your most primal needs are not being met. You cannot always know with 100 percent certainty what to do when your gut-brain speaks up. The process of working with it is like building a muscle; it takes time and practice. Start by examining big decisions you have made in the past, noting when and how your gut communicates with you in the present.

When you are unsure, do a full body and brain scan about an upcoming decision or conversation: What does your head say? What does your heart say? What does your gut say? Your gut acts as the referee between what your head says you *should* do and what your heart most *wants* to do.

PIVOT SCALES: COMFORT VERSUS RISK

Imagine a scale with your comfort zone on one side of the balance and your willingness to take a career risk on the other. As the risk surrounding a new direction starts to outweigh the comfort of staying in place, many pivoters experience the following sequence of inner events leading up to their launch:

- Pivots often start just below the surface of your awareness, with slight dissatisfaction or a whisper in your gut about the desire to change, even if you have not expressed anything outwardly. On the Riskometer, this state falls within the comfort or stagnation zones. Soon, however, staying in place becomes increasingly uncomfortable. You realize it is time to pivot, but are not sure what, when, or how to do something about it. You have started to outgrow your comfort zone.

- At this point, you are ready to Plant: identify what you do want moving forward, and uncover clues from your existing career portfolio of strengths, interests, and experiences.

- In the second stage, you start preparing yourself for risk by Scanning—learning, talking to others, and looking for examples of people who have been successful in the areas you are aiming for. The scale is still tipped toward your comfort zone, but is slowly starting to shift.

- In the third stage, you dip your toe in the water, testing your new direction by Piloting. Fear may be heightened at this point as the option to pivot becomes increasingly real, but so will your sense of anticipation, excitement, and adventure. If you are scanning and piloting strategically, you will be in your stretch zone, not your panic zone. Pull back on pilots that send you into your panic zone and look for smaller next steps. The scale feels relatively even.

- In the fourth stage, the tipping point occurs. You know that no matter what, you are willing to launch in the new direction even if you fail. At this point, you would regret not trying more than trying and not meeting your expectations. Besides, after piloting you will have increased your chances of success. So, as the scale tips and you meet your Launch decision criteria, you close out the former option and . . . *pivot!*

———

After reviewing the Launch timing criteria in this chapter, you will know what critical factors your final Pivot steps hinge on. All that remains is working your way toward those benchmarks, adjusting as you move along, and then *going for it.*

"But, wait!" you say. "What if things don't go as planned?" No person or book can guarantee success. What I *can* do is share how the most agile impacters handle launch-related rejection, failure, dips in motivation, and difficult conversations.

CHAPTER 11: FLIP FAILURE

What Will Move You into Action?

Cut yourself some slack. Remember, one hundred years from now, all new people.

—Message tacked to a tree by monks at Wat Umong,
a 700-year-old temple in Thailand

IT IS IMPOSSIBLE TO TALK ABOUT PIVOTING WITHOUT ADDRESSING THE FEAR of failure.

I am an optimistic realist. As a business and career coach, I do not insult my clients by pretending their fears are not real, or that they can move past them with simple affirmations and positive thinking. I have experienced years of wading knee-deep in my own doubts. So when they tell me their fears, I reply with, "Yep. Those things might happen." Then I follow up with, "But will that stop you? What would you need to do to feel more confident moving forward in spite of these fears?"

These are not rhetorical questions. Ask yourself: *will* those worst-case scenarios stop you? If so, that is okay. It is a signal that you need to develop a game plan that allows you to sidestep paralysis. Although many of us know when it is time to leave our comfort zone, there is a blurrier line between weaving through the stretch zone without tipping into the panic zone.

In many early conversations with clients, before their launch is a sure thing, the word *failure* comes up. *I want to do XYZ, but I am afraid to fail.*

What if I am not cut out for this? To that I ask, "What is your definition of failure?" I do not mean this in a Pollyanna sense, as a loaded question requiring them to reply, "There is no such thing!" Because fear of failure is real. But what does failure actually mean to you?

In some cases, failure is *very* real: losing a job or critical income source, or cashing in all remaining savings. In other cases, reflecting on this question reveals a straw man that is dismantled through further inquiry.

How do *you* define failure? Does your definition of failure focus only on quantitative financial consequences (if at all) or does it include qualitative measures, too?

Beyond not being able to pay my bills or getting to zero financially, a sign I am long overdue to pivot my business, my *qualitative* failure categories are:

- Not giving something my best effort, or overcommitting to the point where I deliver sloppy work.

- Failing to act in my own best interest; steamrolling my own needs to please others, gain approval, or protect the status quo.

- Dishonesty; any situation in which I act without integrity and that conflicts with my values.

- Not trying something new based on an irrational fear, as opposed to a strong instinct that indicates something is not for me.

According to this list, I have failed many times. I also know that I *feel* failure right away, in the sick feeling in my belly, and I take steps to correct it as soon as I can. If what is done is done, I vow to learn from the experience and never do it again. The visceral feeling of disappointing myself or others, or doing something I consider wrong based on my value system, is enough to make me never want to repeat it.

When I dig deeper with people who say they are afraid to fail in terms of losing money, or having to find steady work again even if they do not love it, their true definition of failure is regret. That is certainly mine. Though declining income or a dwindling bank account would certainly point to business blind spots and growth areas, these quantitative measures are not how I define myself. For me, the biggest failure is not trying.

Jeff Bezos, founder of Amazon, shares similar sentiments, and applies what he calls a regret minimization framework to big decisions:

> *I wanted to project myself forward to age 80 and say, "OK, I'm looking back on my life. I want to minimize the number of regrets I have." And I knew that when I was 80, I was not going to regret having tried this. I was not going to regret trying to participate in this thing called the Internet that I thought was going to be a really big deal. I knew that if I failed, I wouldn't regret that. But I knew the one thing I might regret is not ever having tried. I knew that that would haunt me every day.*

Determine your own values around risk and failure, and what failures are acceptable or not. As one of my mentors once asked me, "One year from now, how would you feel if nothing had changed?" What would you regret more: trying and failing, or not trying at all?

Failure is not:

- Uncertainty.

- Trying something new.

- Trying something that doesn't work.

- Doing something imperfectly.

- Making the "wrong" decision.

- Getting rejected.

These are the experiences that make you human, and an adventurous one at that. How can something be a failure if it is a critical building block of your growth?

REJECTION AS A STEPPING-STONE TO SUCCESS

Recall Shawn Henry, the former FBI assistant director we met in the Scan stage. One of the key turning points of Shawn's career came from four consecutive "failures" trying to move up to the next level within the FBI. He was looking for a field desk role and applied for four different supervisor roles across Washington, D.C., and Baltimore. Despite the fact that he was the most qualified candidate, Shawn was turned away each time, and grew increasingly dejected.

Then a job opened up as chief of the computer investigations unit at FBI headquarters. Shawn was not a programmer, but in 1999 he had the foresight to realize that the advent of computer crime was upon us. He got curious: what if we took the techniques that we used in the physical world, such as wiretaps and undercover work, and applied those tactics to online crime? He pitched his ideas to the hiring manager and finally, still weary from the rejections of the last two years, got the job. Shawn pivoted and applied for a role off the typical career ladder, and became the new chief of the computer investigations unit at FBI headquarters.

After fourteen months in that job, Shawn moved up to supervisor of a cybersecurity squad. After seven years, he was promoted to executive director of the Cyber Division. He became widely known as the FBI's "cyber guy," and represented the U.S. government in international cybersecurity forums. Everything sprang from those four rejections. "All because I didn't get a job and was devastated every time I didn't get that job," Shawn says.

Shawn has since retired from the FBI, pivoting to become the president of a cybersecurity start-up called CrowdStrike. This is a role he did not see coming either, given that most of his predecessors left the FBI to work for Fortune 10 companies, but it is one that meets his values of impact, excitement, and smart risk.

On handling rejection as a catalyst for career opportunity, Shawn says, "It is about keeping doors open, constantly persevering, and having confidence and faith in yourself. Just because these circumstances didn't work out it is not a judgment on you as a person; there are other opportunities around the corner."

MINE FAILURE FOR STRENGTHS

Businesses can fail and go bankrupt. There is the remote possibility that you could do something that leads to your death. But barring that, you have the ability to try again, wiser the next time.

Particularly in business, I see most failures as feedback on my skills or what the market wants. If I launch a course that I know will benefit people but that does not sell, I may need to brush up on my copywriting skills. Or it might mean that I did not create the right course for my specific audience, at the right price, and for what they need at this point in their lives. Business is a great platform for learning because it is not personal. I am not a failure as a person, I simply did not hit the mark with my strategy and execution.

If you experience failure fallout, mine the wreckage for underlying strengths and key lessons. Transform failure by returning to the Plant and Scan stages as you evaluate experiences that did not unfold as planned. Perhaps you ran pilots that were not well anchored to your strengths, vision, and work history. When you mine the learning, the experience stops being a failure and becomes the seeds of something new, a strength-in-waiting.

Dave Ursillo had this experience after he published *Lead Without Followers*, a book on personal leadership that did not catch fire as he had hoped. He had recently moved to New York City, and was starting to worry as his finances dwindled.

"I was living in the East Village watching my bank account dry up fast as my modest business as a self-employed entrepreneur and evangelist of personal leadership refused to pick up the momentum I needed," he said. "My first book, published the year before, was a bust in helping me establish myself as a voice of personal leadership. I was slowly realizing that the vision I had been working toward, and quit my job in politics for, was falling flat with people."

Together, Dave and I examined his book launch "failure" as an opportunity to return to his career portfolio—to what *was* working—even if it was only a small percentage of how he was currently spending his time. When we revisited his book launch, we discovered that what Dave really loved and was best at was writing itself, not writing about the meaning of personal leadership, a concept that didn't resonate with his audience. Dave knew many readers and clients who wanted to write their own books but were hitting roadblocks. He had been neglecting his "writerly side" and longed to create an environment where he could build support for it, and encourage others along the way.

We came up with a plan that would optimize for enjoyment *and* consistent revenue. Dave could pilot a community for writers, billing monthly or quarterly for membership, enabling him to better predict his income. He scanned by putting feelers out and listening on social media. Dave asked ideal customers, readers already connected to his work in some way, what they were struggling with as writers and creatives, without any mention of his writers' group. Next, he piloted by setting up an online forum called the Literati Writers, with regular calls and critiques. We brainstormed a $20 monthly price tag. The recurring subscription could mean $400 a month if even twenty people joined, which would help Dave make a dent in his Manhattan living expenses.

This new idea quickly caught fire. Dave settled on a rate of $50 per quarter. This evolved into $225 per quarter over the following two years, as the group grew into "a premier offering for those who wanted a deep, meaningful and personal relationship to their writing."

Dave turned his book failure into a triumph by filtering its lessons for hidden strengths and interests that he was not fully applying in his business, then turning those strengths into a vehicle to help others. True to impacter form, though money was a factor, it was not the primary driver.

"Money was putting a lot of stress on me, but even more so, I knew I was also failing to honor my own calling of writing," Dave said. "This pivot provided me with financial promise but also an instinct about my purpose that would serve me more deeply than pure dollars. I fell in love with my mission again."

YOU CAN'T MAKE EVERYBODY HAPPY— SO STOP TRYING AND START LIVING

You can either go emotionally broke running around trying to please everyone, or you can spend your time creating, being authentic to your own needs and desires, then serving others from that full place.

One Pivot pitfall, particularly approaching a big launch, is obsessing over making everyone *else* happy, including partners, family members, managers, or even hypothetical "others." Although some amount of this is critical for weighing a decision and not burning bridges, *too* much focus on pleasing others clouds Launch decisions and timing.

Although I have made much progress over the years, I continue to learn the following lessons as I juggle my impacter desire to be helpful with my tendency to give *too* much:

- People pleasing is exhausting. It is inauthentic. It means placing everyone else's needs above your own.

- You cannot make everyone happy all the time, and it is futile to try. You are no good to *anyone* if you run yourself ragged trying to please *everyone*.

- You have a choice: you can spend your time ceaselessly worrying about other people or you can bravely follow your own path.

- The universe rewards backbone. Not speaking up or acting authentically may lead to a bigger explosion down the road, when you least want or expect it.

Although Tricia Krohn, who you met in the Launch overview, was clear that she wanted out of her banking job, social concerns still brought great uncertainty. She asked herself, "What would people think if I quit? Coworkers? Family? Could I face the disappointment of feeling less than?" She tackled these concerns through meaningful conversations, first with a coworker, then with her family.

When Tricia sat down with her kids and laid all the possibilities on the table, her daughter was encouraging, and Tricia felt tremendous joy at realizing she had become her daughter's "hero and role model yet again."

Then came the bigger conversation: telling her parents. Tricia was already firm in her choice, but still, their reaction was important. "I was an almost forty-year-old woman about to give up a 401(k), five weeks' paid vacation, and a secure and stable job. Who does that?" she said. "My parents shocked the heck out of me and said, 'Go for it!' D-day was set."

Although her backup plan was to return to working in finance, Tricia knew that was never *really* an option, saying, "Once my decision was made I vowed I would never go back to banking."

One of the best change tactics for impacters is to take comfort in their work ethic and resourcefulness, knowing that they already have the skills to create opportunities, and always have. "I am a workaholic so I knew I would always find work doing *something*," Tricia said. "That was truly my backup plan."

As for Tricia's coworkers, rather than meeting her decision with the scorn and disapproval she anticipated, hers became a story of inspiration within the company. "Once I told the people at work, the news spread like wildfire and I got a lot of, 'Wow, I wish I was brave enough to do what you are doing,'" she said. "It was very encouraging. I have yet to have a moment of looking back with regret. My regret is not doing it sooner."

E List Your MIPs

Author and professor Brené Brown's strategy for dealing with naysayers and unproductive people pleasing is to identify her five Most Important People. She suggests making a short list of those who really matter in your life, or as she puts it, "would help you move a body."

Brown says when you ruffle feathers or do something that invites haters, ask what the people on your MIP short list would say. If they are on board, you can lean on them for the courage to proceed. After you make your MIP list, here are some additional questions to consider:

- How do you scale back and recharge when you are people pleasing in a way that contradicts your core needs, or when you are worrying too much about what others think?

- What is more important to you than merely trying to make others happy? What is at stake if you ignore your instincts about what is best for *you*?

- In her book *Steering by Starlight*, Martha Beck suggests using a "shackles on" versus "shackles off" approach. Does this request, person, or action weigh you down and feel tiresome or draining? Or does it feel energizing and uplifting?

Over the course of the next week, observe your shackles on versus shackles off reaction before making decisions, and after working on projects or interacting with others.

SEPARATE DECISIONS FROM DIFFICULT CONVERSATIONS

In addition to dealing with others' reactions and opinions, and your anticipation of their reactions, another big sticking point in the final Pivot stage is actually *having* the difficult conversations with family, clients, managers, or coworkers that set your launch in motion.

Difficult Launch conversations have five distinct parts:

1. *Making* the decision based on your gut instinct.
2. Figuring out *how* to express the difficult decision in words, clearly and directly.
3. Deciding *when* to have the conversation.
4. *Communicating* the decision to the other(s) involved.
5. *Responding* to their reaction and any ensuing consequences or follow-up.

Many people make the mistake of conflating all five steps, and end up thoroughly confused when facing a tough decision. What may really be happening is that they are clear about number one, the right thing for them to do, but scared or unsure about how to communicate it.

As my friend Julie says, sometimes the initial conversation is like an earthquake; it can be rattling for all involved, and everyone may need time to absorb and reflect. There may be a few aftershocks, or follow-up conversations needed, to finish working through things.

One of my clients, who I will call Sadie, started coaching with me when she felt unsure about what to do: continue working at her small company, where she had a lot of responsibility, or pivot to launch her own related business. In her heart of hearts, she knew all along she wanted to start her own business. She had been harboring a dream of running her own company since childhood.

At first, Sadie felt torn between the difficult decision of giving notice at work and her true desire to launch an idea she had been incubating for years.

Together we worked through the following stages:

- **Plant:** Sadie wrote a mission statement for her new business, and imagined what success would look like one year from launch.

- **Scan:** We created a strategy to work toward that vision, whether or not it was a side gig or her full-time job. We considered tools, skills, and contacts that would be most helpful as she started building her business on nights and weekends.

- **Pilot:** Sadie took small, meaningful steps toward building her business, such as writing website copy and setting up an onboarding guide for new team members. We also determined a checkpoint date at which she would seriously consider leaving her full-time job, which ended up being about three months ahead. We agreed not to debate the issue for the next two months, only to revisit at that later date.

- **Launch:** Together we worked through *how* to have the "I'm leaving" conversation with her boss, whether it was in two weeks or two months. We wrote talking points that felt authentic and would keep their relationship strong, and practiced run-throughs.

Having clarity on each of the steps above gave Sadie tremendous relief. As a result, a few weeks later her gut started speaking to her more loudly and she felt increasingly anxious and bored at work. Even though she had given herself permission to wait three months before resigning, Sadie knew she was ready to give her notice in a few weeks, and she did.

Being able to separate *what* her decision was from *how* to communicate it from *when* to communicate it gave Sadie the space and clarity she needed to move forward on a timeline that worked for her. Even though nothing could change the fact that the conversation with her boss would be uncomfortable, she went in feeling confident and empowered knowing that her choice was the right one.

DON'T WAIT FOR PERFECT CONDITIONS

Decisions are data. You can only spin on a set of questions for so long before the better thing to do is to get *something* in motion, be an observer, and make your next move from a new position. At a certain point, any decision is better than no decision.

When the real estate market tanked, Roxanne Vice and her husband went from 1-percenters to penny-pinchers, counting spare change to buy groceries. Her biggest regret is waiting too long to take even small steps forward. "The worst thing we did was to wait for things to get better instead of taking action," she said. She and her husband watched as six years of savings got whittled away. Roxanne started to feel despondent, but it wasn't until hitting rock bottom that she moved into action.

"I went through stages of panic, sadness, anger, grief, and self-pity—but also discovered that was where my willpower was hidden. When I finally got reacquainted with my desire to live, and remembered that this experience was just that—an experience, a wrinkle—I was able to get through. I got up and got moving," she said. "Focusing on the simple, core routines like self-care, meditation, health cleanses, and rebuilding from the inside out cannot be overstated. The surprising benefit from stepping back in a transformation is that you get to choose a new step forward in any direction, something new and unexpected."

Roxanne pivoted from full-time artist and work-from-home mom to partnering with her husband to launch an artisan manufacturing retail business. To do this, she combined her husband's experience as a land developer with her career portfolio of strengths and experience in business building, publishing, marketing, and operations.

Roxanne's new venture nurtures her creative expression by helping more artists at a time, and continues to reveal new opportunities. Roxanne never predicted that she and her husband would get a chance to work together, but is grateful for the opportunity and sees each new challenge as a blessing, "a Christmas present waiting to be unwrapped."

Pivot Paradox: Shoot the Moon

Our focus so far has been on taking smart risks that will help you make a purposeful shift in a new direction, starting from a foundation of what is already working.

It all sounds so reasonable and pragmatic.

But deep down there may be a part of you that wants to shout, *BO-RING!* For many impacters, small steps are fine, but our lives and most exhilarating memories are defined by the big leaps, the times when the odds were not in our favor but we prevailed. We love a good underdog story, and revere phrases like "No risk, no reward," "You can't cross the Grand Canyon in two small leaps," and "Go big or go home."

I am a firm believer in paying attention to practicalities while not neutering yourself or your dreams. One of the most invigorating things you can do is go for something so outlandishly enormous that just to attempt the feat strengthens your resolve and forces an entirely new dimension of creative thinking.

Many inventions, scientific discoveries, and technological advances follow from the residue of bigger failures. Post-it Notes were an accidental blip from 3M on the way to creating a stronger adhesive. Twitter started as a podcasting service, and YouTube used to be a video dating site. Today they are multibillion-dollar businesses.

In the popular card game Hearts, the goal of each round is to take the fewest points, or cards. However, players can also try a risky strategy called "shooting the moon," by attempting to collect every heart card and the Queen of Spades. The odds of success are quite low, but that is why it is so glorious for a player who shoots the moon successfully—they win the game in one fell swoop. If they fail to shoot the moon, they are stuck with an excess number of cards that would all but guarantee a loss.

Look for opportunities where you can shoot the moon while minimizing your risk. For my brother, Tom, this meant taking on monthly property management accounts while looking for the next great real estate investment opportunity that fit his criteria. Until his most recent pivot, this had only happened twice in a period of four years of scanning, a less than 1 percent hit ratio. But twice was enough to keep going; he knew that where there were two, there would be more. Each property that he passed on helped him refine his search process and become more efficient at making a go or no-go decision, and placing smart bets when those rare "shoot the moon" opportunities surfaced.

HOW DO YOU KNOW YOUR LAUNCH WORKED?

To answer this question, you first need to determine what *worked* means for you. Does it mean financial success? A feeling of exhilaration and freedom? Increasing your time and energy? Working from your biggest strengths for most of the day? For many, a launch worked if they have no regrets about having made that choice. Others may have more specific parameters for declaring success, such as those outlined in their vision or in the Launch timing criteria.

Let some time pass before assessing or analyzing whether your launch was successful. It is natural to experience turbulence following a big decision, particularly once the excitement wears off. Many people emerging from intense work environments need weeks or months to decompress and recharge after years of relentless stress and pressure. It is particularly important to focus on physical fundamentals during this time such as sleep, rest, exercise, and nutrition.

After your new trajectory has stabilized, reflect:

- Do I feel more calm, healthy, and engaged?

- Does this new direction match my core values?

- Do my projects engage my innate strengths and interests?

- Is this new direction sustainable financially? Healthwise? Interestwise? Can I see myself doing this for the next few years?

- Am I able to maintain balance between this career path and other aspects of my life, such as friends, family, and relationships?

Your launch may have worked in the sense that you have no regrets, but still not be perfectly lined up with your long-term career aspirations. It is possible that you will hit a pivot point or plateau again, but each new decision will reveal additional insights. Even if you declare your launch successful, given impacters' innate drive for growth and challenge, you may want to continue piloting soon afterward.

Christian and John, who you met in the High Net Growth chapter, pivoted from working as commodities traders in the open outcry pits to running their own urban farming business, SpringUps. They pooled their money to purchase two shipping containers that were repurposed as hydroponic growing facilities, rented a parking space in Red Hook, Brooklyn, and started growing basil. Soon after, they brought me on as a consultant to help with operations and communications, and I got a front-row seat to watch and help their pivot unfold.

John and Christian had a predetermined pivot runway of two years after leaving the trading floor: one year for exploration to decompress and determine what industry and type of company interested them, then one year to launch and expand SpringUps. After taking the first year off to travel and explore options, John and Christian set their make-or-break marker as the company's profitability after year two, their first full year in business. If they were not profitable or did not see a promising revenue trajectory, they would explore other options.

One year in, although the SpringUps business was successful, having landed some of the biggest retail clients in the region, it no longer seemed like the right fit. As former traders, neither John nor Christian were willing to stick around just because they had sunk costs into the project. They wanted to make sure their career trajectory was on track to a robust financial future, and one that felt like the best match for their strengths. SpringUps came close but ultimately did not fit the bill, which they learned only through hands-on experience.

In reflecting on their pivot, John and Christian realized SpringUps was too sharp a turn from their talents, true interests, and financial goals, so they sold the company. John, who studied probability theory in college, returned to trading on his own, started learning the Python programming language to create trading algorithms, and took a job with an early-stage predictive ana-lytics start-up. Christian pivoted to a sales role in a national technology firm, which played to his love of interacting with others and making deals. It also lowered his risk profile; Christian got engaged shortly after shuttering SpringUps, and deliberately sought a job that would help him create more stability before getting married and starting a family.

Neither of them have regrets about their entrepreneurial pivot. They en-joyed learning about urban farming and the food scene in New York City, and decompressing from the intensity of commodities trading. The SpringUps venture helped John and Christian identify next career moves that were even more aligned. They see their launch as a success even though they changed direction after two years. Both recognize their careers will be ever shifting from this point forward, fluid enough to meet their growth-oriented lives.

THE CONTINUOUS PIVOT

As I mentioned in the introduction, almost none of the pivoters' stories I wrote for the first draft of this book remained the same by the final edit—some by choice, others by circumstance. The people featured are proof in point of what it means to be an impacter living in our dynamic economy.

Some recounted their updated pivot stories with excitement, while oth-ers shared their news with a slightly discouraged tone, as if somehow their initial pivot at the time of our interview had failed.

But when I dug deeper with each person, it was clear that pivoting was always the right move. Even if their launch did not prove fruitful in the ways they were expecting, it taught them valuable lessons about life, business, and what they wanted next in their career. It helped them reconnect to their strengths and build a new bridge toward an even better opportunity. They started to adjust to the fact that Pivot is the new normal, and stopped taking the wins and losses so personally.

Cycle through the first three stages—Plant, Scan, Pilot—as many times as necessary to feel secure when you launch. You can also work through the Pivot process anytime you get stuck, not just during major moves, but also within businesses, side hustles, your current role, and smaller projects and goals. The Pivot Method will help you be a scientist in your life—a steady observer and experimenter—as you direct future changes gracefully, methodically, and with greater confidence, clarity, and insight.

Pivot Cycle

Asking whether a launch worked is a trick question. Launches work no matter what because they get you unstuck. Launches move you out of thinking and into action. They expose your strengths, your grit, your creativity, and when you might be veering off course. Launches reveal blind spots and new insight. Launches catapult you into the next phase of your life.

A launch works because, after making it through the rocky terrain of the Pivot stages that preceded it, you know you wouldn't return to the starting point again even if you could.

Launch: Online Resources

Visit PivotMethod.com/launch for additional tools, templates, and book recommendations for this stage.

STAGE FIVE

LEAD 〉

Create a Pivot-Friendly Culture

PLANT

SCAN

PILOT

LAUNCH

LEAD

LEAD OVERVIEW

YOU NOW HAVE A FIRM GRASP ON THE PIVOT METHOD. YOU CLARIFIED YOUR ONE-year vision, scanned for new opportunities, and identified experiments rooted in your strengths to test your new direction. Pivot as a mindset? *Check.* Pivot as a process for figuring out what's next? *Check.* But what about others you interact with on a daily basis?

Impacters rarely operate in a vacuum. You work with other people regularly, possibly even managing others. You might have two employees reporting to you or twenty. Perhaps you are a president or founder, charged with improving company culture for hundreds or thousands of people. Maybe you do not manage a team yet, but can envision growing into a leadership role. Or you want to create a ground-up movement from within your organization to improve communication and career development opportunities. Perhaps you enjoy coaching and mentoring others and want to learn new skills to formalize your process.

This final stage is for leaders—anyone who wants to apply the Pivot process to help others. The Pivot Method can become a shared language for having expansive career conversations. When used as a coaching framework, you can quickly help others brainstorm solutions to problems, set development goals, and identify ambitious yet achievable next steps. When rolled out on a regular basis, Pivot can create a culture of open communication. Talking about career aspirations can become a welcome experience for managers and employees, rather than something to avoid.

CHAPTER 12: ARE YOU LISTENING?

How Can You Facilitate Engaging Career Conversations?

You have done all this work to create a hiring process that will bring in all these awesome smart creatives, and how do they pay you back? By leaving!! That's right. News flash: When you hire great people, some of them may come to realize that there is a world beyond yours. This isn't a bad thing, in fact it's an inevitable by-product of a healthy, innovative team. Still, fight like hell to keep them.

—Eric Schmidt and Jonathan Rosenberg, *How Google Works*

THE CAREER CONVERSATION I REGRET MOST IS THE ONE I NEVER HAD.

I have given two weeks' notice twice in my career. The first time was at the political polling start-up where I worked for two years while finishing my undergraduate degree. I remember walking into the founder's office with a cup of coffee clutched tightly in my hands as I sat down. I had always been a bit intimidated by his brilliance and, at twenty-one years old, did not have much professional experience to draw upon for situations like these.

My voice wobbled. "I . . . I . . . I have loved working here, but I have accepted a job at Google. This is my two weeks' notice." The conversation lasted fifteen minutes, and he asked me to have my things packed up and taken care of by Friday.

I had been the first employee, and by the time I left, the company had grown to thirty people. I welcomed each new employee, developed vendor agreements, managed our office build-out, and helped recruit our online panel of survey respondents. I was the office manager, webmaster, and marketing assistant. I loved growing so quickly with the company, and our founder often joked that I was "hiding five Jennys" in my office. But as layers of the company were added, my future there got cloudier. Instead of progressing into managerial roles, I was taking direction from three different managers at one point. I was often torn between conflicting assignments, and started feeling frustrated and restless.

What I regret is that our first career conversation was also our last. I wish I had gone to the founder and had the courage to say, "I want to keep growing with the company. Help me map a course here where I can see my development continuing." Or, "I would love to learn more about coding. Can I take classes and increase my responsibilities?" Or even just shooting straight: "I am getting bored, and having three managers is stifling. Is there anything we can do?"

Instead, I started taking phone interviews for Google in my car on lunch breaks. It was the only company I would leave the start-up for, and it was a long shot. I interviewed for four months with twelve different people, and gave a forty-five-minute mock presentation to the entire training team, all while I could have been trying to troubleshoot the job I already had.

After two years at Google, I started itching for change again when I was spending a significant part of my time preparing PowerPoint strategy decks, decidedly *not* my Zone of Genius. During my first stint as a manager at age twenty-four, I was charged with displacing several friends and colleagues who were older than me and had been there longer than I had. My manager and I had meetings to ask each of them to find another role on a different team or leave the company. This crushed me.

I was ready to quit, not knowing if I was cut out for corporate life much longer, when I ran into my good friend Becky Cotton, who I mentioned earlier, and she helped me transition onto the recently formed career development team. Thanks to Becky, the angel on the shoulder of many a Googler, I ended up staying with the company two and a half more years, working with her and a small team to create and launch the global Career Guru coaching program that is still thriving today.

In the first example, I was green. I did not know how to have a career conversation and admit that I had hit a ceiling, and did not know where to go from there. I did not ask for input from the founder. Instead, I avoided the tough conversation and made plans to leave.

In the second scenario, I was able to parlay my strengths and interests into a new role within the company. I confided in an advocate, Becky—who is still working at Google on career development programs after ten years— who helped me navigate the internal job transition process.

I wanted to know, the second time around, that I had given Google every chance to fit before leaving. I was able to have transparent conversations with my manager about what mattered to me. I demonstrated strong performance in my role, and had developed unique skills by attending coach training on nights and weekends. I got approval to dedicate 10 percent time to a drop-in coaching pilot project, Career Guru. It later turned into a full-time role as the company's growth exploded and retention became a bigger focus, allowing me to pivot internally.

"Beckys" are crucial to your organization. Imagine if managers and senior leadership in your company reacted the way Becky did. How many great people could you keep, or at least have open conversations with? How would it enable you to create a coaching culture in which impacters like Becky, who love supporting others, can also thrive? How could you provide resources that allow employees to brainstorm solutions to their hairiest career questions without judgment or fear?

YOUR INTEREST MATTERS MORE THAN YOU THINK

These days, it is likely that an employee who does not feel heard will start looking elsewhere. Money is no longer the only currency for career or life success. High net growth individuals want to feel challenged, collaborative, and like they are able to make a positive impact within their organizations and outside of them.

Jason Shen, from Chapter 3, was working at a start-up when he pivoted internally from content marketing to product management. His primary driver was not money, recognition, or even climbing the ladder. Jason's framework for determining how long to stay in a role and at a company re-flects that of many impacters I speak with: "Am I learning? Am I growing? Are these skills, experiences, and connections going to be valuable in the future? Is this making me a better person, and do I enjoy the people I work with?"

When impacters hit a career plateau, leaving is often *not* their first im-pulse. Many want to stay with the company, ideally expanding their role by pursuing new opportunities. It is when they feel these conversations become a dead end that they start to look elsewhere. If you hire impacters for their entrepreneurial fire and creativity, do not be surprised if they get antsy when they become stymied navigating too many layers of bureaucracy.

That was the case with Courtney John-Reader. CJ felt stuck in her job as a digital communications coordinator at an architectural firm. She was ex-cited about her projects at work, but felt the company she worked for was resistant to change and did not value her efforts.

"They seemed to place such a low priority on what I did that no matter how hard I worked, I felt like I wasn't accomplishing anything," she said. "Af-ter three years, I felt like I had no value and it led me to having daily panic attacks at work, and finally having to take a health leave for a few weeks."

When CJ realized she was sacrificing her health for her job, in addition to not feeling seen or appreciated, she knew she needed to "choose herself." This was not a rash decision, or one made lightly. "I hesitated to leave work for *years* because I had this feeling I would be letting people down if I skipped off," she said. "I was totally invested in the company. But they weren't invested in me."

Are you creating an environment where people feel comfortable sharing their best ideas and career aspirations with you? If your impacters have a growing interest in an innovative field, are you willing to support them in running small pilots to experiment and prove the market? When people ex-press how they would like to grow within your organization, do you provide support, guidance, and internal programs to encourage those goals? Or do you or your managers turn a deaf ear?

Too often, organizations and their managers treat coaching and career development as an afterthought. For some leaders, these are lip service HR terms that have nothing to do with the bottom line, quarterly earnings, or growth reports. But you know better.

In an *Inc.* survey of five hundred CEOs from the fastest-growing private companies, 41 percent of leaders identified "recruiting talent" as the biggest contributor to their company's ability to innovate. Fifty percent said "attracting and retaining skilled employees" is the biggest challenge facing leaders today. It is likely that you have worked hard to find great employees; now it is time to apply equal effort toward keeping them.

Workers whose managers hold regular meetings are three times more likely to be engaged and to feel involved in and enthusiastic about their work. One Gallup study revealed that just 12 percent of workers strongly agreed that "their manager helps set work priorities." This is an issue, given that this cohort tends to be much happier at work than those who scored managers' goal-setting guidance at the lower end of the scale.

Ronnie Mae Weiss, director of MIT's Work-Life Center, has spent twenty-five years working with organizations on employee retention and work-life benefits, and says that managers play a critical role in helping impacters do their best work. She says organizations do best with "managers who see their role as supporting their direct reports stretching, trying new things, taking some risks, and letting go a little bit, allowing them to explore intriguing opportunities."

As the saying goes, "People leave managers, not companies." According to Gallup, among 7,200 adults, 50 percent left a job "to get away from their manager." So why, given the data, don't managers have these conversations more often? Moreover, why don't employees express their dissatisfaction *before* seeking opportunities outside of the organization? One major factor: fear.

Dismantle Manager Roadblocks

Managers hesitate to have career conversations for a variety of reasons, including work pressure and lack of time, uncertainty about how to best facilitate these conversations, fear of not having the answers to an employee's career questions or goals, and fear of losing their best talent.

According to Julie Clow, senior vice president of people development for Chanel, one of the biggest roadblocks is managers' fear of making promises they cannot keep. Managers often do not feel comfortable guaranteeing a role, and it can be easy for individuals to misinterpret the intent of these discussions. Career conversations that focus on five or ten years out are difficult.

"Individuals have a hard time foreseeing where they will be, either vastly underestimating their ability to progress or overestimating where they *should* be, and managers feel uncomfortable projecting ahead to think about possible roles," Clow says. "The best strategy is to focus on what's *next*, a much easier conversation for all involved."

Clow says *next* could involve a timeline of next month or even a few years ahead. If managers fear making promises, they can focus on helping their employees find smaller career steps, experiments, and opportunities. Managers *can* promise things like help finding side projects, approving spending 10 percent of an employee's time with another team, or reimbursing tuition for a class to build up a work-related skill set.

Jennifer Grayeb, talent development manager at Aetna, believes that managers are afraid of losing their best talent by having career conversations, but in fact, this "training people up and out" makes them even more desirable to work for.

"The best managers I know are those who not only have those conversations, but help their directs create a plan to get there," Grayeb says. "Their reputation is shared across the organization and attracts other high performing individuals to want to work for them."

Career Conversations Are a Two-way Street

No matter how much managers take increased responsibility for initiating these career conversations, they are still a two-way street, and should be owned by individuals. Impacters know themselves best, and shouldn't expect others to read their mind or wait to be asked.

"I do believe it is part of the manager's responsibility to support career development, because it means you have a more engaged, productive, happy employee who is thinking of solutions and ways to solve problems all the time, not just in the office," Ronnie Mae at MIT says. "But it is equally important for every one of us to be looking at our career and going after what we need. Both asking our managers for that, and asking other people in the organization."

Jennifer Grayeb suggests that individuals ask their managers about *their* personal career journey, and the choices they had to make along the way.

She also says one of the biggest lessons for younger impacters is balancing their desire for stretch projects and meaningful work with rolling up their sleeves and getting things done. If impacters want to create a growth culture, they should also take the lead in helping others. "For every opportunity you get, help open a door for someone else."

Laura Grose, HR business partner at one of Silicon Valley's fastest-growing start-ups, advocates that impacters keep a realistic and patient view of what roles may be available. She found that many impacters who enjoy the building phase may feel limited when their roles require more process and maintenance.

"In high-growth start-ups, it's common for early employees to wear many hats. But sometimes it takes a different person and more specialization as the company matures. Rock stars at doing everything in the beginning may find themselves less interested over time," Laura said. "Sometimes your company goes through a growth spurt or a decline and it is no longer the right fit for your skills. You might need to figure out at what stage you add the most value and start seeking out those opportunities."

Laura says that when impacters get impatient about getting promoted quickly, they should remember: "The question is not only about *are you ready*, but is the job available to you? There is only one CEO."

One of the most untapped tools for pivoters is proposing a business case for why they would be valuable somewhere else within the company. "You don't always have to go up, you can go across," Laura said. "Make your case: I have knowledge A, if I apply that to business B, here is how I can transfer my skills to add enormous value. It is one of the least known and most effective ways to get new opportunities within an organization."

HOW TO USE THE PIVOT METHOD WITHIN ORGANIZATIONS

Although it is beneficial for individuals in transition, Pivot is also a simple way to hold career conversations with members of your team, helping them expand within their role and pivot internally when they are ready for development opportunities, instead of looking for outside work.

Many coaching and management models are obscured from the person sitting across from you, whereas Pivot is a simple framework that you can discuss and work through *with* employees. It encourages people to be transparent about the ways they want to grow within the organization. It also empowers employees to devise small career experiments that would increase their skills and benefit the company, without waiting for a promotion or a lateral move—neither of which will always be available options. Pivot points and plateaus don't have to be a problem, nor something employees have to hide in conversation; you will both be equipped with language to articulate these moments. Working through the Pivot Method enables you both to explore career options before creating more detailed development plans.

There are several ways to create a strong culture that emphasizes openness and engagement.

1. Casual Conversations

First, you can use the Pivot Method as a way to talk about career development when having one-on-one conversations:

- In its quickest form, share the basic premise: Double down on *what is working* to pivot toward what is next within the role, team, or company. Turn existing strengths and interests into related opportunities and help people shift incrementally, instead of aiming too far ahead to make dramatic career turns that are too sharp.

- Share the basketball player analogy: Focus on strengths and interests (Plant foot) to scan for new opportunities (Pivot foot). From there, identify small pilots to help impacters expand their skills and pursue interests that also benefit the team.

- Review the Career Operating Modes from the introduction: Ask employees to self-assess whether they are in reactive, proactive, or innovative mode, and what would move them into the latter categories if they are not already there.

2. Structured Annual Career Conversations

Setting dedicated time aside for career conversations once or twice per year improves retention, engagement, and internal mobility, and does not require a massive budget or highly sophisticated tools. Simply expressing interest in your team members' development goes further than you might expect.

Although performance reviews seem like a natural time to start a career conversation, many employees dread them. People are often nervous, on guard, and anxious about what the future might hold in terms of promotion or a salary increase. These reviews may be a great time to discuss strengths and areas for development, but they are not times when employees are most open to discussing their most vulnerable hopes and career aspirations.

Instead, I recommend setting up regular career conversations outside of performance reviews, ideally several months apart, to increase the overall frequency of big-picture conversations. Managers do not have to do the heavy lifting here. When you are ready to roll these out, ask each employee to schedule thirty to sixty minutes on your calendar. Suggest they prepare by thinking through each of the Pivot stages in advance, particularly Plant and Scan, reflecting on their greatest strengths and how they would like to add value and develop within their role moving forward.

Do's—Best Practices for Conducting These Meetings

- **Do more listening than talking:** Save your own advice and experience for the end of the conversation, when you will have a better sense of what would be most helpful to share.

- **Ask open-ended questions:** Instead of asking *why* (which can some-times make people feel defensive), ask follow-up questions such as *What is important to you about that? What else?* and *Tell me more.* These will help you both get to the root of what matters most.

- **Focus most on the Plant stage:** Explore what values are most impor-tant to the individual, what their talents and interests are, and what suc-cess looks like one year from now, while also adding your observations about their key strengths and accomplishments.

- **Remain exploratory during the conversation:** The more you help uncover what is working and what is exciting one year from now, with-out skipping ahead to problem solving or specific next steps, the more insight you will both have to scan effectively for potential solutions and pilots later in the conversation.

- **Scan by asking about a range of interesting opportunities as a next move:** Go first for *quantity,* with expansive brainstorming, before narrow-ing down for *quality.* From that list, ask them what one or two pilots would be most promising to pursue, before weighing in with your suggestions.

- **Bonus: Conduct these sessions as walk-and-talks:** Fresh air and movement will revitalize both of you, fostering a better connection and more engaging conversation.

Don'ts—Common Missteps

- **Do not take notes:** It breaks eye contact and takes away from deeper, more active listening. You can both jot down memorable insights and next steps after the meeting.

- **Do not hold these pivot conversations at the same time as perfor-mance reviews:** Employees are likely to be nervous and are often over-whelmed processing information from your assessment of their work.

- **Do not combine them with your usual one-on-one meetings either, if possible:** This way, neither of you will be distracted by loom-ing action items.

- **Do not worry about trying to "solve" an employee's one-year vision in this conversation:** Just get clear on what it is. Regular one-on-ones can be a time to follow up with planning more specific pilots and next steps.

3. Coaching Framework for Managers and Mentors

You can also roll out the Pivot Method as a conversation framework for managers, mentors, and internal coaches. Whether or not you have formalized coaching programs within your organization, Pivot can be taught as a method to hold exploratory conversations, rather than tactical or advice-based ones. It can also be used to guide problem solving anytime someone feels stuck and unsure of what to do next, whether on a project, in their role, or in their career.

Many of the coaches and managers I have trained in the Pivot Method as a coaching tool report a sense of relief that this is a simple process that can be shared directly with the person they are speaking with. Their coachees leave these conversations feeling energized, because the method emphasizes strengths and small experiments, which lead quickly to positive and productive outcomes.

PILOT CREATIVE INTERNAL-MOBILITY PROGRAMS

Establishing a culture of career conversations is a strong start, but not sufficient. Career development must go beyond talk, into the realm of action and real opportunities. Individuals will soon hit a frustrating wall if their desire to develop within the company is met by red tape when they actually try to make a move. One unfortunately common refrain is, "It is harder to find another job *within* my company than it was to get hired in the first place."

Career conversations are most beneficial when accompanied by internal-mobility programs that support them, making employees even more likely to stay long term. If your company does not offer the types of programs you would like to see, take the lead in starting one, or see how you might pilot a smaller version. Do not assume that just because it does not yet exist, it never will.

In keeping with the Pivot Method, consider the following questions:

- **Plant:** What is your organization already doing that is working? What would success look like in terms of creating a culture of engagement and mobility?

- **Scan:** What are other managers, teams, departments, or outside organizations doing that interests you? What ideas stand out as particularly achievable or that would make the biggest impact? Who else could you partner with inside or outside of the organization?

- **Pilot:** What small experiments could you try with one team or department before rolling out to the entire organization? How will you evaluate these pilots?

- **Launch:** What resources would be required for a bigger launch in terms of time, team, and tools? When would you launch this program, and how would you measure its success?

Internal Programs to Support Career Mobility

The chart below shows a handful of examples for how to create a Pivot-friendly development culture. Companies range in size, budget, and resources, so there is no expectation to implement all of the following.

Manager Training	Internal Learning	Internal Mobility	Coaching
How to have career conversations	10 to 20 percent projects	Internal job board, job shadowing	Designated internal and external coaches
Leader-led team-building workshops	Education reimbursement	Rotation programs (home and abroad)	Mentoring and reverse mentoring

Below are a few more creative ideas, many adapted from programs cited in *Fortune*'s "100 Best Companies to Work For":

- **Guest speakers:** Authors, industry experts, prominent public figures, and musicians hosted at lunch-and-learn sessions or special events. Many companies stream these events live to other offices, and record them to post on public channels. Cliff Redeker, who manages the Talks at Google program, has developed a model for this that many companies have since followed. He has hosted over 500 talks in the eight years he has been involved with the program, first as a volunteer, now in a full-time position managing other volunteers who dedicate a small percentage of their time to recruit and host interesting speakers.

- **On-site library:** SAS, a business and analytics software company, has "more than 16,000 books, research resources, business tools and loaner equipment that help employees work toward their professional and personal goals." Zappos also has a library of favorite books in the lobby; employees and visitors are encouraged to take one on their way out, or read and return them. They do this to contribute to one of their core values, "Pursue Growth and Learning," to help employees connect with each other and the outside world.

- **Externships:** Wegmans facilitates externships for employees, hands-on learning opportunities outside of the company.

- **Job-specific certification programs:** Whole Foods provides job-specific development opportunities, such as the American Cheese Society Certified Cheese Professional training and exam, and the Produce Warrior Program.

- **Companywide volunteer initiatives:** Google's GoogleServe encourages all employees to volunteer during the same week of the year, and this time off is company sanctioned. There are directories of thousands of global initiatives to choose from, ranging from donating domain expertise, such as résumé review or training, to environmental cleanup efforts.

- **Fund a Goal program:** Lululemon (a Canadian company, thus not on the Fortune list) promotes a culture of goal setting and accountability, asking all employees to identify business, health, and personal goals for one, five, and ten years. They have created a Fund a Goal program for high performers to contribute money toward aims such as running a marathon or attending yoga teacher training.

- **Reverse mentoring and lunches:** General Electric pairs senior executives with younger employees. The junior employees mentor their counterparts in technology, social media, and emerging trends, and the senior employees provide more traditional career guidance and organizational mentoring in return. Acuity encourages executives to schedule lunch meetings with more junior employees to foster communication and idea exchange at all levels of the company.

- **Experiment with project-based teams that disband when complete:** One midsize defense contractor launched an internal talent market to increase productivity, collaboration, and engagement by connecting employees with excess capacity to leaders who have short-term development opportunities. Laura Grose had the idea for teams to experiment with setting up a fantasy-football–style draft for talent, mirroring the way professional sports teams recruit to make performance management more engaging and effective.

Many of these initiatives can be rolled out in a cost-effective manner, led by anyone with a passion to do so within the organization. Do not wait until you have the perfect solution to try something that sounds interesting; you will probably never feel like you have enough time, budget, or resources.

If you are not sure where to start, *ask*. Return to the grounded theory approach from the Scan stage. Listen to your team members, either in open all-hands meetings, during office hours, or with a suggestion capture tool or internal survey, and choose one key area to tackle first.

Better still: recruit impacters looking for leadership opportunities to lead the charge.

———

During my time at Google, one of the traits recruiters looked for in potential employees was adaptability. Hiring managers would consider how willing and open someone was to change. If new hires were not adaptable, they would surely struggle. Our job roles changed frequently, our teams shifted strategy often to meet the company's rapid expansion, and departments within the company were often reorganizing. During my five years there, the teams I was on were "re-orging" as much as we were "orging."

Dr. Tom Guarriello is a professor at New York's School of Visual Arts and founder of RoboPsych, a platform for exploring the psychology of human-to-robot interaction. When I told him about the ever-changing nature of companies today and asked how it relates to the economic landscape, he said, "The fantasy is that there is org, that there is an 'org' to be 're.' There is no org anymore. The org is an emergent entity that reconfigures itself circumstantially around opportunities."

Coaching conversations are an excellent start toward helping impacters adapt to a world of ever-shifting orgs, and in fact, the best tool we have to collaboratively redefine our roles as often as is now required.

Lead: Online Resources

Visit PivotMethod.com/lead for additional tools, templates, and book recommendations for this stage.

CONCLUSION: CELEBRATE COMPLEXITY

People say that what we're all seeking is a meaning for life.... I think that what we're seeking is an experience of being alive, so that our life experiences on the purely physical plane will have resonances within our innermost being and reality, so that we can actually feel the rapture of being alive.... That's what it's all finally about, and that's what these clues help us to find within ourselves.

—Joseph Campbell, *The Power of Myth*

I REMEMBER SQUEALING WITH DELIGHT WHEN ONE OF MY COACHING CLIENTS, Brian, told me what he thought was an extraneous fact about his past.

Brian was a high-level engineering director who had hit a plateau at a large technology company. After nearly a decade there, he was looking for a career reboot, something new and challenging. Brian had a robust compensation package at his present job and a wife and kids to support, so the choice about when to leave and what to do next was not an easy one.

As we continued talking, Brian mentioned that he pursued a PhD in knot theory for a year and a half. A huge smile spread across my face. Brian's love for knots—and knotty, complex challenges—was the perfect background for navigating this transition. Rather than viewing his current career conundrum as a struggle, he started to see it as just the type of knot he loved to untangle, and one that he *could* solve with the same diligent problem-solving skills that he practiced in graduate school.

Through our work together, Brian grew increasingly clear on his values and vision. Within a month, he was certain that he was ready to leave his job; now it was just a matter of timing. Brian's one-year vision was to work in a smaller organization in an emerging area, and help expand and connect with others in the burgeoning technology community where he lived.

A few weeks later he got a call, seemingly out of the blue, from a venture capitalist looking to hire a senior vice president for a technology start-up in his hometown, in an emerging industry, with great potential for innovation and leadership. After several exploratory conversations, Brian accepted the job and made the move. This all happened within a span of two months.

Hitting a career plateau is not a problem, nor is it a crisis. It is a captivating knot waiting to be untangled, in exchange for accelerated growth. As an impacter, you would not have your work be any other way. Like Brian, you too can become a master knot worker.

High net growth and impact individuals usually have high self-efficacy: they generally believe they can accomplish what they set out to achieve. But when pivoting, they still wonder, "Am I capable of these grand ambitions I am setting out to achieve?" All of us, when we reach even higher than we have previously or bust out of traditional norms, may wonder, *Am I smart enough? Capable enough? Am I the rule or the exception? Am I cut out for this?*

YES. Your biggest vision is worth pursuing. Just as no two people share the same fingerprint, *your* ideas have not yet been tackled with your unique upbringing, worldview, and life experiences, at this moment in time, in the framework of our current economy and technology, for your intended community.

That does not mean that your exact conjecture about what's next is guaranteed to be successful or profitable. But what I can say with absolute conviction is that you are creative, resourceful, and resilient, and will find a way to bounce back from just about anything. *That* is a certainty you can return to.

CHECKING IN AT THE LAST RESORT

There was one particularly low point during the pivot year I described in the introduction, the period of my life that inspired this book, when I looked out the windows of my studio apartment with a mixture of hope, prayer, and slight desperation. "How?" I whispered to the array of lower Manhattan buildings in front of me, as if they could answer me out loud. "How do I do this? How do I make it here? Is there a way out of this muck of uncertainty?"

My money had run out. In order to stay in New York City, I had wiped out the last of my savings to get the apartment in which I was asking these questions. My rent doubled overnight, but my business income did not. Many of my biggest fears about self-employment had come true. I was doing what I loved at a macro level by coaching, speaking, and writing, but I did not know how to best apply these skills in my business moving forward.

At that point the question is not, "What would you do if you knew you couldn't fail?" but *What do you do when your back is up against the wall?*

Two weeks later, I was on the phone with Vanguard, my 401(k) company, ready to move into my worst-case scenario by liquidating part of my retirement account—the final frontier of my remaining cash savings. In my mind, the last resort was always just a paper exercise meant to appease my inner CFO . . . and the leasing office that accepted my rental application despite my being self-employed. As I contemplated the next steps in pickpocketing my future's bank account, a gremlin sat on my shoulder telling me that I was delusional and should just go get a job, throw in the towel on this crazy dream.

But my gut was saying something else: to keep going, that this low moment was a necessary part of my personal development and a critical, pivotal time in my life and business. This was an initiation, another doorway to the career I knew was waiting for me on the other side.

It was oddly reassuring that I was willing to feel so down, so discouraged, so bruised, battered, and exhausted by the journey of solopreneurship, and still not be ready to quit. Feeling that inner fire—with all the realities of my financial uncertainty, not just the hypothetical version from a perch of safety—solidified the knowledge that I still had fight left.

I never dipped into my 401(k). Instead, I stopped looking for answers outside of myself. I studied what worked in prior transitions and with my coaching clients. I redefined my one-year vision. I took the pressure off of having *the* answer and identified small pilots that were anchored in my strengths, increasing their scope in smart succession.

My pivot forced me to step up and do things differently. It was not until I started applying, further refining, and digging deeper into the systems I have shared in this book that my career regained traction, this time stronger and more aligned than ever.

THE COURAGEOUS LIFE

Make no mistake. Even after reducing risk by working through the stages in this book, pivoting still requires courage. Every time.

To show up in the world as an impacter, vigorously pursuing learning, meaning, and growth, is courageous in itself. You are signing up for a life of relentlessly pursuing what matters most. You are signing up for a life of making choices that align with your core values, regardless of how tough those decisions are in the moment, ultimately to benefit many lives beyond your own.

As an impacter, you refuse to phone it in. You ask a lot of yourself and others. You are responsible, not reckless, and for that reason, cautiously optimistic. You do not take blind leaps, because you care about the side effects your choices have on others. You may have tasted failure in the past and be hesitant to expose yourself to that possibility again. But at the same time, you know that the greatest failure is not to try—to settle, to succumb to your fear, and to live as a shell of your truest self.

Impacters are not afflicted with FOMO: Fear of Missing Out. They have FONT: Fear of Not Trying. Connect with that part of you that knows, deep down, that you are *antifragile*—that shocks and setbacks only make you stronger—and that you *can* succeed at whatever you set your mind to, even though success will not always look the way you expect. Life does not give us what we want; it gives us what we need. Pivots work the same way.

Living life as an impacter can be a vulnerable experience, as you are constantly stretching beyond your comfort zone. But it is also exhilarating, and the only way for you to truly thrive. So remember: build first, *then* your courage will follow. Hasn't it always?

————

There is one thing I know for sure: we will all face many more pivots on the road ahead, big and small, planned and unplanned. My aim in this book is to teach you how to *teach yourself* to fish—to persevere and thrive—when navigating these changes.

You will learn to lean into a sense of flow with the seasons of your life and career. Get nimble enough with the Pivot process and it transforms into a fluid movement. The edges of the pivots become smoother and less stressful. Rather than making sharp, jarring turns—shocked at hitting pivot points that you do not see coming—you will generate momentum as you make these turns in succession, continually and naturally.

Operating this way is the adventure and privilege of a lifetime. And it is from *this* place that we can turn our full focus outward and make the impact on the world that is waiting for us.

Pivot is the new Plan A, and that's good news. Learn to love the knots.

Prevent trouble before it arises.
Put things in order before they exist.
The giant pine tree
grows from a tiny sprout.
The journey of a thousand miles
starts from beneath your feet.
Rushing into action, you fail.
Trying to grasp things, you lose them.
Forcing a project to completion,
You ruin what was almost ripe.
Therefore the Master takes action
by letting things take their course.
He remains as calm
at the end as at the beginning.

—Lao Tzu, *Tao Te Ching*

ACKNOWLEDGMENTS

Every book . . . has a soul. The soul of the person who wrote it and of those who read it and lived and dreamed with it. Every time a book changes hands, every time someone runs his eyes down its pages, its spirit grows and strengthens.

—Carlos Ruiz Zafón, *The Shadow of the Wind*

First and foremost, to you, dear reader: thank you for investing your time and energy with me. May you embrace your fear as fuel to tackle anything you set your mind to. I look forward to hearing how your current and future pivots unfold!

There are no words to capture my enormous gratitude to my family, not just for supporting me unconditionally, but for their invaluable role in helping me thoroughly hash through the ideas presented here. Enormous thanks to my brother, Tom Blake, for brainstorming many of the concepts and sticking points over phone calls and massive cups of coffee. To my dad, Jim Blake, for his thought-provoking ideas and laser-sharp edits throughout the writing and revision processes. It was so inspiring to read your essays about evolutionary theory and jam about all the parallels to *Pivot*! To my mom, Cathy Blake, for her wise perspective and ongoing input. Congratulations on your ASLA fellowship and twenty year workiversary at Stanford! You are an inspiration. And to my grandma, Janice Deino, who has been and always will be an angel and kindred spirit in my life. Much love to my extended and second families: Blake, Deino, Harrington, Quinn, Knox, Schwartz, Walker, White, Dray, and Chaloeicheep. To the immensely talented Mark Hanauer, thank you for another round of author portraits, thirty-one years after the first ones you took when I was a baby. To Zoë, Aivey, and Eva—it is an honor to be your Auntie J. I love you all!

To the publishing pit crew that made this book possible: Sarah Lazin, my agent—you gave much needed tough love when this book was just the seedling of an idea; the proposal I resubmitted to you one year later was for a far more powerful message. Adrian Zackheim, the president of Portfolio, and Natalie Horbachevsky, my exceptional editor, thank you for believing in me and betting on *Pivot*—I have been thankful every day since for your vision, input, and support. Working with Portfolio on this project is the privilege of a lifetime; it surpasses my wildest *jump-out-of-bed-with-glee* dreams. To Roger Scholl and Porscha Burke, thank you for the energizing meetings and votes of encouragement—they meant the world to me.

Natalie, your brilliant observations, insightful questions, and challenging feedback have shaped this book immeasurably. You rolled up your sleeves and treated the book as your own, never letting up on our shared mission to bring out the best *Pivot* can offer the world. You are insanely good at what you do. Thank you to the entire team of highly talented people at Portfolio, who I was also fortunate to work with: Hannah Kinisky, Merry Sun, Will Weisser, Tara Gilbride, Stefanie Rosenblum, Daniel Lagin, Megan Gerrity, Chris Sergio, Karl Spurzem, Henry Nuhn, Eric Nelson, Annie Hollands, Joel Rickett, and Richard Lennon. Big thanks also to *Pivot*'s copy editors, Jane Cavolina and Jim Blake, whose skill at catching and improving upon every last detail astounds me.

Adam Chaloeicheep, my trusted thought partner and genius brand strategist, you kicked off much of my thinking for this book when you said that my coaching process was "like a rocket launcher to the moon" for people going through career transitions. Thank you for helping me figure out what's next at every step. Big thanks also to the ABC Design Lab team (*Pivot*'s secret weapons!) for visually bringing this concept to life, and for all the brand strategy and creative direction along the way.

Tara Adams, your wisdom is sharp and grounding, and you have been a rock for so many of my pivots. Julie Clow, dinners over these last ten years of our friendship, not to mention following our Yellow Brick Road to Manhattan together and all the experiences that have come with it, have been an oasis in the madness, a little—who are we kidding, huge ol' heaping—slice of heaven. Inna Aizenstein, I cherish our Friday dinners and am so grateful for your fashion counsel! Ann "NYC Angel" Turi, thank you for showing us the way at every fabulous Louboutin-clad step. Elisa Doucette, from blogs to besties, I am so grateful that trading a few comments many years ago would turn into regular phone calls, accountability e-mails, and workcations around the world. Becky Cotton, I love being the "J" to your "P"! Working with you again has been a dream; your huge heart lights up so many lives, and we are all better for knowing you. Laura Garnett, I cherish our weekly walk-and-talks on all things life, love, and business. John Scaife, you came into my life when I was mid-pivot myself and made me an offer I couldn't refuse, to be the 1/3 to your and Kit's 0.667; thank you for all the morning laughs while driving over the Brooklyn Bridge, and for the great meals, coffee talks, and conversations. Dorie Clark, it's an honor to be business-author doppelgängers; I am so grateful for your friendship and all of our New York City adventures!

Marisol, I could not do what I do without you. I am thrilled we found each other, and beyond lucky to have you at the helm of all things Jenny Blake Enterprises, Pivot, Momentum, and Life After College. You are a job category all your own, given that so many of my friends are looking for "a Marisol" for their business. I look forward to watching and helping your career unfold! Lou Ann Alberts and Mandi Holmes, thank you for keeping all the nuts and bolts on track while I worked on this book.

Anyone crazy enough to live in New York City knows that friends become family here. Many of us have moved far away from home—to a literal and figurative island—to pursue our wildest Pivot ambitions. My NYC family has been an abundant source of joy, support, and idea sharing. From Friday dinners, to picnics in the park, to brunches and potlucks, to walk-and-talks, to Dorie's author dinners, I am deeply grateful for all of you: Allie Mahler, Kristin Glenn, Monica "MonBon" McCarthy, Christian Golofaro, Bob Gower, Alexandra Jamieson, Dan Schawbel, Jenn Racioppi, Jacquette Timmons, Lauralee Kelly, Petra Kolber, Sarah and Alex Peck, Willie Jackson, and Daniel Jarvis. To the Wolveri family who pop in and out: Nick Reese, Kyle Durand, Nicky Halal, and Sean Ogle, I am always grateful for your domain expertise and epic hugs. Big thanks also to the Young Entrepreneur Council (shout-out to Ryan Paugh, Scott Gerber, Jeff Gabel, and Morgan Brady) for the ongoing connections and community.

My JB mentor and friendtor crew: no matter how often we talk, you are beacons of light and leadership that inspire me to keep going. Thank you for your warmth, work ethic, kindness, generosity, and good humor. This list does not do your impact on my life justice, but here goes. To my mentors—Lynn Vavreck, Marianne Chowning-Dray, Susan Biali, Pamela Slim, Michael Bungay Stanier, James Altucher, Seth Godin, Christina Rasmussen, Steve Maxwell, Mike Robbins, Michael Port, Jenna Buffaloe, Scott Stratten, and Chris Guillebeau. Tosha Silver—your books taught me the priceless practice of outrageous openness. Penney Peirce, your writing on intuition and frequency opened many doorways of insight and delight. Martha Beck, you are one of my very brightest North Stars and have inspired me from afar to grow in countless ways as a writer and wayfinder. Daniel Pink, thank you for paving the way for *Pivot* with books like *Free Agent Nation* and *A Whole New Mind*, and for accepting my Pixar Pitch with your wonderful cover endorsement. I wasn't kidding when I said an e-mail from you was as exciting to this bookworm as one from the president. To my friendtors—Ryan Stephens, Alexis Grant, Chris Taylor, John Hill, Ben Casnocha, ChaChanna Simpson, Sally Hope, Derek Shanahan, Melissa Foster, Jenny Ferry, Melissa Anzman, Molly Mahar, Melani Dizon, Thomas Edwards, Nate St. Pierre, J-Money, Buford

Barr, Ando Mierzwa, and Nicole Antoinette—thank you for all the support and camaraderie over the years.

My yoga teachers have provided solace, spiritual support, and regular sweat sessions that have kept me sane: Ari Halbert; Ariel Karass; Teri Steele (Pilates guru extraordinaire); Tara Stiles and Mike Taylor; Phillip Askew, Ivy Kaminer, Nevine Michaan, and the Katonah team; Pashupa Goodwin; and Rodney Yee, whose DVDs unleashed this life passion nearly fifteen years ago. Thank you for the studios and classes you run with such heart, my homes away from home.

Similar thanks to McNally Jackson, my corner bookstore and coffee shop, an anchor of inspiration, awesome author talks, and binge book buying; and Grey Dog, whose unlimited coffee refills in those great ceramic diner mugs fueled many morning writing and editing sessions.

My California family of friends: Sara Plummer, Shaun Carrigan (who I promised on a napkin contract at the Meatball Shop that I would finish the proposal for this book), Laura Grose, Jeremy Orr, Cliff Redeker, Susan RoAne, Adrian Klaphaak, Tucker Warner, and Lori Newman (and Emily and Maddie). To my Gunn High '01 ladies: Vanessa Zarrilli, Laura "LBOBP" Vivona, Katy Stoner, Emily "Scooms" Schuman, Lauren Stone, Diana Neill, Nerissa Gaspay, Krista Cioffi, Tracy Tripp, Maura Ruzhnikov, Amy Costello, Erin Ventura, and Megan Stichter. I love our reunions and am so grateful to still be in touch!

To all the courageous pivoters who generously shared their stories: thank you for bringing this book to life. To my coaching clients, you are a huge source of inspiration for me. You are insanely smart, talented, and generous. I will not name names for privacy reasons, but you know who you are! It is the highest honor to help organize your brain. Enormous thanks to the Momentum Crew, who gave ongoing feedback at critical points throughout the book process; it's so much fun to "hang out" with you online and during our calls.

If I forgot anyone—or for new soul-traveler friends who I met after this book went to press, and therefore left your name out of these acknowledgments—forgive me!

Most of all, I want to end where I started: thank you to the JennyBlake.me and LifeAfterCollege.org readers and Pivot Podcast listeners, some of whom have been with me for ten years and counting. You are the reason I do what I do. I know that I am doing something right because of you.

Thank you for reading—I will be cheering you on wherever you go from here. May you be happy, healthy, and free. May your pivots exceed your wildest dreams, and may you savor all the small moments in between. Finally, may you shoot the moon whenever you get the chance. :)

Much love,

Jenny

POST PIVOT: ONLINE RESOURCES

Ways to Keep in Touch:

- Questions, success stories, or feedback to share? I would love to hear from you! E-mail Jenny@PivotMethod.com, and share your Pivot story at PivotMethod.com/share or with the hashtag #mypivot or #nextmove on social media.
- Access the book's full toolkit at PivotMethod.com/toolkit, and a glossary at PivotMethod.com/glossary.
- For ongoing blog posts visit JennyBlake.me, and subscribe to the Pivot Podcast at JennyBlake.me/podcast.
- Subscribe to my twice-monthly behind-the-business newsletter at JennyBlake.me/updates, where I share curated lists of the latest Pivot-related tips, tools, books, and resources.
- For more personalized ongoing support, join our private community of solopreneurs and side hustlers at MomentumCrew.com.

Want to Help Spread the Word?

As my first book mentor Michael Larsen told me, "Authors don't keep books alive, readers do." If you enjoyed *Pivot* and think others could benefit, I would be grateful for your help in any of the following ways:

- Write a review, on the retailer's site where you purchased the book and/or on Goodreads, to help others decide whether to purchase a copy.
- Gift a copy to a friend or coworker.
- Share your pivot story on social media with the hashtag #mypivot or #nextmove.

PIVOT METHOD QUICK REFERENCE

STAGE ONE: PLANT
33

- **Values:** What are your guiding principles? 39
- **Vision:** What does success look like one year from now? 53
- **Strengths:** What is working? Where do you excel? 65
- **Finances:** What is your timeline? How can you earn extra income? 75

STAGE TWO: SCAN
87

- **Connect:** With whom can you exchange expertise and support? 91
- **Learn:** How can you grow? What research can you conduct? 107
- **Discern:** How can you add unique value and build visibility? 123

STAGE THREE: PILOT
139

- **Identify:** What small experiments can you run? 143
- **Implement:** What real-world data are you collecting? 143
- **Evaluate:** What worked? What didn't? What could you do differently? 161

STAGE FOUR: LAUNCH
169

- **Launch:** When will you make the big move? What are your linchpin decision criteria? 173
- **Flip Failure:** What will move you into action? 197

STAGE FIVE: LEAD
215

- **Communications Culture:** How can you facilitate engaging career conversations? What programs can you pilot within your organization to engage and retain top talent? 219

LAUNCH CRITERIA CHECKLIST

Financial Benchmarks

- [ ] Money saved
- [ ] Money earned
- [ ] Stay until OBO (Or Better Offer)
- [ ] Specific size compensation
- [ ] Stock or bonus incentive tied to a date
- [ ] Acquire funding, loan, or scholarship

Date-Based Timing

- [ ] Launch X project at work
- [ ] Take X months to explore, or take a sabbatical
- [ ] Make a launch decision by X date
- [ ] Leave/change no later than X date

Progress Milestones

- [ ] Build X prototype
- [ ] Land X new clients
- [ ] Planning readiness in new direction
- [ ] Platform reaches a certain size

Instinct/Intuition

- [ ] Gut feeling
- [ ] Gave the last gig my all
- [ ] Maxed out; health symptoms flaring up
- [ ] Willing to go all in toward new direction

In Others' Hands

- [ ] Gatekeeper industry approval or offer
- [ ] Accepted to application-only program
- [ ] When my partner earns X, or completes Y
- [ ] Full or partial agreement from family

One-Hour Pivot Lunch-and-Learn Workshop

I have created a one-hour Pivot workshop that anyone on your team can lead in addition to, or in place of, a kickoff keynote with your organization. You will have everything you need to facilitate the workshop at your fingertips, with a dashboard to track group participation and follow-up. This workshop is a great tool for office book clubs, leadership development, and team building.

Six-Month, Six-Workshop Pivot Follow-Up Series

The Pivot workshop can be run as a stand-alone team-building exercise, or you can pair it with a curated monthly follow-up series of additional leader-led workshops that reinforce each of the Pivot core concepts, such as expansive thinking, problem solving, riding out dips, and experimenting frequently to drive innovation. These six workshops help sustain the initial workshop takeaways, and allow teams to continue having powerful individual and group conversations in the months that follow.

Manager Training: How to Career Coach

Pivot Career Coach Training is an interactive workshop that empowers managers to better engage and retain top talent by learning how to hold exploratory career conversations. Using the simple structure of the Pivot Method, managers will walk away with coaching tools for working with direct reports to reveal resonant next steps and areas for development, and for helping employees pivot within their role, team, or broader organization. Managers will learn how to ask powerful questions, effectively structure sessions, and align individual career aspirations with team and company goals.

Career Conversation Toolkit

In keeping with the workshop-in-a-box format, the Career Conversation Toolkit has everything you need to roll out career conversations quickly, easily, and regularly within your organization. You and your managers will get instant access to template e-mails with session overviews and scheduling instructions for your team, and worksheets for individuals to fill out before and after career conversations with their manager.

Interested in Bringing Any of These Programs to Your Organization?

Learn more at PivotMethod.com/workshops.

PIVOT 201: RECOMMENDED READING

Pivot stands on the shoulders of giants. Below are books for each stage that have been instrumental in my life, business, and career. These books provide in-depth coverage of areas where I just scratched the surface. I encourage you to dig deeper into anything that grabbed you. *For the full reading list, visit PivotMethod.com/toolkit.*

Introduction

- *A Whole New Mind* by Daniel H. Pink
- *Antifragile* by Nassim Nicholas Taleb
- *The Second Machine Age* by Erik Brynjolfsson and Andrew McAfee
- *The Antidote* by Oliver Burkeman
- *The Start-Up of You* by Reid Hoffman and Ben Casnocha

Plant

- *The Power of Full Engagement* by Jim Loehr and Tony Schwartz
- *Finding Your Own North Star* by Martha Beck
- *The Big Leap* by Gay Hendricks
- *Body of Work* by Pamela Slim
- *Choose Yourself* by James Altucher

Scan

- *So Good They Can't Ignore You* by Cal Newport
- *The First 20 Hours* by Josh Kaufman
- *Tribes* by Seth Godin
- *Stand Out* by Dorie Clark
- *Essentialism* by Greg McKeown

Pilot

- *The Lean Startup* by Eric Ries
- *Eat That Frog!* by Brian Tracy
- *Business Model You* by Tim Clark, with Alexander Osterwalder and Yves Pigneur
- *Making Ideas Happen* by Scott Belsky
- *The War of Art* by Steven Pressfield

Launch

- *Smartcuts* by Shane Snow
- *The Dip* by Seth Godin
- *Outrageous Openness* by Tosha Silver
- *The Intuitive Way* by Penney Peirce
- *Playing Big* by Tara Mohr

Lead

- *Conscious Business* by Fred Kofman
- *The Work Revolution* by Julie Clow
- *How Google Works* by Eric Schmidt and Jonathan Rosenberg
- *The Alliance* by Reid Hoffman, Ben Casnocha, and Chris Yeh
- *The Coaching Habit* by Michael Bungay Stanier

NOTES

INTRODUCTION

Pivot Is the New Normal

4 **People are no longer working:** Tyler Cowen, "A Dearth of Investment in Young Workers," *New York Times*, September 7, 2013, www.nytimes.com/2013/09/08/business/a-dearth-of-investment-in-young-workers.html.

4 **average tenure drops to three years:** Bureau of Labor Statistics, "Employee Tenure in 2014," September 18, 2014, www.bls.gov/news.release/pdf/tenure.pdf.

4 **either "not engaged":** Barry Schwartz, "Rethinking Work," *New York Times*, August 28, 2015, www.nytimes.com/2015/08/30/opinion/sunday/rethinking-work.html.

4 **project-based economy:** Adam Davidson, "What Hollywood Can Teach Us About the Future of Work," *New York Times Magazine*, May 15, 2015.

7 **defines a business pivot:** Eric Ries, *The Lean Startup: How Today's Entrepreneurs Use Continuous Innovation to Create Radically Successful Businesses* (New York: Crown Business, 2011).

11 **program still cited as one of the benefits:** (a) *Fortune*, "25 Best Global Companies to Work For," Fortune.com, November 14, 2012, http://fortune.com/2012/11/14/25-best-global-companies-to-work-for/.

　(b) Lance Whitney, "Google Named 2nd Best Company to Work For in the World." CNET, November 14, 2014. http://www.cnet.com/news/google-named-2nd-best-company-to-work-for-in-the-world/.

High Net Growth

19 **A study by Daniel Kahneman and Angus Deaton:** Daniel Kahneman and Angus Deaton, "High Income Improves Evaluation of Life but Not Emotional Well-being," Proceedings of the National Academy of Sciences of the United States of America 107(38): 16489–93.

19 **(in today's dollars):** Saving.org, "Inflation Calculator," http://www.saving.org/inflation/.

20 **Maintaining a growth mindset:** Carol Dweck, *Mindset: The New Psychology of Success* (New York: Ballantine Books, 2007), 7.

20 **boredom itself can induce stress:** Alina Tugend, "The Contrarians on Stress: It Can Be Good for You," *New York Times*, October 2013, www.nytimes.com/2014/10/04/your-money/the-contrarians-on-stress-it-can-be-good-for-you-.html.

20 **In her 1997 study:** Amy Wrzesniewski, Clark McCauley, Paul Rozin, and Barry Schwartz, "Jobs, Careers, and Callings: People's Relations to Their Work," *Journal of Research in Personality* 31:21–33.

25 **"thrive and grow":** Nassim Nicholas Taleb, *Antifragile: Things That Gain from Disorder* (New York: Random House, 2012).

STAGE ONE: PLANT

35 **According to Tom Rath:** Tom Rath, *StrengthsFinder 2.0* (Washington, D.C.: Gallup Press, 2007), ii–iii.

Chapter 1: Calibrate Your Compass

45 **creatively named values:** Jenny Blake, *Life After College* (Philadelphia: Running Press, 2011).

47 **You can even write this out:** Bill Connolly, *The Success Disconnect: Why the Smartest People Choose Meaning over Money* (New York: Self-published, 2015).

48 **Willpower is a limited resource:** Kelly McGonigal, *The Willpower Instinct: How Self-Control Works, Why It Matters, and What You Can Do to Get More of It* (New York: Avery, 2011).

49 **Peace of mind is the dividend we collect:** Jim Blake, *The Bliss Engine* (Nashville: Two Steps Publishing, 2013).

49 **In a *Harvard Business Review* article:** Roger L. Martin, "Rethinking the Decision Factory," *Harvard Business Review*, October 2013, hbr.org/2013/10/rethinking-the-decision-factory.

49 **"Virtually no one has a gut-level sense of just how tiring it is to decide":** John Tierney, "Do You Suffer from Decision Fatigue?" *New York Times*, August 17, 2011.

49 **There is a reason Steve Jobs:** Walter Isaacson, *Steve Jobs* (New York: Simon & Schuster, 2011).

51 **ten to twelve minutes a day:** Dan Hurley, "Breathing In vs. Spacing Out," *New York Times*, January 14, 2014, www.nytimes.com/2014/01/19/magazine/breathing-in-vs-spacing-out.html.

Chapter 2: Put a Pin in It

54 **quite ineffective at predicting:** Daniel Gilbert, *Stumbling on Happiness* (New York: Vintage, 2007).

Chapter 3: Fuel Your Engine

66 **their viral manifesto video, "This Is Your Life":** Holstee, "The Holstee Manifesto," Holstee.com, last modified 2014, https://www.holstee.com/pages/manifesto.

67 **unique "Zone of Genius":** Gay Hendricks, *The Big Leap: Conquer Your Hidden Fear and Take Life to the Next Level* (New York: HarperOne, 2010), 33–34.

69 **He describes each one as follows:** Ibid., 29–34.

70 **such as Myers-Briggs:** The Myers & Briggs Foundation, www.myersbriggs.org/my-mbti-personality-type/mbti-basics/; for a free test, visit www.humanmetrics.com/cgi-win/jtypes2.asp.

70 **such as . . . StrengthsFinder:** Tom Rath, *StrengthsFinder* 2.0 (Washington, D.C.: Gallup Press, 2007). Assessment code comes with book purchase.

70 **such as . . . the Enneagram:** Don Richard Riso and Ross Hudson, *The Wisdom of the Enneagram: The Complete Guide to Psychological and Spiritual Growth for the Nine Personality Types* (New York: Bantam, 1999).

Chapter 4: Fund Your Runway

78 **average unemployment duration:** Michele Lerner, "How Big Should Your Emergency Fund Be?" Bankrate.com, March 6, 2012, www.bankrate.com/finance/savings/how-big-should-emergency-fund-be.aspx.

79 ***burn rate* is defined as:** *Investopedia*, "Definition of Burn Rate," www.investopedia.com/terms/b/burnrate.asp.

83 **According to Sendhil Mullainathan:** Sendhil Mullainathan and Eldar Shafir, *Scarcity: Why Having Too Little Means So Much* (New York: Times Books, 2013), 13.

STAGE TWO: SCAN

Chapter 5: Bolster Your Bench

91 **One study revealed that the word:** Melissa Dahl, "Networking Is Literally Disgusting," *New York Magazine*, September 3, 2014, nymag.com/scienceofus/2014/09/networking-is-literally-disgusting.html.

98 **"the Church of Oprah":** Mark Oppenheimer, "The Church of Oprah Winfrey and a Theology of Suffering," *New York Times*, May 27, 2011, www.nytimes.com/2011/05/28/us/28beliefs.html.

103 **In a study of a thousand:** "How to Live the Freelance Life," Freelancers Union.org, 2014, fu-web-storage-prod.s3.amazonaws.com/content/filer_public/8f/d7/8fd7d4ce-f714-486e-b2d5-80e190b0ce70/fu_surveyinfographics_workandlife_v3.pdf.

Chapter 6: Bridge the Gaps

107 **I hope that:** Neil Gaiman, "My New Year Wish," NeilGaiman.com, December 31, 2011, journal.neilgaiman.com/2011/12/my-new-year-wish.html.

109 **The dip:** Seth Godin, *The Dip: A Little Book That Teaches You When to Quit (and When to Stick)* (New York: Portfolio/Penguin, 2007).

111 **Building new skills:** Jason Shen, "Why Practice Actually Makes Perfect: How to Rewire Your Brain for Better Performance," *Buffer App* Blog, May 28, 2013, blog.bufferapp.com/why-practice-actually-makes-perfect-how-to-rewire-your-brain-for-better-performance.

111 **Albert Einstein called this:** Maria Popova, "How Einstein Thought: Why 'Combinatory Play' Is the Secret of Genius," BrainPickings.org, August 14, 2013, www.brainpickings.org/2013/08/14/how-einstein-thought-combinatorial-creativity/.

111 **"Forget being a comedian":** Frank Rich, "In Conversation: Chris Rock," *New York Magazine*, December 1, 2014.

112 **"Yes, and" technique:** Matt Besser, Ian Roberts, and Matt Walsh, *The Upright Citizens Brigade Comedy Improvisation Manual* (New York: Comedy Council of Nicea, 2013).

114 **"The secret is to take yourself":** Tripp Lanier, *The New Man Podcast with Tripp Lanier*, "The Rise of Superman—Steven Kotler," June 17, 2014, www.thenewmanpodcast.com/2014/06/tnm-158-steven-kotler-the-rise-of-superman/.

114 **Brown shared her approach:** Jonathan Fields, *Good Life Project*, "Brené Brown: On Gratitude, Vulnerability and Courage," podcast audio: 51:59, November 25, 2014, www.goodlifeproject.com/brene-brown-radio/.

117 **called *empathy interviews*:** Institute of Design at Stanford University, "Method: Interview for Empathy," dschool.stanford.edu/wp-content/themes/dschool/method-cards/interview-for-empathy.pdf, and "Use Our Methods," dschool.stanford.edu/use-our-methods/.

118 **This is the Downing effect:** Janet E. Davidson and C. L. Downing, "Contemporary Models of Intelligence," in *Handbook of Intelligence*, ed. Robert J. Sternberg (Cambridge: Cambridge University Press, 2000).

119 **In his 1951 book:** Alan W. Watts, *The Wisdom of Insecurity: A Message for an Age of Anxiety* (New York: Vintage, 1951), 32.

119 ***complement* technology, rather than compete:** Erik Brynjolfsson and Andrew McAfee, *The Second Machine Age: Work, Progress, and Prosperity in a Time of Brilliant Technologies* (New York: W. W. Norton, 2014), 153–54, 189–200.

120 ***Leverage* refers to:** Ibid.

120 **it is futile to ask:** Geoff Colvin, *Humans Are Underrated: What High Achievers Know That Brilliant Machines Never Will* (New York: Portfolio/Penguin, 2015), 42, 44; Oliver Burkeman, "Are Machines Making Humans Obsolete?" *Guardian*, September 18, 2015.

Chapter 7: Make Yourself Discoverable

124 **"Well-being is enhanced":** Brian R. Little, *Me, Myself, and Us: The Science of Personality and the Art of Well-Being* (New York: PublicAffairs, 2014), 196.

126 **suggests aiming for "1,000 True Fans":** Kevin Kelly, "1,000 True Fans," KK.org, March 4, 2008, kk.org/thetechnium/1000-true-fans/.

129 **"data is the new oil":** Michael Palmer, "Data Is the New Oil," *ANA Marketing Maestros*, November 3, 2006, ana.blogs.com/maestros/2006/11/data_is_the_new.html.

STAGE THREE: PILOT

142 **"Making assumptions and then taking them personally":** Don Miguel Ruiz with Janet Mills, *The Voice of Knowledge: A Practical Guide to Inner Peace* (San Rafael, CA: Amber-Allen Publishing, 2004).

Chapter 8: Get Scrappy

143 **the concept of the MVP:** Eric Ries, *The Lean Startup: How Today's Entrepreneurs Use Continuous Innovation to Create Radically Successful Businesses* (New York: Crown Business, 2011), 93.

149 **the principle of "optionality":** Nassim Nicholas Taleb, *Antifragile: Things That Gain from Disorder* (New York: Random House, 2012), 158.

150 **Theodor Geisel was a cartoonist:** Donald E. Pease, *Theodor SEUSS Geisel* (New York: Oxford University Press, 2010).

Chapter 9: Pause, Review, Repeat

162 **Seinfeld said, "It just seems":** Rob Brunner, "Jerry Seinfeld," FastCompany.com, May 12, 2014, www.fastcompany.com/3029462/most-creative-people-2014/jerry-seinfeld.

162 **In an interview with David Letterman:** Paley Center for Media, "Jerry Seinfeld and David Letterman (Full Program)," June 9, 2014, YouTube video, 1:05:13, published on July 11, 2014.

164 **appearance on national TV:** Fox Business, "Recent College Grad Plans to Retire by Age 40," FoxBusiness.com, video, 4:06, March 10, 2015, video.foxbusiness.com/v/4103938151001/recent-college-grad-plans-to-retire-by-40.

STAGE FOUR: LAUNCH

Chapter 10: Build First, Courage Second

173 **"the rapture of being alive":** Joseph Campbell, *The Power of Myth* (New York: Anchor, 1991), 4.

183 **the Project Management Triangle:** Michael W. Newell and Marina N. Grashina, *The Project Management Question and Answer Book* (New York: AMACOM, 2003).

186 **"The Gambler":** Song, written by Don Schlitz, recorded by Kenny Rogers (1978).

186 **Career Roomba Syndrome:** Brad Zomick, "Career Roomba Syndrome: How to Cure Your Lack of Passion and Find Direction in Your Career Path," ThoughtCatalog.com, May 15, 2015, thoughtcatalog.com/brad-zomick/2015/05/career-roomba-syndrome-how-to-cure-your-lack-of-passion-and-find-direction-in-your-career-path/.

190 **our addiction to new ideas:** Scott Belsky, *Making Ideas Happen: Overcoming the Obstacles Between Vision and Reality* (New York: Portfolio/Penguin, 2012), 71.

191 **average life span of human cells:** Institute for Stem Cell Biology and Regenerative Medicine, Stanford Medicine, "Research," stemcell.stanford.edu/research/; Nicholas Wade, "Your Body Is Younger Than You Think," *New York Times*, August 2, 2005, www.nytimes.com/2005/08/02/science/your-body-is-younger-than-you-think.html.

191 **Our bodies cycle through circadian rhythms:** National Institute of General Medical Sciences, "Circadian Rhythms Fact Sheet," last modified October 1, 2015, www.nigms.nih.gov/Education/Pages/Factsheet_CircadianRhythms.aspx.

191 **the average attention span:** Statistic Brain Research Institute, "Attention Span Statistics," last modified April 2, 2105, www.statisticbrain.com/attention-span-statistics/.

Chapter 11: Flip Failure

199 **regret minimization framework:** Zach Bulygo, "12 Business Lessons You Can Learn from Amazon Founder and CEO Jeff Bezos," *KISSmetrics* Blog, January 19, 2013, blog.kissmetrics.com/lessons-from-jeff-bezos/.

208 **Post-it Notes:** "Post-it note," Wikipedia, en.wikipedia.org/wiki/Post-it_note.

STAGE FIVE: LEAD

Chapter 12: Are You Listening?

219 *You have done all this work:* Eric Schmidt and Jonathan Rosenberg, *How Google Works* (New York: Grand Central Publishing, 2014).

223 **In an *Inc.* survey:** *Inc.* staff, "How the Top CEOs Really Think (Infographic)," *Inc.* magazine, September 2014, www.inc.com/magazine/201409/inc.500-2014-inc-500-ceo-survey-results.html.

223 **One Gallup study revealed:** Lauren Weber, "What Do Workers Want from the Boss?" *Wall Street Journal*, April 2, 2015, blogs.wsj.com/atwork/2015/04/02/what-do-workers-want-from-the-boss/?mod=e2tw.

223 **50 percent left a job:** Ibid.

230 *Fortune's* **100 Best Companies:** *Fortune*, "100 Best Companies to Work For," last modified February 2015, fortune.com/best-companies/.

231 **"more than 16,000 books":** Ibid.

231 **contribute to one of their core values:** "Zappos Library List," Zappos.com, zapposinsights.com/about/library-list.

231 **Fund a Goal program:** Mark Walker, "Lululemon Athletica—Driving a Culture of Individual and Organizational Development, Accountability and Innovation," HRMToday.com, September 29, 2011, www.hrmtoday.com/featured-stories/lululemon-athletica-driving-a-culture-of-individual-and-organizational-development-accountability-and-innovation/.

231 **Reverse mentoring and lunches:** Leslie Kwoh, "Reverse Mentoring Cracks Workplace," *Wall Street Journal*, November 28, 2011, www.wsj.com/articles/SB10001424052970203764804577060051461094004.

INDEX

Adams, Tara, 2, 5
adaptability, 232–33
agility, 13, 72
Allen, David, 128
analysis paralysis, 89, 156
Anderson, Marques, 2, 6, 115
antifragile, 25, 238
Anzman, Melissa, 188
assumptions: hypothesis versus, 142
asymmetric upside, 149–50

bartering, 103–4
basketball analogy, 13, 226–27
Beck, Martha, 204
Belsky, Scott, 190–91
Bezos, Jeff, 199
Biali, Susan, 95
Bilanich, Bud, 3, 6
Bisong, Gigi, 156–57
board of advisors, 97–98, 100
body: and Plant stage, 47–49, 52
boiling frog, 188
Bourke, Joanna, 67
bridge income, 79–80, 81, 84, 85
Brilliance Barter, 116–17
Brown, Brené, 114–15, 117, 204
Brynjolfsson, Erik, 119
Build-Measure-Learn feedback loop, 143
Burch, Noel, 109
burn rate, 79

calfee, 101
Campbell, Joseph, 9, 173, 235
career conversations/coaching, 10, 219–21,
    223–25, 226–32
career karma, 104–5

career portfolio, 66, 146, 150, 155
Career Roomba Syndrome, 186
careers
    in age of app and smartphone analogy, 8–9
    operating modes for, 23–25
    plateaus in, 24, 190–91, 222, 226, 235, 236
Carr, Peter, 180–81
Chaloeicheep, Adam, 2, 5, 50, 51, 102, 131–32
change
    and duration of pivot, 15
    fear of, 8–9, 119
    and mindset, 20, 22, 23
    as opportunity, 20, 22
childhood interests, 67–68
Chödrön, Pema, 10
Clark, Dorie, 126
Clow, Julie, 3, 6–7, 127, 224
collective brainpower, 94
Colvin, Geoff, 120
combinatory play and hobbies, 110–11
comfort zone, 27–28, 47, 60, 89, 111, 118, 158,
    194, 197, 238
complexity, 235–39
connecting the dots, and looking backward,
    10–13
Connolly, Bill, 47, 147
continuous pivot, 211–12
Cotton, Becky, 187–88, 220, 221
courage: and Launch stage, 173–95
Covey, Stephen R., 39

Dahl, Marisol, 154–55
Danckert, James, 20
Danylchuk, Lisa, 105
Deaton, Angus, 19

decision fatigue (ego depletion), 49–50, 52
decision
    to launch, 172, 174-82, 185, 209
    as separate from difficult conversations,
        205–6
Decision Tracker (exercise), 166
Decoda, Tara, 181–82
Deffley, Andrew, 75, 76, 98, 99
difficult conversations, 205–6
diminishing returns, 186, 188–91
discoverable, 89–90, 123–37
Dizon, Melani, 145
Doucette, Elisa, 102, 158
Downing effect (illusory superiority), 118
drafting, career, 98–99
"Drop the Bucket" game, 114
Durand, Kyle, 2, 6, 22, 155
Dweck, Carol, 19, 20

entrepeneurs: mindset of, 17
exercise(s)
    linear logic, 113
    listening, 117–18
    meditation, 51–52
    mentor, 96–97
    Pivot Hexagon, 185
    platform, 128–29
    skills/expertise, 108
    "sliding-doors" careers, 59–60
    strengths, 68, 70, 128–29
    success, 58–59
    30-Day Decision Tracker, 166
    values mining, 41–45
    vision, 57–62
    Zone of Genius, 70
experts, 126–27, 128–29. See also reputation;
    skills/expertise; thought leadership expert

failure
    and courageous life, 238
    definition of, 198–99
    fear of, 197–213, 238
    as feedback, 201–2
    regret and, 198–99
    and risk, 173, 180
    and values, 198, 199
family, 182. See also other people
fauxspiration, 156–57
fear
    of change, 8–9, 20, 119
    as consuming thinking, 113
    of failure, 197–213, 238
    and finances, 83
    FOMO (Fear of Missing Out) and, 238
    FONT (Fear of Not Trying) and, 238
    and mindset, 20, 23, 28, 29
Ferriss, Tim, 20, 108

Ferry, Jenny, 166
Fields, Jonathan, 114, 117
finances
    and bridge income, 79–80, 81, 84, 85
    burn rate and, 79
    as constraint on pivot, 35
    and duration of pivot, 15
    and emergency fund, 78
    and income-anxiety seesaw awareness,
        84–85
    last resort and, 237–38
    mindset and, 18, 21, 26, 29–30, 83–84
    and monthly nut, 77–78, 85
    risk and, 76, 78, 81
    runway for, 78, 79, 157, 174
    and savings, 79–80
    side hustles and, 80–82
    and yearly nut, 78
folding: and knowing when to fold, 185–91
Frank, Thomas, 163–64
friendtors, 100–101, 146

Gaiman, Neil, 107
Garnett, Laura, 69–70
Gaspay, Nerissa, 124
Geisel, Theodor, 150–51
get scrappy, 143–44
Gillian (sister-in-law), 56–57
Give-Receive-Achieve framework, 58–59
givers, 23, 58, 94, 104–5, 116–17, 125,
        126–27, 217
Gladwell, Malcolm, 60
Godin, Seth, 81
Golofaro, Christian, 21, 22, 210–11
Gower, Bob, 148–50
Gramaglia, Casey, 51, 52
Grant, Adam, 94
Grant, Alexis, 102–3
Grayeb, Jennifer, 224, 225
greener grass, 135–36
Grey, Nick, 129
Grose, Laura, 225, 232
Grosz, Stephen, 8
grounded theory, 114–15, 116, 232
Guarriello, Tom, 233

happiness, 39, 46–47, 52, 124, 135, 202–5
happiness formula, 47
Harold (grandfather), 151–52
Harris, Dan, 51
Heller, Rachel S.F., 190
Hellstrom, Travis, 21–22
Hendricks, Gay, 69
Henry, Shawn, 93, 200
high net growth, 18–30, 221, 236
high net worth, 18–30
Hill, John, 3, 6, 54

hobbies, 110–11
hotter/colder, 41, 167
hypothesis: assumptions versus, 142

illusory superiority, 118
impacters
    aim/purpose of, 18, 70
    and career operating modes, 68–69
    characteristics of, 19–23
    and courageous life, 238–39
    and discoverability, 126, 132
    as givers, 94
    and mindset, 19–23, 24–25, 28
    self-doubt of, 118–19
    strengths of, 68–69
income-anxiety seesaw, 84–85
incremental pilots, 152–53
Insight Timer app, 50
instinct and intuition, 174, 179–81, 192–93,
    205, 206, 237
interests: importance of, 221–23
internal mobility and programs, 229–32
intrapreneurs, 17

Jacobson, Jeff, 55
JennyBlake.me (website), 11, 23, 29, 116
jobs
    disengagement from, 4
    impact of technology on, 4
    reasons for leaving, 219–23
    See also careers
Jobs, Steve, 11, 49
John-Reader, Courtney "CJ," 222
Jones, Brian (alias), 3, 6–7, 177–78, 235–36
Justin (client), 40–41

Kahneman, Daniel, 19
Kaufman, Josh, 108
Kelleghan, Daniel, 127–28
Kelly, Kevin, 126
Kit (friend), 81
knots, 235–36, 239
known and unknown variables, 62–63
Koenig, Lora, 102
Kondo, Marie, 128
Kotler, Steven, 114
Krishnamurti, J., 173
Krohn, Tricia, 171–72, 203–4

last resort, 237–38
Launch stage
    approvals in, 182
    and "being scrappy," 143–44
    benchmarks in, 17
    courage and, 173–95
    and evaluation of launch, 209–11
    and failure, 173, 179, 180, 195, 197–213

and fear, 171, 182, 184–85, 197–213
and finances, 171, 174–76, 177, 184–85, 187,
    190, 202
and other people, 174, 181–82,
    202–6
overview of, 13, 14, 171–72
perfect conditions for, 207
and Pivot Scales, 194–95
progress milestones in, 174, 178–79
and risk, 173, 180, 182, 184–85, 188,
    194–95, 208–9
and success, 171, 200, 209–11
launch timing criteria, 174–82, 185, 209
Lead stage
    and career development, 219–33
    listening during, 219–33
    overview of, 15, 217
leadership
    and mindset, 23
    and "servant leader" perspective, 115
    thought, 60, 93, 126
lean pilots, 148–49
leapfrog approach, 130–32
learning
    discernment about, 119–20
    and evaluation of Pilot stage, 167
    failure and, 111, 201
    and how to learn, 108–9
    importance of, 137
    levels of, 109–10
    mindset and, 21, 25, 28
    and MVP, 143
letting others know you are looking, 133–35
leverage existing strengths, 7, 8, 14, 29–30,
    61–62, 65–73, 89, 112, 119, 128–29
Levine, Amir, 190
Life After College (Blake), 3, 11, 18, 26, 29,
    45, 154
listening
    active, 118
    exercise about, 117–18
    to gut, 135, 136
    investigative, 114–18
    and networking, 117
Little, Brian R., 124
Lucius Seneca, 91

make-or-break marker, 82–83
managers, career conversations with, 223–25
Marbin, Seth, 152–53
marketable skills, 71–72
Martin, Roger, 49
Martin, Steve, 18
Maslow, Abraham, 8
mastermind groups, 101–3, 146
McAfee, Andrew, 119
McCarthy, Monica, 9, 65–66

meditation, 50–52
Meitner, Amanda and Tom, 176
mentors, 94–97, 99, 100–101, 146, 232
Miceli, Carlos, 134–35
mind map, 43–44, 45, 62
mindset
    abundance, 84
    and finances, 18, 21, 26, 29–30, 83–84
    growth, 18–30, 221, 236
    pivot, 16–17
MIPs (Most Important People), 204–5
Momentum (online community), 116–17
monthly nut, 77–78, 85
Mullainathan, Sendhil, 83
MVP (minimum viable product), 143, 144,
    148. *See also* get scrappy

Nash, Jennie, 179
networking
    and bartering, 103–4
    board of advisors and, 97–98, 100
    collective brainpower and, 94
    discoverability and, 129, 132, 133–35
    and drafting, 98–99
    and expanding sphere of influence, 93
    friendtors and, 100–101
    and letting others know you are looking,
        133–35
    mastermind groups and, 101–3
    and mentors, 94–97, 99, 100–101
Newport, Cal, 128
Nguyen, Davis, 154

Oka, Marvin, 193
180s, 28,
one-off mentors, 94–97
operating modes, career, 23–25, 68–69, 227
opportunities
    and career conversations, 228
    and organizational change, 233
    sources for, 91–92
organizations
    changing nature of, 232–33
    pilots within, 152–53
    Pivot Method within, 226–29
other people
    happiness of, 202–5
    and letting others know you are looking,
        133–35
    as MIPs, 204–5

panic zone, 27–28, 163, 174, 194, 197
Pell, Dave, 129
Pennington, Casey, 133–34, 165
performance reviews, 227, 228
personality assessments, 70
Pham, Julien, 61–62, 125

Pilot stage
    aim/purpose of, 14, 136, 141, 163, 167
    and being wrong, 142
    characteristics of, 146–150, 158
    evaluation of, 161–67
    and failure, 201
    and fear, 158, 194
    and finances, 146, 157, 162
    and "getting scrappy," 143–59
    and MVP, 143, 144
    overview of, 13, 14, 141–42
    and risk, 141, 145, 146, 148, 149, 151, 152,
        153–55, 164–65, 171, 194
pilots
    incremental, 152–53
    lean, 148–49
    list of common, 145
    in organizations, 152–53
    size of, 148–50
    strong, 146-50
    vision, 146
Pink, Daniel, 60
Pivot Cycle, 14, 15, 86, 138, 168, 211–12
Pivot Hexagon, 183–85
Pivot Method
    aim/purpose of, 226
    benefits of, 212, 217
    as coaching tool, 15, 217, 229
    overview and stages in, 13–17
    within organizations, 226–29
pivot paradox
    Don't Push the River, 191–92
    Embrace the Slow Build, 150–52
    Fauxspiration, 156–57
    finances and, 82, 83–84
    Ignorance Is Bliss, 118–19
    Make Short-Term Trade-Offs if
        Necessary, 183
    Scarcity Versus "The Secret," 83–84
    Shoot the Moon, 208–9
    When the Grass Really is Greener, 135–36
pivot points, 3, 226, 239. *See also* plateau,
    career
Pivot Scales, 194–95
PivotMethod.com, 15, 23, 50, 85, 137, 167,
    213, 233
pivots/pivoting
    business, 7, 15
    characteristics of, 9–10
    crisis compared with, 9–10
    culture for, 217, 219–33
    definition of, 7
    degree of, 28, 161
    duration of, 15
    fear of, 8, 17
    or getting pivoted, 4–8
    mindset for, 16–17

motivation for, 1–3, 4–8
plateaus versus, 24
risk in, 9
Plant stage
    aim/purpose of, 14, 35, 89, 107
    finances and, 75–85
    guiding principles and, 39–52
    overview of, 13, 14, 35–37
    project-based purpose in, 69–70, 124–25
    and strengths, 35–37, 61–62, 65–73, 107, 118
    values and, 35, 39–45, 52, 66
    and vision, 35, 53–63, 66
plateau, career, 24, 190–91, 222, 226, 235, 236
platform, 93, 120, 125–29, 163–64, 178
progress milestones, 174, 178–79
project-based purpose, 69–70, 124–25
Project Management Triangle, 183–84

quantity/quality issues, 145, 150, 183, 228

Rapple, Rebecca, 97
Rasmussen, Christina, 10
Rath, Tom, 35–36
reciprocal transformation, 105
Redecker, Cliff, 231
redundancy, 153–55, 164
Reese, Nick, 77, 78
regret, 172, 198–99, 207, 210, 211
rejection, 130, 181–82, 195, 200
reputation
    of best managers, 224
    capital, 92
    and discoverability, 123, 125,
        127, 130
    and duration of pivot, 15
    networking and, 94
    and strengths, 71, 72–73
results, 72
Ries, Eric, 7, 143, 148
risk
    and courageous life, 238
    and duration of pivot, 15
    and failure, 173, 180
    and finances, 76, 78, 81
    incremental, 164–65
    and Pivot Scales, 194–95
    in pivots, 9, 17
    and redundancy, 153–55
    riskometer for, 27–29, 194
    tolerance for, 25–27
Riskometer, 27–29, 194
Roberts, Christian, 147
Rock, Chris, 111
Rosenberg, Jonathan, 219
routines: importance of, 49
Ruiz, don Miguel, 142
runway, 78, 79, 157, 174

Sadie (client), 205–6
Sam (friend), 92
Saramago, José, 1
savings, 79–80
Scaife, John, 21, 22, 210–11
Scan stage
    aim/purpose of, 14, 89–90, 115
    and discoverability, 89–90, 123–37
    frustration during, 136–37
    and networking, 89, 91–105, 115, 132, 133–35
    overview of, 13, 14, 89–90
    and skills/expertise, 107–21
scarcity, 83–84
Schmidt, Eric, 77, 219
Schoenberger, Amy, 2, 5, 130
Schrotberger, Luke, 101
Seinfeld, Jerry, 161–62
Seneca, Lucius, 91
"servant leader" perspective, 115
shadowing, 95–96
Shafir, Eldar, 83
Shen, Jason, 67, 221–22
shoot-the-moon, 208–09
short-term trade-offs, 183
side hustles, 80–82, 148, 152, 165, 175, 176
Silver, Nate, 129
Sims, Stacy, 126
skills/expertise
    building new, 82, 107–21
    closing the gap in, 108–21
    hobbies and, 110–11
    marketable, 71–72, 146
    technology and, 107, 119–20
    transitional, 132
    See also strengths
"sliding-doors" careers, 59–60
Slim, Pamela, 144
slow build (incremental) pilots, 152–53
Snow, Brooke, 62–63
Soosalu, Grant, 193
sphere of influence, 93
stagnation zone, 27–28, 194
strengths
    aim/purpose of, 69–70
    and career conversations, 228
    and characteristics of strong pilot,
        146–48
    and finances, 82
    leveraging existing 7, 8, 14, 29–30, 61–62,
        65–73, 89, 112, 119, 128–29
    and marketable skills, 71–72
    mining failure for, 201–2
    reputation and, 71, 72–73
    and results, 72
    and timing of pivots, 17
    and work-history highlights, 70–73
    See also skills/expertise

stretch zone, 27–28, 55, 158, 163, 180, 194, 197
structured annual career conversations,
      227–29
success
   Career Karma and, 104–5
   defining, 58–59
   mindset and, 23
   rejection as stepping stone to, 200
   "white picket fence" ideal of, 118–19
Sullivan, Stacy, 152
sweet spots, 23, 26–27, 68, 69

Taleb, Nassim Nicholas, 25, 149
talent, 20, 23, 67–70, 71, 147, 161, 223–24, 232.
      See also strengths
technology, 4, 107, 119–20
"then what" questions, 112–13
thinking
   fear as consuming, 113
   linear, 111–13, 176
   stagnant, 157–59
   strategic, 119–20
thought leadership, 60, 93, 126
Tierney, John, 49
Tom (brother), 95–96, 101, 208–9
travel pilots, 157–59
tyranny of the hows and the whole how,
      55–56, 113

Uhrig, Scott, 4
unrealized gains, 186, 187–88, 189–91
Ursillo, Dave, 201–2

values
   aim/purpose of, 39–40, 53
   career conversations and, 228
   clarification of, 39–45

clusters of, 43
   ranking of, 44, 45
   shifting of, 40
   vision and, 53, 57
   visual reminder of, 45
Vice, Roxanne, 207–9
vision
   aim/purpose of, 53–55
   clarification of, 60, 62–63
   as cloudy, 56–57
   importance of, 53–55
   and knowns/unknowns, 62–63
   and leapfrog approach, 132
   one-year statement of, 57, 58–59, 60–62, 66
   and purpose, 124
   time-range for, 54–55
   values and, 53, 57

Waitzkin, Josh, 108
Walker, Alice, 161
warm connections, 92. See also networking
Watson, Thomas, 65
Watts, Alan, 119
Weiss, Ronnie Mae, 223, 224–25
White, Ryan (aka Bob Gower), 148–50
why: defining your project-based purpose,
      124–25
Whyte, David, 54
willpower, 48, 49
work history, 70–73
Wrzesniewski, Amy, 20–21

yearly nut, 78
"Yes, and" technique, 112, 113

Zomick, Brad, 186
Zone of Genius, 67, 68–70, 72